KW-272-018

*EVERYMAN, I will go with thee,*

*and be thy guide,*

*In thy most need to go by thy side*

# The Paston Letters

IN TWO VOLUMES · VOLUME ONE

EDITED WITH AN INTRODUCTION BY
JOHN WARRINGTON

WANDSWORTH PUBLIC LIBRARIES

DENT: LONDON
EVERYMAN'S LIBRARY
DUTTON: NEW YORK

*All rights reserved*
*Made in Great Britain*
*at the*
*Aldine Press · Letchworth · Herts*
*for*
*J. M. DENT & SONS LTD*
*Aldine House · Bedford Street · London*
*First included in Everyman's Library 1924*
*Revised edition 1956*
*Last reprinted 1966*

200152419

942·04 PAS
D 1775 75

857-00307

NO. *752*

# INTRODUCTION

THE Paston Letters consist of more than one thousand items—private correspondence, copies of State papers, and legal documents—covering a period of almost ninety years (1418–1506). A large majority of these are letters written by or to members of the Paston family. The collection as a whole forms a most valuable source for English social history in the late fifteenth and early sixteenth centuries; but so much of it is devoid of interest to the general reader that selection is necessary. I have accordingly chosen those letters which describe most vividly the political and religious background, which best reveal the characters of those who dominate the scene, and which throw most light upon the manners and customs of the age.

The genealogy of the Pastons is clear from the table on pages xiv–xv; the geographical situation of their lands may be seen by reference to the map on page xii. But a brief sketch of the main features of their story during the years in question will help to guide the reader through that shifting scene, and some comment upon certain general aspects of the letters will enhance their many-sided interest. A succession of unwonted accidents to which we owe their preservation deserves also to be recorded.

I

The Pastons were a Norfolk family, owing what little eminence they achieved to William Paston, an able lawyer, who added to his modest patrimony first by marriage (*circa* 1420) with Agnes, daughter and heiress of Sir Edmund Berry, and afterwards by the purchase of lands—including the manor of Gresham—in and around his ancestral home at Paston. He was appointed a Judge of the Common Pleas in 1429, but, contrary to what has often been assumed, was never knighted. The jealousy stirred up by his success appears to have been restrained as much by respect for his character as by fear of his influence in high places. But after his death in 1444 both his widow and his heir paid the penalty of his advancement.

Relatively few of the documents fall within this early period. It must be remembered that the writing and transmission of letters was a more tedious and costly business than it is to-day: men and women communicated with one another in this fashion only when necessary for the conduct of urgent business, though on such occasions they might touch upon matters of less importance.

v

After 1444, however, and for reasons that are not far to seek, the amount of correspondence increases a hundredfold. At the time of his death, Judge Paston was preparing to build a new manor house, and agreement had been reached as to consequent interference with the highway; but within twelve months of his burial disputes arose between Agnes and her neighbours, and the animosity thus engendered lasted for several years. His son and heir, John Paston, had married (*circa* 1440) Margaret, daughter of John Mauteby, Esq., of Mauteby. John had followed in his father's footsteps, and soon had cause to be thankful for his legal training. In 1448 he was dispossessed of Gresham by Robert Hungerford, Lord Moleyns, upon grounds that no court could possibly have upheld. Then, in 1449, an ex-friar, one John Hauteyn, laid claim to another of the family properties at Oxnead. The Gresham affair dragged on for three years, during which time Paston re-entered the manor, learned of his wife's forcible expulsion therefrom, and finally regained possession in 1451. But Moleyns and his men, though brought to trial, were acquitted by order of the King, and Paston was unable to recover damages. Hauteyn's claim to Oxnead was ultimately abandoned.

Meanwhile, the incompetence of the royal government aroused much discontent and gave free rein to cupidity, lawlessness, and violence. The ensuing disorders, of which Cade's rebellion is one example, were particularly serious in Norfolk, as appears not only from such episodes as that at Gresham, but also from the outrages committed by Charles Nowell and others in 1452. These upheavals continued during the next three years, and culminated in a period of civil strife known as the Wars of the Roses, to the principal events of which the Letters contain numerous references.

In 1453 we obtain a glimpse of Sir John Fastolf's building operations at Caister Castle, where that wealthy but avaricious and cantankerous knight took up his residence in August 1454. Between 1455 and 1459 many of the Letters are concerned with his anxieties, his business affairs, and sometimes with his outbursts of ill-humour, until at length we come to that crucial date in the Paston story, 5th November 1459, when Fastolf died, leaving John Paston virtual owner of his great estates in Norfolk and Suffolk. These included the manors of Caister, Drayton, Hellesdon, and Cotton—to name only the most important.

The state of the law governing trusts and testamentary dispositions, not to mention the suspicious circumstances in which Fastolf's will was drawn up and the prevailing chaos due to civil war, invited litigation and recourse to less peaceable measures. On 4th March 1461, Edward IV was proclaimed King, and two

months later the storm broke over John Paston's head.   Caister
was coveted by the Duke of Norfolk, Drayton and Hellesdon
by the Duke of Suffolk, while Yelverton and other enemies
allowed him no rest elsewhere.   These contentions and the
protracted lawsuit arising out of Fastolf's will were not ended
with his death.

John Paston breathed his last on 22nd May 1466, worn out
with anxiety and poor health.   Business and litigation had kept
him much from home, and had involved him in three terms of
imprisonment.   During these long absences his estates were
managed, to the best of their ability, by his wife and a group of
loyal though ill-requited servants.   Margaret Paston saved the
family from an early and irretrievable fate: her ability, her
strength of character, her solid piety, and her wealth of common
sense justify us in considering her as the central figure of this
little drama.   Indeed, the women who cross the Paston stage
put their menfolk to shame.   John himself appears as a self-
centred, dour, and grasping creature, devoid of affection and, it
would seem, of gratitude.

His two elder sons were both named John.   The heir, who
had all his father's defects (*plus* a repellent streak of coarseness)
without his caution and determination, inherited a legacy of
misfortune to which his meanness and ineptitude, his fickleness
and irresponsibility, rendered him altogether unequal.   That he
managed to survive disaster was due to chance rather than to his
own gifts, the lack of which his father had frequently lamented
and which his mother would have cause on more than one
occasion to regret.

Young John Paston had been attached to the King's household
from 1461 until the beginning of 1463, in which latter year he
received the honour of knighthood.   He took some part in
looking after his father's interests in Norfolk during the next
three years; but the general picture of him at this time gave
small encouragement to those who had the family's welfare at
heart.

When Sir John Paston succeeded his father in 1466, the
litigation begun five years earlier showed no sign of ending; it
had indeed made very little headway in either direction.   For
the present, however, he was in the King's good grace, and
attended the Princess Margaret at her wedding to Charles of
Burgundy in the summer of 1468.   It was on the occasion of
this journey that he met Anne Hawte, a relation of the Wood-
villes, and was soon afterwards engaged to her.

Two events in 1469 shook the house of Paston.   First, Sir
John's sister Margery was clandestinely betrothed to his bailiff,
Richard Calle, and in spite of determined and cruel opposition

they were married in the early days of 1470. Calle remained in Paston's employ; but the family clung to their futile snobbery, and he was never acknowledged as one of its members. Both he and Margery were ignored in Margaret Paston's will. Meanwhile, however, the King had been taken prisoner and confined at Middleham. The last vestiges of law and order having disappeared, the Duke of Norfolk was able to enforce his claim to Caister by laying siege to the castle in August 1469. Sir John was in London, handling affairs with his usual inefficiency, though the attack had been expected for some time; and although the castle was bravely defended by his younger brother John, it was obliged to capitulate on 26th September following. Notwithstanding prolonged negotiations and the good offices of the Duchess, it was not recovered until after Norfolk's death in January 1476.

Sir John Paston fought on the Lancastrian side at Barnet in April 1471, and did not receive his pardon until January in the next year. The lawsuit had been terminated in his favour during the summer of 1470; but from then until his death in November 1479, he suffered from the chronic lack of money which afflicted even the largest landowners at that time. Nevertheless, his difficulties were aggravated by his own extravagance, against which his mother did all she could to warn him. He spent some time abroad on military service; when in England, he resided for the most part in London where he imagined his interests to lie and where he bungled most matters to which he put his hand. He broke off his engagement to Anne Hawte, fancied himself as a gallant *sans pareil*, but died a bachelor with one bastard child, a girl.

John Paston the youngest, who succeeded his brother in 1479, was more level-headed, more generous, more human, and a far more attractive personality than the departed knight. He had been educated in the household of John Mowbray, third Duke of Norfolk; but his superior refinement, which is reflected in some of the concluding letters, did not detract from the value of his service in helping Margaret with the administration of her husband's affairs. He cannot have been blind to his brother's miserable weakness, but he never failed him as a loyal friend and counsellor, as witness his defence of Caister in 1469. After months of wrangling, which nearly failed on account of her father's greed, he married Margery, daughter of Sir Thomas Brews, in 1477.

From 1479 onwards the letters become fewer; those that we possess breathe a new atmosphere, a faint air of elegance prophetic of a somewhat later age. Margaret Paston, whose character became more gentle, as her piety became more marked, in her declining years, died on 4th November 1484. John, who had been knighted after the battle of Stoke (16th June 1487), lost his first wife about 1495. He was married soon afterwards to Agnes, daughter of Nicholas Morley, Esq., of Glynde in Sussex, and died in the late summer of 1503. From him were descended the earls of Yarmouth.

Such, in broad outline, is the story with which the bulk of these Letters is concerned. The remainder are incidental thereto, or touch in some other way upon the lives, the interests, and the background of the Paston family. Footnotes supply more detailed information wherever this has seemed desirable.

II

Three facts in particular are likely to impress themselves upon the reader of these letters. First, there is what I may call the absence of rancour, whether at the political or personal level. The Pastons were Lancastrian in sympathy, but you will nowhere discover a trace of abuse; there is no libelling of the other side, no pretence, no suggestion of 'my party right or wrong.' They suffered much, not only indirectly, as did the whole of their class, through the disorders of civil war, but also from the intrigues and violence of individual enemies. Yelverton and Jenney, for example, as well as the dukes of Norfolk and Suffolk, did all they could to bring about their ruin. But here again you will meet no trace of personal recrimination. It is, in fact, remarkable how many of the bitterest antagonisms quickly turned, if not to friendship, at least to polite and rational intercourse. The reason for this is not at once apparent, but one cause suggests itself: the heavenly virtue of mutual respect, notwithstanding violent differences, arose in bygone ages from the roots of feudal society and had not yet been eradicated by the cynicism and amorality of a later age.

We must, on the other hand, confess that the evidence of these letters tends to show that the Pastons and others of their contemporaries were singularly blind to the more remote causes of their problems and their sufferings. At any rate, there is nothing to suggest that they stopped to consider causes, remedies, or probable results. They had, in fact, no sense of history. And this same narrowness of outlook—I bear in mind, of course, the 'local' character and uneven distribution of the letters—is reflected in their *apparent* indifference to events outside the strait confines of their world. There are references to English affairs in France and Flanders, but these are little more than odd pieces of gossip. It is worth while noticing that we have no reference to the invention of printing, which fell within this period. The capture of Constantinople by Mahomet II (1453) calls for no comment any more than does the arrival of Turkish advance-guards in the West (1471–80). The letters, as we have remarked, become less frequent after 1479, which may account for the fact that no writer mentions the taking of Granada and the discovery of America in 1492. It is not suggested that these omissions are convincing in the sense that they can be used to *prove* ignorance or indifference; our evidence is far too slender for that. But the omissions themselves are just worthy of remark, if only to emphasize the limited area of that bright-lit stage on which the Pastons move.

The third striking fact is this: notwithstanding attempts by many historians and imaginative writers to present the Christian faith as an outworn creed—or at least a medley of idle, and sometimes beastly, superstition—after, say, 1350, that faith was still very much alive. It was part and parcel of men's everyday existence. A great number of the Paston Letters are dated by reference to the ecclesiastical calendar, and there is scarcely one document from which the name of God is absent, whether by way of introduction or farewell. The generosity of the faithful towards their Church was unexhausted; such religious as we meet appear to have enjoyed the respect of those with whom they dealt; while the secular clergy, having regard to the less exacting standard of canonical discipline imposed by the Church upon her ministers at that time, do not appear in the horrid light with which modern authors have surrounded them.

The letters contain several references to pilgrimage and other devout practices, the sincerity of which there is no good reason to suspect. Nor is it without interest that the Duke of Norfolk, writing in August 1485, informs John Paston that Richard III delayed his march against the rebel Henry Tudor in order to celebrate the feast of the Assumption: 'the King wold hafe set forthe as uppon Monday but only for Howre Lady Day.' Christendom as a living unity had long since ceased to be, and with it much that was of value had passed away. But the Christian faith was still a force by which men lived and moved and had their being.

### III

The Paston muniments descended in the course of generations to William, second Earl of Yarmouth. After his death in 1732, some of these manuscripts came into the possession of Thomas Martin, Esq., of Palgrave, and were acquired in 1775 by John Fenn who published a two-volume annotated selection in 1787. For this service he was knighted on 23rd May of the same year by George III, to whom he presented the corresponding originals.

Having published another two volumes in 1789, Sir John Fenn died in 1794; but his nephew, Sergeant Frere, issued a fifth and final volume (prepared from his uncle's transcripts) in 1823. The manuscripts of vols. iii–v were not presented to the King; but by some almost inconceivable accident they, *together with the originals of vols. i and ii*, were lost. The most careful searches failed to reveal their whereabouts, and all hope of their recovery had been abandoned when the originals of vol. v, with some others not published by Fenn, came to light in 1865 at Dungate, Cambridgeshire, the home of Philip Frere. He sold them to the British Museum where they are contained in four volumes: Add. MSS. 27, 443–6.

In 1875 the originals of vols. iii and iv, together with ninety-five hitherto unpublished letters, were found at Roydon Hall near Diss. They were acquired by the British Museum in 1896, and occupy two volumes: Add. MSS. 34,888, 34,889. By some unknown and now undiscoverable means, the originals of vols. i and ii had been taken from the royal library and deposited at Orwell Park, where they were found in 1889. Other manuscripts of the Paston collection are in the following British Museum: Add. MSS.: 27,447–27,455; 33,957; 35,251. Besides these, there are a few in the Bodleian Library at Oxford and at Pembroke College, Cambridge. Gairdner, in his complete edition (1904), prints a number of documents from originals in the tower of Magdalen College, Oxford. These never formed part of the Paston correspondence, but their subject-matter is closely related to the fortunes of that family.

The present edition is based on that of Fenn; but I have added a number of letters and other papers from Gairdner's definitive edition (6 vols., 1904). These are indicated by the initials J. G. in brackets at the head of each. For permission to use them I am indebted to Messrs Chatto & Windus. Modern spelling and punctuation have been used throughout, except that a number of proper names and all obsolete words have been left as they are found in the manuscripts. The footnotes are mine, adapted in many cases from Fenn and Gairdner. At the end of each volume will be found a glossary of words and phrases to explain those terms the meaning of which is not apparent from the context. Each volume likewise contains an Index of Letters grouped under writers' names. A general Index of Names and Places concludes the second volume.

JOHN WARRINGTON.

1956.

# SELECT BIBLIOGRAPHY

EDITIONS. Sir J. Fenn, 5 vols., 1787–1823; edited in condensed form by A. Ramsay, 2 vols., 1840–1; J. Gairdner (with additions), 3 vols., 1872–5; reissued with further additions and corrections, 3 vols., 1896; 4 vols., 1900–1; 6 vols., 1904. The first volume of this last edition consists of an Introduction which must be considered the most authoritative work on the subject as a whole.

GENERAL. H. Bennett, *The Pastons and their England*, 1922; E. C. Robbins, *William Paston, Justice, 1378–1944*, 1932.

SKETCH-MAP OF EASTERN ENGLAND

# PEDIGREE OF THE FAMILY OF PASTON, OF NORFOLK

Clement Paston, of Paston, died 1419. = Beatrice, daughter of John de Somerton, died before 1419. Buried at Paston.

Buried at Paston.

William Paston, Esq., born 1378. Brought up to the law, and = Agnes, daughter and co-heiress of Sir Edmund Berry, of Harling-became a Judge of the Common Pleas. His will is dated 20th bury Hall, in Therfield, Herts, by Alice, daughter and heiress of Sir June 1443, and he died 13th August 1444, aged 66. He was Thomas Garbridge. Died 1479. Both she and Sir William are called the Good Judge. buried at Norwich Cathedral, in Our Lady's Chapel.

| | | | |
|---|---|---|---|
| John Paston, Esq., born 1420. Married before 1440, when he studied the law in the Inner Temple. He was one of the executors of the will of Sir John Fastolf, to which his cousin Hugh Fenn was supervisor. His estates were seized by Edward IV., and he was committed to the Fleet just before his death, which happened in London on 26th May 1466. He was buried very sumptuously at Bromholm Priory in Norfolk. = Margaret, daughter and heiress of John Mauteby, Esq., by Margaret, daughter of John Berney, Esq., of Reedham. Her will is dated 4th Feb. 1481, and proved 18th Dec. 1484. She was buried at Mauteby. | Edmund Paston, Esq., born 1425. His will is dated 21st Mar. 1448.<br><br>Walter Paston. | William Paston had disputes with his nephews concerning their estates, etc. | Clement Paston, born 1442. Was at London under the care of Master Grenefeld in 1457. | Elizabeth Paston, born about 1429. She lived with Lady Pole in 1457, and was alive in 1485. Married, first, Robert Poynings; second, Sir George Browne, Kt., of Beechworth Castle, in Surrey. |

| | | | | |
|---|---|---|---|---|
| Sir John Paston, Kt, born about 1440. He took possession of his father's estates by a warrant from Edward IV., dated 6th July 1466; was a brave soldier; performed many gallant actions in the French wars, and was the king's champion at Eltham. He died unmarried on 15th November 1479, 19 Edward IV, aged nearly forty years, and was buried in London. He left a natural daughter named Constance. | John Paston, Esq., appears = Margery, daughter to have been brought up in the family of the Duke of Norfolk; was a soldier, and engaged in the French wars. He attended the Princess Margaret to Bruges in 1468; was heir to his brother in 1479, and in 1485 High Sheriff of Norfolk. He was knighted, and made a knight banneret at the battle of Stoke by Henry VII in 1487, and died in 1503. | of Thomas Brews, of Stinton Hall, in Salle. She was married in 1477, and, dying in 1495, was buried in the White Friars in Norwich, where her husband was afterwards interred. | William Paston was at Eton in 1467. | Clement Paston. | Walter Paston took a degree, and died at Oxford in 1479. | Edmund Paston was in the garrison at Calais in 1473. He was twice married, and died about 1504. | Anne Paston, married Wm Yelverton, son of John, son of Sir William Yelverton, the judge. | Margery Paston, married Richard Calle. |

Sir William Paston, Kt., an eminent counsellor at law, born about 1479 or 1480, and died in 1554. === Bridget, daughter of Sir Henry Heydon, of Baconsthorpe.

Christopher Paston, born 1478, and probably died in his infancy.

Clement Paston, Esq., a great sea commander. He built Oxnead Hall, and, dying in 1597, was buried at Oxnead.

Erasmus Paston, died during his father's life, in 1538, and was buried at Paston. === Mary, daughter of Sir Thomas Windham, of Felbrigg, Kt., died in 1596, and was buried at Paston.

Sir William Paston, Kt., was born in 1528, died in 1610, aged 82, and was buried at North Walsham. He was heir to his uncle, Clement Paston. === Frances, daughter of Sir Thomas Clere, of Stokesby, Kt.

Christopher Paston, Esq., born in 1554. Married in 1577. Adjudged an idiot in 1611, 9 Jac. I, when the jury found that he had been so from about 1587. === Anne, daughter of Philip Audley Esq., of Palgrave, near Swaffham.

Sir Edmund Paston, Kt., born 1585. Died 1632, aged 48. Married 1603. Buried at Paston. === Catharine daughter of Sir Thomas Knevet, of Ashwelthorpe, Kt. She died in 1628, and lies buried at Paston.

Sir William Paston, Bart., an antiquary and collector, was High Sheriff of Norfolk in 1636, created a baronet in 1641, and, dying in 1662, was buried at Paston. === Catharine, daughter of Robert Bertie, Earl of Lindsey, died 1636, and is buried at Oxnead, where there is an elegant mural monument with her bust, etc.

Robert Paston, Earl of Yarmouth, etc., created Baron Paston in 1679, and Viscount Yarmouth, 1673, and Earl of Yarmouth in 1682, was buried at Oxnead. He was shot at in his coach in 1676; and, dying in 1682, was buried at Oxnead. === Rebecca, daughter of Sir Jasper Clayton, Kt, a citizen of London.

William Paston, Earl of Yarmouth, etc., encumbered his inheritance, and having survived all his male issue, died in 1732, when his titles became extinct, leaving his estates to be sold for the payment of his debts, etc. === First wife, Lady Charlotte Boyle, alias Fitzroy, a natural daughter of Charles II by Elizabeth Viscountess Shannon. She died in 1684. Second wife, Elizabeth, daughter of Dudley Lord North.

Charles Lord Paston, born 1673. Died unmarried.

William, born 1677. Died an infant.

William Lord Paston, 1682. Died unmarried.

Charlotte, born 1677. married Thos Hyrne, Esq., of Heverland.

Rebecca, married Sir John Holland, of Quidenham, Bart.

# INDEX OF LETTERS

*The references are to numbers preceding the letters.*

# CONTENTS

## VOLUME I

## VOLUME II

# HENRY VI (1430–1461)

## 1. William Paston to the Abbot of Cluny's Vicar [J. G.]

My right worthy and worshipful lord, I recommend me to you. And as forasmuch as I conceive verily that ye are Vicar-General in England of the worthy prelate, the Abbot of Cluny, and have his power in many great articles, and among other in profession of monks in England of the said Order. And in my country, but a mile [1] fro the place where I was born, is the poorhouse of Bromholm of the same Order, in which are divers virtuous young men, monks clad and unprofessed, that have abiden there about nine or ten year; and by longer delay of their profession many inconveniences are like to fall. And also the prior of . . . [2] hath resigned into your worthy hands by certain notable and reasonable causes, as it appeareth by an instrument, and a simple letter under the common seal of the said house of Bromholm, which the bearer of this hath ready to show you. Whereupon I pray you with all my heart, and as I ever may do you service, that it like to your grace to grant of your charity, by your worthy letters to the prior of Thetford in Norfolk, of the said Order of Cluny, authority and power as your minister and deputy to profess in due form the said monks of Bromholm unprofessed. And that it like you overmore to accept and admit the said resignation by your said authority and power, with the favour of your good lordship in comfort and consolation of your poor priests, the monks of the said house of Bromholm, and thereupon to grant your worthy letters, witnessing the same acceptation and admission of the said resignation, and all your said letters to deliver to my clerk, to whom I pray you to give faith and credence touching this matter, and to deliver it him in all the haste reasonable. And I am your man, and ever will be by the grace of God, which ever have you in His keeping. Written at Norwich the . . . of April.

Yours,

WILL. PASTON.

[*Circa* 1430]

---

[1] Nearer two modern statute miles.     [2] Missing in the original.

1

2.     JOHN GYNE TO JOHN[1] PASTON [J. G.]

*To the worthy and worshipful sir and my good master, John Paston,*
*of Trinity Hall in Cambridge.*

Right worthy and worshipful sir, and my good master, I commend me to you.   Like it you to wete that on the Sunday next after the Ascension of our Lord, in the highway between Cambridge and Becontree toward Newmarket, I found a purse with money therein.   The intent of this my simple letter is this, that it please to your good Mastership by way of charity, and of your gentleness, to wete if any of your knowledge or any other, such as you seemeth best in your discretion, have lost such a purse; and, the tokens thereof told, he shall have it again, what that ever he be, by the grace of our Lord, who ever have you in His blessed keeping.   Written at Snailwell the Monday next after the said Sunday.   By your poor servant,

JOHN GYNE.

[*Circa* 1435–6]


3.     AGNES PASTON TO WILLIAM PASTON

*To my worshipful husband, W. Paston,[1] be this letter taken.*

Dear husband, I recommend me to you, etc.   Blessed be God, I send you good tidings of the coming and the bringing home of the gentlewoman [2] that ye weten of from Reedham this same night, according to appointment that ye made there for yourself.

And as for the first acquaintance between John Paston [3] and the said gentlewoman, she made him gentle cheer in gentle wise, and said he was verily your son; and so I hope there shall need no great treaty betwixt them.

The parson of Stockton told me, if ye would buy her a gown, her mother would give thereto a goodly fur.   The gown needeth for to be had; and of colour it would be a goodly blue, or else a bright sanguine.

I pray you do buy for me two pipes [4] of gold.   Your stews do well.   The Holy Trinity have you in governance.

---

[1] Judge of the Common Pleas; born in 1378, died in 1444.
[2] Margaret, daughter and heiress of John Mauteby, of Mauteby in Norfolk, by Margaret, daughter of John Berney, of Reedham, Esq., and who, soon after the writing of this letter, became wife of John Paston.
[3] Eldest son of William and Agnes Paston, was born about 1420, and died in 1466.
[4] Gold thread on pipes or rolls, for needlework or embroidery, etc.

Written at Paston, in haste, the Wednesday next after *Deus qui errantibus*; [1] for default of a good secretary, etc.

Yours,

AGN. PASTON.[2]

[Before 1440]

## 4.   ROBERT REPPS TO JOHN[1] PASTON

*To my right reverend and right honourable master, John Paston, be this given.*

*Salvete*, etc. Tidings, the Duke of Orleans hath made his oath upon the Sacrament, and used it, never for to bear arms against England, in the presence of the King and all the lords, except my Lord of Gloucester; and in proving my said Lord of Gloucester agreed never to his deliverance, when the Mass began he took his barge, etc.

God give grace the said Lord of Orleans be true, for this same week shall he toward France.

Also Frenchmen and Picards a great number came to Arfleet,[3] for to have rescued it. And our lords with their small puissance manly beat them and put them to flight; and, blessed be Our Lord, have taken the said city of Arfleet, the which is a great jewel to all England and especially to our country.

Moreover, there is one come into England, a knight out of Spain, with a kerchief of pleasaunce [4] wrapped about his arm; the which knight will run a course with a sharp spear for his sovereign lady's sake, whom either Sir Richard Woodville [5] or Sir Christopher Talbot,[6] shall deliver, to the worship of England and of themselves by God's grace.

Furthermore, ye be remembered that an esquire of Suffolk called John Lyston recovered, in assize of novel disseisin, 700 marks in damages against Sir Robert Wingfield, etc. In avoiding of the payment of the said 700 marks, the said Sir Robert

---

[1] The words beginning the Collect on the third Sunday after Easter.

[2] Agnes, daughter and co-heiress of Sir Edmund Barry, or Berry, of Harlingbury Hall in Hertfordshire, by Alice, daughter and heiress of Sir Thomas Garbridge, Kt, and wife of William Paston. She died in 1479, and was buried beside her husband in the Lady Chapel at Norwich Cathedral.

[3] Harfleur, in Normandy.

[4] A scarf, or rich embroidered handkerchief, presented him by his lady, and which, in her honour, he wore tied upon his arm.

[5] Afterwards Earl Rivers, and father to Elizabeth, Queen of Edward IV. He was beheaded at Banbury in 1469.

[6] Third son of John, the famous Earl of Shrewsbury. He was slain at the battle of Northampton in July 1460, fighting for the House of Lancaster.

Wingfield subtlely hath outlawed the said John Lyston in Nottinghamshire, by the virtue of which outlawry all manner of chattel to the said John Lyston appertaining are accrued unto the King, etc. And anon as the said outlawry was certified, my Lord Treasurer [1] granted the said 700 marks to my Lord of Norfolk [2] for the arrears of his sowde whilst he was in Scotland. And according to this assignment aforesaid, tallies were delivered, etc. And my Lord of Norfolk hath released the same 700 marks to Sir Robert Wingfield.

And here is great heaving and shoving by my Lord of Suffolk [3] and all his council for to espy how this matter came about, etc. Sir, I beseech, recommend me unto my mistress your mother, to my mistress your wife, and to my mistress your sister, *et omnibus aliis quorum interest*, etc.

Sir, I pray you, with all mine heart, hold me excused that I write thus homely and briefly unto you, for truly convenable space sufficed me not.

No more at this time, but the Trinity have you in protection, etc.; and when your leisure is, resort again unto your college, the Inner Temple, for there be many which sore desire your presence—Welles and others, etc.

Written on the feast of All Saints, between Mass and matins *calamo festinante*, etc.

Your,

ROB. REPPS.

[1st November 1440]

5. MARGARET PASTON TO JOHN[(1)] PASTON

*To my worshipful husband, John Paston, abiding at Peterhouse, in Cambridge.*

Right reverend and worshipful husband, I recommend me to you with all my simple heart, and pray you to wete that there came up eleven hundred Flemings at Waxham, whereof were taken and killed and dronchyn eight hundred; an' they had not have been, ye should have been at home this Whitsuntide, and I suppose that ye should be at home ere aught long be.

I thank you heartily for my letter, for I had none of you since

[1] Ralph, Lord Cromwell.
[2] John Mowbray, third Duke of Norfolk. He succeeded his father in 1432, and died in 1461.
[3] William de la Pole, Earl of Suffolk. He was afterwards Marquis (1444) and Duke (1448) of Suffolk; beheaded at sea in 1450. (*See* No. 35, footnote 1, page 38, and No. 36, page 40.)

I spoke with you last of for the matter of John Mariot; the quest passed not off that day, for my Lord of Norfolk was in town for Wetherby's [1] matter, wherefore he would not let it pass off, for further of I know Finch nor Bylbys maketh no purveyance for his good.

No more I write to you at this time, but the Holy Trinity have you in keeping. Written at Norwich, on Trinity Sunday.

Your,

MARGARET PASTON.

[After 1440]

6.     MARGARET PASTON TO JOHN[(1)] PASTON

*To my right worshipful husband, John Paston, dwelling in the Inner Temple at London, in haste.*

Right worshipful husband, I recommend me to you, desiring heartily to hear of your welfare, thanking God of your amending of the great disease that ye have had. And I thank you for the letter that ye sent me, for by my troth my mother and I were nought in heart's ease from the time that we wist of your sickness, till we wist verily of your amending.

My mother behested another image of wax of the weight of you, to our Lady of Walsingham, and she sent four nobles to the four orders of friars at Norwich to pray for you, and I have behested to go on pilgrimage to Walsingham and to St Leonard's [2] for you. By my troth, I had never so heavy a season as I had from the time that I wist of your sickness till I wist of your amending; and yet my heart is in no great ease, nor nought shall be till I wete that ye be very hale. Your father [3] and mine [4] was this day se'nnight at Beccles, for a matter of the Prior of Bromholm, and he lay at Gelderstone that night, and was there till it was nine of the clock and the other day. And I sent thither for a gown, and my mother said that I should have then, till I had been there anon, and so they could none get.

My father Garneys [5] sent me word that he should be here the next week and my eme also, and play them here with their hawks, and they should have me home with them; and so God

---

[1] Mayor of Norwich, 1432–3.
[2] The Church of the priory of St Leonard at Norwich.
[3] William Paston, the Judge.
[4] Whenever Margaret refers in these letters to her father or her mother she is always speaking of her husband's parents.
[5] Probably her godfather.

help me, I shall excuse me of my going thither if I may, for I
suppose that I shall readilier have tidings from you here than
I should have there.   I shall send my mother a token that she
took me, for I suppose that the time is come that I should send
it her, if I keep the behest that I have made; I suppose I have
told you what it was.   I pray you heartily that ye will vouchsafe
to send me a letter as hastily as ye may, if writing be none
dis-ease to you, and that ye will vouchsafe to send me word how
your sore doth.   If I might have had my will, I should have
seen you ere this time; I would ye were at home (if it were your
ease, and your sore might be as well looked to here as it is there
ye be now) lever than a gown, though it were of scarlet.   I pray
you, if your sore be whole and so that ye may endure to ride
when my father come to London, that ye will ask leave and come
home when the horse should be sent home again; for I hope ye
shall be kept as tenderly here as ye be at London.   I may none
leisure have to do write half a quarter so much as I should say
to you if I might speak with you.   I shall send you another
letter as hastily as I may.   I thank you that ye would vouchsafe
to remember my girdle, and that ye would write to me at the
time, for I suppose that writing was none ease to you.   Almighty
God have you in His keeping, and send you health.   Written
at Oxnead, in right great haste, on St Michael's even.

Yours,

M. PASTON.

[28th September 1443]

My mother greet you well, and sendeth you God's blessing
and hers; and she prayeth you, and I pray you also, that ye be
well dieted of meat and drink, for that is the greatest help that
ye may have now to your healthward.   Your son [1] fareth well,
blessed be God!


7.        ANONYMOUS: FRIAR HAWTEYN AND
             OXNEAD MANOR [J. G.]

This day at ten of the clock Edmund Paston and the parson of
Oxnead went out of the manor [2] down to the Wantown Gap, for
they heard tidings that the friar was coming; and with the said

---

[1] John Paston, his eldest son.
[2] The manor of Oxnead was purchased by William Paston, the Judge,
from William Clopton of Long Melford.   After his death, the ownership
was disputed by an ex-Carmelite friar, John Hawteyn; but about 1451 he
with others released his right to Agnes Paston.

friar came John Cates and one Walter Herman of Wheyth, and William Yemmys of Burgh, the friar's man. And Edmund Paston said to John Cates: 'Welcome!' and he asked them what their cause was in coming. The friar said he came for to speak with the good lady,[1] and Edmund said that he should speak with her. At this time she was so occupied he might not speak with her. And he said that he should assay, and he came riding from the Wantown Gap to the great gate; and there he 'lighted and knocked on the gate, and we followed as yarn as we might. And there was within John Jaallere and John Edmunds, and asked the friar what he would; and he said that he would come in for to speak with the good lady of the house. And they said nay, he should not come in. And then came on Edmund Paston and the parson, and asked him what was cause of his coming at this time. And he said for to enter in the manor of Oxnead, the which his father was possessed of, and his ancestors from King Edward the Third unto Colby's time, and that he had found a tally thereof in the King's books. And then Edmund Paston answered him and said that it were best declaring of his evidence in Westminster Hall, and he said again so he should when he might. And he said to them that came with him: 'Sirs, I charge you bear record how that I am kept out with strong hand and may not take possession.' And even forthwith he pressed to the gate-ward to have laid hand on the gate. And then the said Edmund put him from the gate and said: 'Ne were for reverence for thy lord and mine, an' thou layest any hand on the gate I shall see thy heart bleed or thou mine.' And then the said friar said scornfully that he might thank his master; and then the said Edmund said that he might say his lord right well. And then he stooped down and took up earth and delivered to his man, saying to them that came with him: 'I charge you all of the King's behalf ye bear record that I take here possession of mine inheritance.' And Edmund said that this taking of possession skilled nought. And then the friar said that since he might not have it now, he should come again another time. Edmund is ridden forth to Heydon. It was told us this afternoon that there were three men come from Skeyton and met with the friar in the field and spoke with him a good while, and then riding the same way that they came.

[Between 1443 and 1439]

---

[1] Agnes Paston.

## 8.        JAMES GRESHAM[1] TO WILLIAM PASTON

*To my right worthy and worshipful lord, William Paston, Justice,
in haste.*

Please it your good lordship to wete that the chief justice of the
King's Bench[2] recommendeth him to you, and is right sorry of
the matter that is cause of your none coming hither; but he will
do all that he can or may for you.   He hath had a sciatica that
hath letted him a great while to ride, and dare not yet come on
none horse's back, and therefore he hath spoke to the lords of
the Council and informed them of your sickness and his also,
that he may not ride at these next assizes to East Grinstead; and
though those assizes discontinue *pur noun venu dez Justicez*, he
hopeth to be excused, and ye also.   And as for the remnant of
the assizes, he shall purvey to be there by water.   And Almighty
Jesu make you hale and strong.
    Written right simply, the Wednesday next tofore the Feast of
the Purification of our Lady, at London.

By your most simple servant,

JAMES GRESHAM.

[29th January 1444]

## 9.  THE DUCHESS OF NORFOLK TO JOHN[(1)] PASTON

*To our right trusty and heartily well-beloved John Paston, Esquire.*

### KATHERINE, DUCHESS OF NORFOLK[3]

Right trusty and entirely well-beloved, we greet you well,
heartily as we can.   And forasmuch as we purpose with grace
of Jesu to be at London within brief time, we pray you that your
place there may be ready for us, for we will send our stuff
thither tofore our coming.   And such agreement as we took
with you for the same, we shall duly perform it with the might
of Jesu, who have you in His blessed keeping.
    Written at Epworth, the 2nd day of October.

[?after 1444]

---

[1] He was clerk to Judge Paston, and continued in the service of John[(1)].
[2] Sir John Fortescue.
[3] Katherine, Duchess of Norfolk, widow of John Mowbray, second Duke
of Norfolk, who died in 1432.

10.     JOHN HAWTEYN TO THE
        ARCHBISHOP OF CANTERBURY

*To the most reverend Father in God, the Archbishop of Canterbury,
Chancellor of England.*[1]

Beseecheth meekly your gracious Lordship your own servant
and orator John Hawteyn, chaplain, that whereas he hath divers
suits and actions in law to be sued against A[gnes] that was the
wife of W. Paston, of the manor of Oxnead, in the county of
Norfolk; and forasmuch as your said beseecher can get no
counsel of men of court to be with him in the said matters,
because that the said W. P. was one of the King's justices, and
John P[aston], son and heir to the said W. P., is also a man of
court; that it please your good Lordship to assign and most
strictly to command John Heydon, Thomas Lyttelton, and John
Olston to be of counsel with your said beseecher in the said
matters, and other that he hath to do against the said Agnes and
other, and your said beseecher shall content them well for their
labour, and that this be done in the reverence of God and way of
charity.

                        JOHN HAWTEYN, *Chaplain.*

[1444–7]


11.     AGNES PASTON TO EDMUND PASTON

*To Edmund Paston, of Clifford's Inn, in London, be this letter take.*

To mine well-beloved son, I greet you well, and advise you to
think once of the day of your father's [2] counsel to learn the law,
for he said many times that whosoever should dwell at Paston
should have need to con defend himself.

The vicar of Paston [3] and your father, in Lent last was, were
thorough and accorded, and doles [4] set how broad the way should
be; and now he hath pulled up the doles, and saith he will make
a ditch from the corner of his wall right over the way to the new
ditch of the great close. And there is a man in Trunch, hight
Palmer, too, that had of your father certain lands in Trunch

[1] John Stafford, Archbishop of Canterbury, and a cardinal, was Lord
Chancellor from 1443 to 1447.
[2] William Paston, the Judge, lately deceased.
[3] John Partrick, of Swathfield, was vicar of Paston from 1442 to 1447.
[4] On 6th July 1443, William Paston, the Judge, had licence to enclose
part of the highway at Paston (Patent Roll, 21 Henry VI, p. 1, m. 10).   After
his death, exception was taken to the proposal, and the dispute is referred to
again in Nos. 52–4, 57, pages 57–8, 62.

over seven years or eight years ago, for corn, and truly hath paid all the years; and now he hath suffered the corn to be withset for eight shillings of rent to Gimmingham, which your father paid never.    Geoffrey asked Palmer why the rent was not asked in mine husband's time, and Palmer said, for he was a great man, and a wise man of the law, and that was the cause men would not ask him the rent.

I send you the names of the men that cast down the pits, that was Genney's Close, written in a bill closed in this letter.

I send you not this letter to make you weary of Paston, for I live in hope; and ye will learn that they shall be made weary of their work, for in good faith I dare well say it was your father's last will to have done right well to that place, and that can I show of good proof, though men would say nay.    God make you right a good man, and I send God's blessing and mine.    Written in haste at Norwich, the Thursday after Candlemas-day.

Wete of your brother John how many joists will serve the parlour and the chapel at Paston, and what length they must be, and what breadth and thickness they must be; for your father's will was, as I ween verily, that they should be nine inches one way and seven another way.    And purvey therefore that they may be squared there and sent hither, for here can none such be had in this country.    And say to your brother John, it were well done to think on Stansted church;[1] and I pray you to send me tidings from beyond sea,[2] for here they are afraid to tell such as be reported.

By your mother,

AGNES PASTON.

[4th February 1445]

## 12.   SIR ROGER CHAMBERLAIN TO AGNES PASTON

*To my right worshipful cousin, Agnes Paston.*

Right worshipful cousin, I commend me to you.    And as for the matter that ye sent to me for, touching the manor called Walshams, in Walsham, the truth is, your husband sold it to my mother upon condition that she should never sell it but to your sons John or William.    And for the surety of the said condition, your said husband, as I conceive, did the said manor be charged with a greaty annuity upon the same condition, ere the time that my said mother took estate; of the which I suppose ye shall find

---

[1] Stanstead Church in Suffolk.   Dame Agnes had possessions in that parish.

[2] These tidings relate to the English surrender of Maine, truces, etc., on the King's marriage, which had taken place in November 1444.

sufficient evidence, if ye search your evidences therefor. And I beseech Almighty God keep you.

Written at Gedding, the 15th day of September.

Your cousin,

SIR ROGER CHAMBERLAIN.

[After 1444]

## 13. THE DUKE OF BUCKINGHAM TO VISCOUNT BEAUMONT

*To the right worshipful, and with all mine heart right entirely beloved brother, the Viscount Beaumont.*[1]

Right worshipful, and with all mine heart right entirely beloved brother, I recommend me to you, thanking right heartily your good brotherhood for your good and gentle letters, the which it hath liked you to send unto me now late; and like it you to know I perceive by the tenor of the said letter, your good desire of certain debt that I owe unto you.

In good faith, brother, it is so with me at this time that I have but easy stuff of money within me, for so much as the season of the year is not yet grown; so that I may not please your said good brotherhood, as God knoweth my will and intent were to do, an' I had it.

Nevertheless, an' it like you, I send you by my son Stafford an obligation, whereof of late time I have received part of the debt therein comprised; the residue of which I pray you to receive by the said obligation, and that I may have an acquittance thereof, and to give credence unto my said son in such things as he shall say unto your good brotherhood on my behalf.

Right worshipful, and with all mine heart right entirely beloved brother, I beseech the Blessed Trinity preserve you in honour and prosperity.

Written at my Castle of Maxtock, the 17th day of March.

Your true and faithful brother,

H. BUCKINGHAM.[2]

[1442–55]

---

[1] John, first Viscount Beaumont (created February 1440), was killed at the battle of Northampton, 1460, fighting for the House of Lancaster.

[2] Humphrey Stafford, Earl of Stafford, etc., was created Duke of Buckingham in 1441. His mother was Anne, daughter and heiress of Thomas of Woodstock, youngest son to Edward III. Buckingham was killed in 1460 at the battle of Northampton where he jointly commanded with the Duke of Somerset. His son Stafford, mentioned in this letter, was most probably Humphrey, Earl of Stafford, who died in 1455 of wounds received at the first battle of St Albans.

### 14. WILLIAM YELVERTON TO JOHN[1] PASTON

*To my right worshipful cousin, John Paston, Esquire.*

Right worshipful cousin, I recommend me to you, thanking you as heartily as I can for myself, etc., and specially for that ye do so much for Our Lady's House of Walsingham, which I trust verily ye do the rather for the great love that ye deem I have thereto. For truly if I be drawn to any worship or welfare, and discharge of mine enemies' danger, I ascribe it unto Our Lady.

Praying you, therefore, that ye will be as friendly to Our Lady's House as I wot well ye have always been, and in especial now, that I might have of you the report certainly by your letter of that that Naunton your cousin informed you, and told you by mouth of all matters touching Our Lady's house of Walsingham. For methinketh by that I have heard by Our Lady's priest of Walsingham, if I understood well that matter, that it should be much to the good speed of the matter; and doubt you not Our Lady shall quit it you, and her poor prior hereafter as he may, etc.

Praying you also, cousin, and advising for the ease of us both, and of our friends, and of many other, that ye be at London betimes this term. And if we speed well now, all well all this year after; for I know verily there was never made a greater labour than shall be made now, and therefore I pray to Our Lady help us, and her blessed Son, which have you in His holy keeping.

Written at your poor place of Bayfield, on St Francis's day, in haste.

Your cousin,

WILLIAM YELVERTON, *Justice*.[1]

[4th October 1444–60]

### 15. JAMES GRESHAM TO JOHN[1] PASTON [J. G.]

*To my right worshipful master, John Paston.*

Worthy and worshipful sir, and my right good master, I recommend me to you and do you wete that this night, at supper, I was with my mistress your wife, at my mistress Clere's. And, blessed be God, they fare well and hope that ye shall send them good tiding of your matter when ye know the certainty thereof,

---

[1] In 1440 William Yelverton, son of John Yelverton, was appointed king's serjeant, and in 1444 a justice of the King's Bench. In 1460 he was created a Knight of the Bath. This letter, therefore, was most probably written before 1460, otherwise he would have signed himself knight as well as justice.

etc. And my mistress your mother came thither, and fareth well, and sendeth you God's blessing and hers. And she bade me write to you that she hath very knowledge by a true and trusty man, whose name she shall tell you by mouth at your next meeting, that there was purposed a great meny of a wonder gathering of shipmen about Conorhithe for to have come to Oxnead, and put me out there in a worse wise than ye were put out at Gresham.[1] And this was purposed for to have been at Oxnead and a-rifled and put in the priest [2] there; but this purpose held not, for they were countermanded, by what means I cannot know yet. And it is done her to wete that they be purposed to be at Oxnead about mid-Lent; and I am promitted that I shall have two days' warning by a good friend. And therefore she prayeth you that ye espy busily if the priest come into their country or not. For if aught shall be done, I trow the friar will be there at doing. And if ye can espy that he come hither, send my mistress word as hastily as ye may, and of your advice and of all other things as ye seem, etc. And God have you in His keeping. Written at nine on the clock at even the Monday next tofore Saint Gregory, in haste.

My brother Beck and his fellowship shall tell you more by mouth than I can tell you now. Your servant,

J. GRESHAM.

[11th March 1448]

16.      MARGARET PASTON TO JOHN[(1)] PASTON

*To my right worshipful husband, John Paston, be this letter delivered in haste.*

Right worshipful husband, I recommend me to you, desiring heartily to hear of your welfare; praying you to wete that I was with my Lady Morley [3] on the Saturday next after that ye departed from hence, and told her what answer that ye had of John Butt. And she took it right strangely, and said that she had told you and showed you enough, whereby ye might have knowledge that the relief ought to be paid to her; and she said she wist well that ye delay it forth that she should not have that longeth to her right. And she told me how it was paid in

---

[1] See No. 31, page 31.
[2] Friar John Hawteyn.
[3] Isabel, daughter of Michael de la Pole, Earl of Suffolk, and widow of Thomas, Lord Morley, who died in 1435.

Thomas Chambers's time, when her daughter Hastings [1] was wedded; and she said, since that ye will make none end with her, she will sue therefore as law will.

I conceived by her that she had counsel to labour against you therein within right short time. And then I prayed her that she would vouchsafe not to labour against you in this matter till ye come home; and she said nay by her faith, she would no more days give you therein. She said she had set you so many days to accord with her, and ye had broke them, that she was right weary thereof; and she said she was but a woman, she must do by her counsel, and her counsel had advised her, so she said she will do. Then I prayed her again that she would tarry till ye come home, and I said I trusted verily that ye would do when ye came home as it longeth to you to do; and if ye might have very knowledge that she ought of right for to have it, I said I wist well that ye would pay it with right good will, and told her that ye had searched to have found writing thereof, and ye could none find in none wise. And she said she wist well there was writing thereof enough, and she hath writing thereof how Sir Robert of Mauteby, and Sir John, and my grandsire, and divers other of my ancestors paid it, and said never nay thereto. And in no wise I could not get no grant of her to cease till ye come home; and she bade me that I should do an errand to my mother, and when I came home I did mine errand to her. And she asked me if I had spoken to my Lady of this foresaid matter, and I told her how I had done, and what answer I had; and she said she should go to my Lady Morley's on the next day, and she should speak to her thereof, and essay to get grant of her to cease of the foresaid matter till that ye come home. And truly my mother did her devoir right faithfully therein, as my cousin Clere [2] shall tell you when that he speaketh with you; and she got grant of my said lady that there should nought be done against you therein, and ye would accord with her and do as ye ought to do, betwixt this time and Trinity Sunday.

Laurence Reed of Mauteby recommendeth him to you, and prayeth you that ye will vouchsafe to let him buy of you the farm barley that ye should have of him, and if ye will let him have it to a reasonable price, he will have it with right good will. And he prayeth you, if ye will that he have it, that ye will vouchsafe to send him word at what price he should have the comb as hastily as ye may, and else he must be purveyed in other place.

As touching other tidings, I suppose John Damme [3] shall

---

[1] Anne, wife of John Hastings.

[2] William, son of Robert Clere of Ormesby.

[3] Friend and adviser of John Paston; elected M.P. for Norwich, October 1450.

send you word in a letter. As it is told me verily, Heydon [1]
shall not come at London this term.

It is said in this country that Daniel [2] is out of the King's
good grace, and he shall down, and all his men, and all that be
his well willers. There shall no man be so hardy to do neither
say against my Lord of Suffolk, nor none that longeth to him;
and all that have done and said against him, they shall sore
repent them. Katharine Walsham shall be wedded on the
Monday next after Trinity Sunday, as it is told me, to the gallant
with the great chain.[3] And there is purveyed for her much good
array of gowns, girdles, and attires, and much other good array;
and he hath purchased a great purchase of five marks by the
year to give her to her jointure.

I am afraid that John of Sparham is so schitel witted, that he
will set his goods to mortgage to Heydon, or to some other of
your good friends, but-if I can hold him in the better, ere ye
come home. He hath been arrested since that ye went, and
hath had much sorrow at the suit of Master John Stokes of
London for ten marks that Sparham owed to him. And in good
faith, he hath had so much sorrow and heaviness that he wist
not what he might do. I feel him so disposed that he would
have sold and have set to mortgage all that he hath, he had not
rowth to whom, so that he might have had money to have
holpen himself with. And I entreated him so that I suppose he
will neither sell nor set to mortgage neither cattle nor other
goods of his, till he speak with you. He supposeth that all that
is done to him is at the request of the parson of Sparham and
Gnateshale. I suppose it is alms to comfort him, for in good
faith he is right heavy, and his wife also. He is not now under
arrest, he hath paid his fees, and goeth at large; he was arrested
at Sparham, of one of Gnateshale's men.

Hodge Feke told me that Sym Shepherd is still with Willy,[4]
and if ye will I shall purvey that he shall be brought home ere
ye come home. It is told me that he that kept your sheep was
outlawed on Monday at the suit of Sir Thomas Tuddenham, and
if it be so, ye are not like to keep him long. And as touching
that that ye bade me speak for to Bacton, he saith he is well
advised that she said she would never have to do withal, nor
he cannot pick that she hath none right to have it, and he will
say like as he hath heard her say; and if she speak to him thereof,
he will rather hold with you than with her. I pray you that ye

---

[1] John Heydon, a lawyer and Recorder of Norwich.
[2] Thomas Daniel of Castle Rising, Norfolk.
[3] Presumably a chain of gold worn round the neck, apparently in this case
of abnormal size.
[4] William Paston, son of the Judge and Margaret's brother-in-law.

will vouchsafe to send me word how ye speed in your matter touching Gresham, and how Daniel is in grace. Harry Goneld hath brought to me 40*s.* of Gresham since ye went, and he saith I shall have more ere Whitsuntide if he may pick it up.

I suppose James Gresham have told you of other things that I have sped since ye went hence. If I hear any strange tidings in this country, I shall send you word. I pray you that I may be recommended to my lord Daniel.

The Holy Trinity have you in His keeping, and send you health and good speed in all your matters touching your right. Written at Norwich, on the Wednesday next after that ye parted hence.

Yours,

MARGARET PASTON.

[April 1448]

## 17.　JOHN NORTHWOOD TO VISCOUNT BEAUMONT

*To my worshipful and reverend Lord John, Viscount Beaumont.*

Right worshipful, and my reverend and most special Lord, I recommend me unto your good grace in the most humble and lowly wise that I can or may, desiring to hear of your prosperity and welfare, as to my most singular joy and special comfort.

And if it please your Highness, as touching the sudden adventure that fell lately at Coventry, please it your Lordship to hear that, on Corpus Christi[1] even last passed, between eight and nine of the clock at afternoon, Sir Humphrey Stafford[2] had brought my master, Sir James of Ormond,[3] toward his inn from my Lady of Shrewsbury,[4] and returned from him towards his inn, he met with Sir Robert Harcourt[5] coming from his mother's towards his inn, and passed Sir Humphrey; and Richard his son came somewhat behind, and when they met together they fell in hands together, and Sir Robert smote him a great stroke on the head with his sword, and Richard with his dagger hastily went toward him. And as he stumbled, one of Harcourt's men smote him in the back with a knife; men wot not who it was readily. His father heard noise and rode toward

---

[1] The Thursday after Trinity Sunday.

[2] He was a collateral branch of the family of the Duke of Buckingham; and in June 1450 commanded a detachment of the royal army sent out against the rebel Jack Cade: his party fell into an ambush, and he was killed.

[3] Probably Sir James Butler, first Earl of Ormond; created Earl of Wiltshire in 1449.

[4] Wife of John Talbot, the famous Earl of Shrewsbury.

[5] A Knight of the Garter, he was murdered by the Staffords in November 1470.

them, and his men ran before him thitherward; and in the going down off his horse, one, he wot not who, behind him, smote him on the head with an edged tool (men know not, with us, with what weapon), that he fell down, and his son fell down before him as good as dead. And all this was done, as men say, in a Paternoster while.

And forthwith Sir Humphrey Stafford's men followed after, and slew two men of Harcourt's, one Swinnerton and Bradshaw, and more be hurt; some be gone, and some be in prison in the jail at Coventry.

And before the coroner of Coventry, upon the sight of the bodies, there be indicated as principals for the death of Richard Stafford, Sir Robert Harcourt and the two men that be dead. And for the two men of Harcourt's that be dead, there be indicted two men of Sir Humphrey's as principals. And as yet there hath been nothing found before the justice of the peace of Coventry of this riot, because the sheriff of Warwickshire [1] is dead, and they may not sit unto the time there be a new sheriff. And all this mischief fell because of an old debate that was between them for taking of a distress, as it is told.

And Almighty Jesu preserve your high estate, my special Lord, and send you long life and good health.

Written at Coventry on Tuesday next after Corpus Christi day, etc.

By your own poor servant,

JOHN NORTHWOOD.

[28th May 1448]

## 18. LORD MOLEYNS TO THE BISHOP OF WINCHESTER

*To the worshipful Father in God, and my right good Lord, the Bishop of Winchester.* [2]

Worshipful father in God, and my right good lord, as heartily as I can I recommend me to your good Lordship; to the which please it to wete that I have received your letter, by the which I understand the daily suit to your Lordship as of Paston, as for the matter betwixt him and me, wherein also I feel that he is willed that communication and treaty should be had betwixt his counsel and mine, now at midsummer. To the which, my Lord, I am at the reverence of your Lordship well agreed, and have sent to my counsel at London, after the seeing of this your last letter, as for the treaty betwixt him and me, and that they should give full attendance to the end of the matter between the said Paston and me, as though I were present with them.

[1] Thomas Porter.      [2] William Waynflete.

And, my Lord, it were too great a thing, an' it lay in my power, but I would do at the reverence of your Lordship, unless that it should hurt me too greatly; which I wot well your Lordship would never desire.

And God for His mercy have you, right worshipful father in God, and my right good Lord, in His blessed keeping.

Written with mine own chancery hand in haste, the 13th day of June, at Teffont.

Very heartily, your

MOLEYNS.

[1448]

19. JAMES GLOYS[1] TO JOHN[(1)] PASTON [J. G.]

*To my right worshipful master John Paston be this delivered in haste.*

Right reverend and worshipful sir, I recommend me to you, desiring to hear of your welfare, the which gracious God continually preserve and keep to your ghostly health and bodily welfare; praying you to wete that as for the broke silver that my mistress weened for to have sent you when she did write her letter, there is none in your forcer; she supposed that she left it at Norwich in your coffer, whereof ye have the key. Also, my mistress your mother greets you well, and prays you to send her word how she shall do with Edward Whode of Paston; for she did seize his corn on the land the last harvest, and he led it away after that it was seized, without licence and leave of her or any of her officers. Item, my mistress your sister [2] recommends her heartily to you, and prays you that ye would vouchsafe to speak to my master Edmund and pray him if that he hath both her gear that she sent to him for, that he would send it her home; in case that he have not bought it, that he would buy it and send it her in all haste that he may goodly. Furthermore, if it please you to hear of my master Berney, he was at Gresham with my mistress on the Tuesday next after Hallowmas day, the same day that we distrained James Rokkysson; and I had met a little afore with Partrich, and he threatened me and said that we should not long keep the distress, and therefore my mistress did us do on our jacks and our saletts.[3] My master Berney came in, and the parson of Oxnead with him, and saw us in our jacks, and

---

[1] A cleric in Paston's employ.
[2] Elizabeth Paston.
[3] The jack, or jacket, was a protective garment made of linen stuffed with cotton, wool, or hair, quilted and covered with leather. The salett was a light helmet.

he waxed as pale as any herd, and would right fain have been thence; so my mistress did him dine. And while they were at dinner, Harry Collis told my mistress openly among us all that the same time that Partrich entered again upon you, his master was at Cawston to-you-ward; and there it was told him that Partrich had put you out and all your men, and that ye and my mistress were riding again to Norwich, and all your household, and that caused him that he came no farther that time; and my master Berney confirmed that it was so. When they had eaten, he had much haste to have be thence, so my mistress desired and prayed him that he would come again ere aught long; and so with much praying he behest her if he might. And Harry Collis stood therebeside and said to my fellowship: 'What should my master do here?' quoth he. 'Let your master send after his kinsmen at Mauteby, for they have nought that they maun lose.' And so they rode their way. And, within a se'nnight after, my master Berney sent Davy to my mistress, and prayed my mistress that she would hold his master excused. For he had hurt his own horse that he rode upon, and he did Davy saddle another horse; and he stood by and made water while he saddled him, and as Davy should have girt the horse he slinked behind and took his master on the hip such a stroke that never man may trust him after, and brake his hip. And he had sent Harry Collis to Norwich for medicines, so he must ride home the same night; for his master had no man at home. So my mistress was right sorry, and weened that it had been truth, but I know well that it was not so. It happened that I rode the next day to Norwich, and I rode in to my mistress your mother, and she did ask me after my master Berney, and I told her how he was hurt. And she asked the parson of Oxnead if he were hurt, and he said nay; for Davy lay with him the same night afore and told him that he was hale and merry, and prayed him that he would be with him the Sunday next after; and so Davy lay the same night after that he had told my mistress the tale with the parson of Oxnead. I beseech you of your good mastership that ye would not do wreyth this letter; for, an' my mistress knew that I sent you such a letter, I were never able to look upon her nor to abide in her eyesight. My mistress your mother hath sent you two letters; she hath endorsed them to my master Edmund, and she would wete if ye had them or not. The Holy Trinity have you in keeping. Written at Norwich on St Clement's eve. In haste. Your servant,

JAMES GLOYS.

[3rd December 1448]

## 20.    MARGARET PASTON TO JOHN[1] PASTON

*To my right worshipful husband, John Paston, be this delivered in haste.*

Right worshipful husband, I recommend me to you, praying you to wete that I have received your letter this day that ye sent me by Yelverton's man. As for your signet, I found it upon your board the same day that ye went hence, and I send it you by Richard Heberd, bringer hereof. As for your errands that ye wrote to me for, Richard Charles is out about your errands about Gresham, and for his own matters also, and I suppose he cometh not home till it be Tuesday or Wednesday next coming; and as soon as he cometh home he shall go about your errands that ye wrote to me for.

I sent you a letter written on Tuesday last past, which, as I suppose, Roger Ormsby delivered you. I took it to Alson Partridge; she rode with Clippesby's wife to London.

I pray you if ye have another son that ye will let it be named Harry, in remembrance of your brother Harry.[1] Also I pray you that ye would send me dates and cinnamon as hastily as ye may. I have spoken with John Damme of that ye bade me say to him to say to Thomas Note, and he says he was well paid that ye said, and thought therein as ye did. Nevertheless, I bade him that he should say to the said Thomas therein, as it were of himself, without your advice or any other's; and he said he should so, and that it should be purveyed for this next week at the furthest. The Blessed Trinity have you in His keeping.

Written at Norwich in haste the Friday next before Candlemas day.

By your groaning wife,<br>
MARGARET PASTON.

[31st January ?1449]


## 21.       ROBERT PRIOR OF BROMHOLM TO JOHN[1] PASTON

*To my sovereign John Paston.*

I recommend me heartily, thanking you for the tidings and the good advice that ye sent me by the parson of Thorpe;[2] letting you weten that the bishop of the other side of the sea[3] sent late

---

[1] There is no other record of a Harry Paston.
[2] Robert Rogers.
[3] Probably Walter Lyhart of Norwich, who had been sent to Savoy by Henry VI to persuade the anti-pope Felix V to renounce his claim in favour of Nicholas V.

to me a man, the which would abide upon my leisure, for to have had me over with him to the said bishop, and so forth to the court.[1] So the said man and I are appointed that he shall come again on purpose from the bishop, to be my guide over the sea; and so I purpose me fully forth anon after this Easter. I make me every day fully ready as privily as I can, beseeching you, as I trust on you, and as I am your true beadsman, to labour for me here that I might have a writ of passage directed unto such men as you think that should best give me my charge.

The best taking of shipping is at Yarmouth or Kyrley, or some other place in Norfolk side. I shall have favour enough with their searchers; but all my good speed and all my weal lieth in you here, for thereon I trust fully.

Some counsel me to have a letter of exchange, though it were but of 40s. or less; but I commit all my best in this matter to your wisdom, and what at ever ye pay in this matter, I shall truly at our meeting repay again to you. But for God's love purvey for my speed here, for else I lose all my purveyance, and thereto I should jape the bishop's man and cause him to come into England and lose all his labour. For God's love send me down this writ, or else bring it with you, that I might have from you a letter of tidings and comfort; for I had never very need of your labour till now, but my heart hangeth in great languor.

All my brethren weeneth that I should no farther go than to the bishop, and under that colour shall I well go forth to the court. I have great study till I have tidings from you. Evermore Almighty God have you in keeping, body and soul.

Written in haste, the Wednesday in the first week of clean Lent.[2]

Your orator,

ROBERT, *P. of B.*

I sent you a letter, but I had no answer again.

[?1449]

## 22. LORD MOLEYNS TO THE GRESHAM TENANTS

*To my trusty and well-beloved, the vicary and tenants of my lordship of Gresham.*

Trusty and well-beloved friends, I greet you well, and put you all out of doubt for all that ye have done for me; and the money that ye pay to my well-beloved servant John Partrich, I will be your warrant as for your discharge, and save you harmless against all those that would grieve you, to my power.

[1] i.e. to the court of Rome.
[2] i.e. the Wednesday after the first Sunday in Lent.

And, as heartily as I can, I thank you of the good will ye have had and have towards me. And as to the title of right that I have to the lordship of Gresham, it shall within short time be known, and by the law so determined, that ye shall all be glad that hath owed me your good will therein.

And Almighty God keep you, and by His grace I shall be with you soon after the Parliament is ended.

Written at London, on Our Lady's eve last past.

ROBERT HUNGERFORD, LORD MOLEYNS.

[24th March 1449]

## 23. MARGARET PASTON TO JOHN[(1)] PASTON [J. G.]

*To my right worshipful master, John Paston, dwelling in the Inner Temple, be this delivered in haste.*

Right worshipful husband, I recommend me to you, praying you to wete that my cousin Clere [1] dined with me this day; and she told me that Heydon was with her yestereven late, and he told her that he had a letter from the Lord Moleyns, and showed her the same letter praying him [Heydon] that he would say to his [Moleyns's] friends and well-willers in this country that he thanketh them of their goodwill and for that they have done for him; and also praying Heydon that he would say to Richard Arnold of Cromer that he was sorry and evil paid that his men made the affray upon him, for he said it was not by his will that his men should make affray on no man in this country without right great cause. And as for that was done to you, if it might be proved that he had done otherwise than right would as for the moveable goods, ye should be content, so that ye should have cause to con him thank; and he prayed Heydon in the letter that it should be reported in this country that he would do so, if he had done otherwise than he ought to do.

The friar [2] that claimeth Oxnead was in this town yesterday and this day was lodged at Berry's; and this afternoon he rode, but whither I wot not. He said plainly in this town that he shall have Oxnead, and that he have my Lord of Suffolk's good lordship,[3] and he will be his good lord in that matter. There was a person warned my mother within this two days that she should beware, for they said plainly she was like to be served as ye were served at Gresham within right short time. Also the Lord Moleyns wrote in his foresaid letter that he would mightily,

[1] Elizabeth, widow of Robert Clere of Ormesby.
[2] John Hawteyn.
[3] This phrase occurs many times; it means good will, assistance, approval, backing, etc.

with his body and with his goods, stand by all those that had been his friends and his well-willers in the matter touching Gresham, and prayed Heydon that he would say to them that they should not be afraid in no wise, for that was done it should be abiden by.

My mother prayeth you that ye will send my brother William to Cambridge a *nominale* and a book of sophistry of my brother Edmund's,[1] the which my said brother behested my mother the last time he spake with her, that he should have sent to my brother William.    The blissful Trinity have you in His keeping.

Written at Norwich in haste, on the Wednesday next before Palm Sunday.

Yours,

M.  P.

[2nd April 1449]


### 24.    MARGARET PASTON TO JOHN[(1)] PASTON [2]

Right worshipful husband, I recommend me to you, and pray you to get some crossbows and windacs to bind them with, and quarrels; for your houses here be so low that there may none man shoot out with no long bow, though we had never so much need.[3]

I suppose ye should have such things of Sir John Fastolf if ye would send to him; and also I would ye should get two or three short pole-axes to keep with doors, and as many jacks, and ye may.

Partrich and his fellowship are sore afraid that ye would enter again upon them, and they have made great ordinance within the house, as it is told me.    They have made bars to bar the doors crosswise, and they have made wickets on every quarter of the house to shoot out at, both with bows and with hand-guns: and the holes that be made for hand-guns, they be scarce knee high from the plancher, and of such holes be made five.    There can none man shoot out at them with no hand-bows.

Purry fell in fellowship with William Hasard at Quarles's, and told him that he would come and drink with Partrich and with him, and he said he should be welcome.    And after noon he went thither for to espy what they did, and what fellowship they had with them; and when he came thither the doors were fast sperred, and there were none folks with them but Mariot,

---

[1] Edmund Paston, who had died a few days earlier.
[2] The original of this letter is neither signed nor addressed.
[3] Margaret is evidently referring to plans for the first re-entry upon Gresham.

and Capron and his wife, and Quarles's wife, and another man in a black hood somewhat halting; I suppose by his words that it was Norfolk of Gimmingham. And the said Purry espied all these foresaid things.

And Mariot and his fellowship had much great language that shall be told you when ye come home.

I pray you that ye will vouchsafe to do buy for me one lb. of almonds and one lb. of sugar, and that ye will do buy some frieze to make of your children's gowns, ye shall have best cheap and best choice of Hays's wife as it is told me. And that ye will buy a yard of broad cloth of black for an hood for me of 44d. or four shillings a yard, for there is neither good cloth nor good frieze in this town. As for the children's gowns, and I have them, I will do them maken.

The Trinity have you in His keeping, and send you good speed in all your matters.

[?1449]


25. WILLIAM COTYNG TO JOHN[1] PASTON [J. G.]

*To the right reverend sir, my most worshipful master, my master John Paston.*

Right reverend and my most worshipful master, I recommend me to you. Please it you to wete that the man which I would have had to have been your farmer at Snailwell hath told me that he will not thereof. And this he maketh his excuse: he saith that he shall dwell with his wife's father and find him for his good as long as he liveth, and he will no longer meddle in the world. I feel well by him that he hath inquired of the manor, for he could tell me well that old Bridgeman owed my master your father, whom God assoil, much good, and how that he had all that was there when Bridgeman was dead; and that this Bridgeman oweth you much good at this time. I answered thereto: as for old Bridgeman, I said that it was his will that my master should have his good, because he was a bondman and had no children. And as for this Bridgeman, I said that he hath bought a fair place since he was your farmer, and payed therefor; but from this I cannot turn him. Wherefore, an' it like you to send to me a bill of the value of the manor, I shall inquire if any other may hap to be got, and send you word thereof; and in this and what ye will command me also I shall do my part by the grace of our Lord, who ever have you in His keeping. Amen.

Written at Cambridge the Sunday next before the feast of St George.

My master your brother[1] recommendeth him to you, as meseemeth he is in right feeble health. He will not tell me why, save he saith he complained once and had no remedy, and therefore he saith he shall suffer for a season. Forsooth, I suppose he is not entreated as he ought to be.

Your servant and beadsman,

W. COTYNG.

[20th April 1449]

### 26. ROBERT WENYNGTON TO THOMAS DANIEL

*To my reverend master, Thomas Daniel, squire for the King's body, be this letter delivered in haste.*

Most reverend master, I recommend me unto your gracious mastership, ever desiring to hear of your worshipful estate, the which Almighty God maintain it, and increase it unto His pleasance.

Pleasing you to know of my welfare, and of all your men, at the making of this letter we were in good health of body, aye blessed be God.

Moreover, master, I send you word, by Rawly Pickering, of all matters; the which I beseech you give him credence, as he will inform you of all. So, sir, I beseech you in the reverence of God that ye will inform our sovereign lord the King of all matters that I send you in this letter, like as I have sent a letter to my lord and all my lords by your own hands, and let the said Pickering declare all things as he hath seen and knoweth.

First, I send you word that when we went to sea, we took two ships of Brest coming out of Flanders. And then, after, there is made a great arming in Brittany to meet with me and my fellowship, that is to say, the great ship of Brest, the great ship of the Morlaix, the great ship of Vannes, with other eight ships, barges, and balingers to the number of 3,000 men; and so we lay on the sea to meet with them.

And then we met with a fleet of an hundred great ships of Prusse, Lubeck, Campe, Rostock, Holland, Zealand, and Flanders, betwixt Guernsey and Portland; and then I came aboard the admiral, and bade them strike in the King's name of England, and they bade me skite in the King's name of England. And then I and my fellowship said, but he will strike down the sail, that I will oversail them by the grace of God, and God will send me wind and weather; and they bade me do my worst, because I had so few ships and so small, that they scorned with me.

[1] William Paston.

And as God would, on Friday last was, we had a good wind, and then we armed us to the number of 2,000 men in my fellowship, and made us ready for to oversail them; and then they launched a boat, and set up a standard of truce, and came and spoke with me. And there they were yielded all the hundred ships to go with me into what port that me list and my fellows; but they fought with me the day before, and shot at us a 1,000 guns, and quarrels out of number, and have slain many of my fellowship, and maimed also.

Wherefore methinketh that they have forfeited both ships and goods at our sovereign lord the King's will.

Beseeching you that ye do your part in this matter, for this I have written to my Lord Chancellor and all my lords of the King's council; and so I have brought them, all the hundred ships, within Wight, in spite of them all.

And ye might get leave of our sovereign lord the King to come hither, it shall turn you to great worship and profit to help make our appointment in the King's name; for ye saw never such a sight of ships taken into England this hundred winters; for we lie armed night and day to keep them in, to the time that we have tidings of our sovereign and his council. For truly they have done harm to me and to my fellowship and to your ships, more than £2,000 worth harm; and therefore I am advised, and all my fellowship, to drown them and slay them, without that we have tidings from our sovereign the King and his council. And therefore, in the reverence of God, come ye yourself, and ye shall have a great avail and worship of your coming to see such sight; for I dare well say that I have here at this time all the chief ships of Dutchland, Holland, Zealand, and Flanders, and now it were time for to treat for a final peace as for these parts.

I write no more to you at this time, but Almighty Jesu have you in His keeping.

I write in haste within Wight, on Sunday at night after the Ascension of Our Lord.

By your own servant,

ROBERT WENYNGTON.

[25th May 1449]

27.　　　AGNES PASTON TO JOHN[(1)] PASTON

*To John Paston be this letter delivered.*

Son, I greet you well, with God's blessing and mine, and I let you wete that my cousin Clere [1] writted to me that she spake

¹ See footnote 2, page 14.

with Scrope [1] after that he had been with me at Norwich, and told her what cheer that I had made him; and he said to her he liked well by the cheer I made him.

He had such words to my cousin Clere, that, less than ye made him good cheer and gave him words of comfort at London, he would no more speak of the matter.

My cousin Clere thinketh that it were a folly to forsake him less-than ye know of one other as good or better; and I have assayed your sister, and I found her never so willing to none as she is to him, if it be so that his land stand clear.

I sent you a letter by Brawnton for silk, and for this matter before my cousin Clere wrote to me, the which was written on the Wednesday next after midsummer day.

Sir Harry Inglose is right busy about Scrope for one of his daughters.

I pray you forget not to bring me my money from Orwellbury, as ye come from London, either all or a great part. The due debt was at Christmas last past, nothing allowed, £7 14s. 8d., and at this midsummer it is £5 more; and though I allow him all his asking, it is but £1 6s. 6d. less, but I am not so advised yet. As for the friar,[2] he hath been at Saint Benet's and at Norwich, and made great boast of the suit that he hath against me, and bought many boxes, to what intent I wete never. It is well done to beware at London, in dread if he bring any syse at St Margaret's time.[3]

I can no more, but Almighty God be our good Lord, who have you ever in keeping. Written at Oxnead in great haste, on the Saturday next after midsummer.

By your mother,

A. P.

[*Circa* 1449]

28.     Elizabeth Clere to John[(1)] Paston

*To my cousin, John Paston, be this letter delivered.*

Trusty and well-beloved cousin, I commend me to you, desiring to hear of your welfare and good speed in your matter, the which I pray God send you to His plesaunce and to your heart's ease.

Cousin, I let you wete that Scrope hath been in this country to see my cousin your sister; and he hath spoken with my cousin

---

[1] Stephen Scrope, stepson of Sir John Fastolf. He was at this time a suitor for the hand of John Paston's sister.
[2] John Hawteyn.
[3] The feast of St Margaret is celebrated on 20th July.

your mother, and she desireth of him that he should show you the indentures made between the knight that hath his daughter and him, whether that Scrope, if he were married and fortuned to have children, if those children should inherit his land, or his daughter, the which is married.

Cousin, for this cause take good heed to his indentures, for he is glad to show you them, or whom ye will assign with you. And he saith to me he is the last in the tail of his livelode, the which is three hundred and fifty marks and better, as Watkin Shipdam saith, for he hath taken account of his livelode divers times. And Scrope saith to me, if he be married and have a son and heir, his daughter that is married shall have of his livelode fifty marks and no more. And therefore, cousin, meseemeth he were good for my cousin your sister without that ye might get her a better. And if ye can get a better, I would advise you to labour it in as short time as ye may goodly; for she was never in so great sorrow as she is nowadays, for she may not speak with no man, whosoever come, ne not may see nor speak with my man, nor with servants of her mother's, but that she beareth her on hand [1] otherwise than she meaneth. And she hath since Easter the most part been beaten once in the week or twice, and sometimes twice on one day, and her head broken in two or three places. Wherefore, cousin, she hath sent to me by Friar Newton in great counsel, and prayeth me that I would send to you a letter of her heaviness, and pray you to be her good brother, as her trust is in you. And she saith if ye may see by his evidences that his children and hers may inherit, and she to have reasonable jointure, she hath heard so much of his birth and his conditions that, an' ye will, she will have him, whether that her mother will or will not, notwithstanding it is told her his person is simple; [2] for she saith men shall have the more duty of her if she rule her to him as she ought to do.

Cousin, it is told me there is a goodly man in your Inn, of the which the father died lately; and if ye think that he were better for her than Scrope, it would be laboured, and give Scrope a goodly answer, that he be not put off till ye be sure of a better. For he said when he was with me, but-if he have some comfortable answer of you he will no more labour in this matter, because he might not see my cousin your sister. And he saith he might have seen her and she had been better than she is; and that causeth him to deem that her mother was not well willing, and so have I sent my cousin your mother word. Wherefore, cousin, think on this matter, for sorrow oftentime causeth women to beset them otherwise than they should do; and if she were in

---

[1] Attributes something to her.
[2] There is evidence that Stephen Scrope was sickly and deformed.

that case, I wot well ye would be sorry.   Cousin, I pray you
burn this letter, that your men nor none other man see it; for,
and my cousin your mother knew that I had sent you this letter,
she should never love me.   No more I write to you at this time,
but the Holy Ghost have you in keeping.   Written in haste, on
Saint Peter's day, by candle light.

By your cousin,

ELIZABETH CLERE.

[29th June 1449]


29.   JOHN DAMME TO JOHN[(1)] PASTON [J. G.]

*To my right worshipful master, John Paston, at London, in the
Inner Temple.*

Please it your good mastership to know that my mistress your
wife recommendeth her to you and fareth well, blessed be God,
and all your meny fare well also and recommend them to you, etc.
I was with my Lord of Oxford [1] and did mine errand; and I
found his good Lordship well disposed towards you, for he said
if he were sent to for to come to, etc., if it keep fair weather he
would not tarry, and if it rained he would not spare.   Moreover,
I spake with Partrich as touching the letter sent to my Lord
Moleyns.   He saith that he was privy to the writing and will
avow it by record of twenty persons, but he would name to me
no person; and so he and I accorded not fully.   And I bade him
remember that he might not abide there if ye would have him
out.   And he said he knew well that.   But he said, if ye put
him out, ye should be put out [2] soon after again.   And I said
if it hap it so they should not longer rest there.   And Mariot
stood by and said that were no marvel while they were but two
men, but it should not be best so.   And I said that I let them
wete it should be so if ye would, though they made all the
strength that they could make.   And thereto Mariot said
stately, that might not be performed; and more language there
was, too long to write at this leisure.   Partrich and his fellow
bear great visage, and keep great junkers and dinners, and say
that my Lord Moleyns hath written plainly to them that he is
lord there and will be, and shall be, and ye not to have it; but I
trust to God's righteousness of better purveyance.   Like it you
to remember what Heydon doth and made by colour of justice
of the peace, being of my Lord's counsel and not your good
friend nor well-willer, and to commune with your said counsel

---

[1] John de Vere, twelfth Earl of Oxford.
[2] i.e. from Gresham, which Paston had reoccupied some weeks earlier.

what ye must suffer by the law, and wherein ye may resist. On Sunday last passed, Gunnor and Mariot and John Davy and others dined with Partrich, etc. And after evensong Gunnor spake to my mistress that she should make her men to leave their wifels and their jacks. And she answered that they purposed to hurt no man of their own seeking, but for it was said that she should be plucked out of her house, she were loth to suffer that; and therefore she said they should go so till ye come home. And he said stately, but-if they left their array it should be plucked from them. I trust he must have a better warrant, from his stately language, or else he shall not have it from them easily. All this I remit to your good remembrance with God's help, to whom I pray to guide you right to His worship and your heart's desire.

Written at Sustead on St Andrew's day, etc.

Yours,

J. DAMME.

[30th November 1449]

Were but well, as meseemeth, that ye might ordain now a fetis jack defensible for yourself, for there con they do best and cheap.

30. RICHARD, EARL OF WARWICK, TO SIR THOMAS TUDDENHAM

*To our right trusty and well-beloved friend, Sir Thomas Tuddenham.*[1]

Right trusty, and well-beloved friend, we greet you well, heartily desiring to hear of your welfare, which we pray God preserve to your heart's desire. And if it please you to hear of our welfare, we were in good health at the making of this letter; praying you heartily that ye will consider our message which our chaplain, Master Robert Hopton, shall inform you of. For, as God knoweth, we have great business daily, and have had here before this time. Wherefore we pray you to consider the purchase that we have made with one John Southcote, Esquire, of Lincolnshire of £88 by the year, whereupon we must pay the

[1] Sir Thomas Tuddenham, born in 1399, was the second son of Sir Robert Tuddenham but, by the death of his elder brother, became his heir, and resided at Oxburgh in Norfolk. In February 1461, John, Earl of Oxford, Aubrey, his son and heir, this Sir Thomas Tuddenham, John Clopton, John Montgomery, and William Tyrrel, Esqs., were arrested by John, Earl of Worcester, Constable of England, on suspicion of having received letters from Margaret, queen of Henry VI; and being convicted in court before the said Earl of Worcester, were all beheaded (except Clopton) on Tower Hill, on 22nd February 1462.

last payment the Monday next after St Martin's Day,[1] which sum is £458. Wherefore we pray you with all our heart that ye will lend us ten or twenty pounds, or what the said Master Robert wants of his payment, as we may do for you in time for to come; and we shall send it you again afore New Year's day with the grace of God, as we are a true knight.

For there is none in your country that we might write to for trust so well as unto you; for, as we be informed, ye be our well-willer, and so we pray you of good continuance.

Wherefore we pray you that ye consider our intent of this money, as ye will that we do for you in time to come, as God knoweth, who have you in His keeping.

Written at London, on All Souls' day, within our lodging in the Grey Friars, within Newgate.

RICHARD, EARL OF WARWICK.

[2nd November ?1449]

31.      JOHN[(1)] PASTON'S PETITION:
         GRESHAM MANOR [J. G.]

*To the King, our Sovereign Lord, and to the right wise and discreet Lords, assembled in this present Parliament.*

Beseecheth meekly your humble liegeman, John Paston, that whereas he, and others enfeoffed to its use, have been peaceably possessed of the manor of Gresham, within the county of Norfolk, twenty years and more, till the 17th day of February, the year of your noble reign xxvi [1448], that Robert Hungerford, Knight, the Lord Moleyns, entered into the said manor. And howbeit that the said John Paston, after the said entry, sued to the said Lord Moleyns and his counsel, in the most lowly manner that he could, daily from time of the said entry on to the feast of Michaelmas then next following, during which time divers communications were had betwixt the counsel of the said Lord and the counsel of your beseecher. And forasmuch as in the said communications no title of right at any time was showed for the said Lord but that was fully and clearly answered, so that the said Lord's counsel remitted your said beseecher to sue to the said Lord for his final and rightful answer. And after suit made to the said Lord by your said beseecher, as well at Salisbury as in other places to his great cost, and none answer had but delays, which caused your said beseecher the 6th day of October last past to inhabit him in a mansion within the said town, keeping still there his possession, until the 28th day of

---

[1] The feast of St Martin falls on 11th November.

January last past, the said Lord sent to the said mansion a riotous people, to the number of one thousand persons, with blanket bands of assault as risers against your peace, arrayed in manner of war, with cuirasses, briganders, jacks, sallets, glaives, bows, arrows, pavises, guns, pans with fire and teynes burning therein, long cromes to draw down houses, ladders, picks with which they mined down the walls, and long trees with which they broke up gates and doors, and so came into the said mansion, the wife of your beseecher at that time being therein, and twelve persons with her; the which persons they drove out of the said mansion, and mined down the wall of the chamber wherein the wife of your said beseecher was, and bare her out at the gates, and cut asunder the posts of the houses and let them fall, and broke up all the chambers and coffers within the said mansion, and rifled, and in a manner of robbery bare away all the stuff, array, and money that your said beseecher and his servants had there, to the value of £200, and part thereof sold, and part thereof gave, and the remnant they parted among them, to the great and outrageous hurt of your said beseecher, saying openly, that if they might have found there your said beseecher and one John Damme, which is of counsel with him, and divers other of the servants of your said beseecher, they should have died. And yet divers of the said misdoers and riotous people unknown, contrary to your laws, daily keep the said manor with force, and lie in wait of divers of the friends, tenants, and servants of your said beseecher, and grievously vex and trouble them in divers wise, and seek them in their houses, ransacking and searching their sheaves and straw in their barns and other places with boar-spears, swords, and giserings, as it seemeth, to slay them if they might have found them; and some have beat and left for dead, so that they, for doubt of their lives, dare not go home to their houses, nor occupy their husbandry, to the great hurt, fear, and dread as well of your said beseecher as of his said friends, tenants, and servants. And also, they compel poor tenants of the said manor, now within their danger, against their will, to take feigned plaints in the courts of the hundred there against the said friends, tenants, and servants of your said beseecher, which dare not appear to answer for fear of bodily harm, nor can get no copies of the said plaints to remedy them by the law, because he that keepeth the said courts is of coven with the said misdoers, and was one of the said risers, which by colour of the said plaints grievously amerce the said friends, tenants, and servants of your said beseecher, to their outrageous and insupportable hurt.

Please it Your Highness, considering that if this great insurrection, riots, and wrongs, and daily continuance thereof so

heinously done against your crown, dignity, and peace, should
not by your high might be duly punished, it shall give great
boldness to them and all other misdoers to make congregations
and conventicles riotously, unable to be seised, to the sub-
version and final destruction of your liege people and laws:
and also how that your said beseecher is not able to sue the
common law in redressing of this heinous wrong, for the great
might and alliance of the said Lord: and also that your said
beseecher can have none action by your law against the said
riotous people for the goods and chattels by them so riotously
and wrongfully take and bore away, because the said people be
unknown, as well their names as their persons, unto him; to
purvey, by the advice of the Lords spiritual and temporal
assembled in this present Parliament, that your said beseecher
may be restored to the said goods and chattels thus riotously
take away; and that the said Lord Moleyns have such commandment that your said beseecher be not thus with force, in manner
of war, held out of his said manor, contrary to all your statutes
made against such forcible entries and holdings; and that the
said Lord Moleyns and his servants be set in such a rule, that
your said beseecher, his friends, tenants, and servants, may be
sure and safe from hurt of their persons, and peaceably occupy
their lands and tenements under your laws without oppression
or unrightful vexation of any of them; and that the said risers
and causers thereof may be punished, that others may eschew to
make any such rising in this your land of peace in time coming.
And he shall pray God for you.

[1450]

## 32. MARGARET PASTON TO JOHN[(1)] PASTON [J. G.]

*To my right worshipful master, John Paston, be this delivered
in haste.*

Right worshipful husband, I recommend me to you, desiring
heartily to hear of your welfare, praying you to wete that I
commanded Harry Goneld to go to Gunnor to have copies of the
plaints [1] in the hundred. And Gunnor was not at home; but
the said Harry spake with his clerk, and he told him plainly he
wost well his master would not let him have no copies, though
he were at home, till the next hundred. Wherefore I send you
that bill that was wound about the reliefs. Custance, Mak,
and Kenting would have disavowed their suits right fain the last
hundred, as I heard say of right thrifty men; but the Lord
Moleyns's men threatened them that both they should be beaten

---
[1] Referring to the feigned plaints mentioned in No. 31, page 32.

and lose their houses and lands and all their goods, unless they would avow it. And after that Osbern was gone, Hasard entreated Kenting and Mak to avow the suits after that they had disavowed it, and gave them money to give to the clerks to enter again the plaints. Unless ye seek a remedy in haste, for to remove it, I suppose they will distrain for the amercements ere the next hundred.

As for Mak, he gat respite that he should not sue till the next hundred. As for Harry Goneld, he was distrained yesterday for rent and farm, and he must pay it to-morrow, 22s., or else lose his distress. They gather money fast of all the tenants; all the tenants be charged to pay all their rent and farm by Fastingong Sunday.[1] It is told me that the Lord Moleyns should keep his Fastingong [2] at John Winter's place.

The said Lord's men had a letter on Thursday last past. What tidings they had I wot not; but on the next morning betimes, Thomas Bampton, a man of the Lord Moleyns, rode with a letter to his lord, and they that be at Gresham wait after an answer of the letter in haste. Barrow and Hegon, and all the Lord Moleyns's men that were at Gresham when ye departed hence, be there still, save Bampton, and in his stead is come another; and I hear say they shall abide here still till their lord come . . . [3] to Barrow as ye commanded me to wit what the cause was that they threaten men . . . Goneld and other your servants and well-willers to you, the which were named to him that were threatened . . . swore plainly that they were never threatened. But I know verily the contrary, for some of his own fellowship laid in wait sundry days and nights about Goneld's, Purry's, and Beck's places; and some of them went into Beck's and Purry's houses, both in the halls and the barns, and asked where they were, and they were answered that they were out; and they said again that they should meet with them another time. And by divers other things I know, if they might have been caught, either they should have been slain or sore hurt.

I sent Katherine on this foresaid message [4] (for I could get no man to do it), and sent with her James Halman and Harry Holt. And she desired of Barrow to have an answer of her message, and if these foresaid men might live in peace for them, and said there should else be purveyed other remedy for them. And he made her great cheer, and them that were with her, and said that he desired for to speak with me, if it should be none displeasance to me; and Katherine said to him that she supposed

---

[1] The first Sunday of Lent.
[2] Shrove Tuesday.
[3] Dots here and in the following lines indicate gaps in the manuscript.
[4] i.e. the message to Barrow, referred to in line 22 above.

that I desired not to speak with him. And he said he should come forby this place on hunting after noon, and there should no more come with him but Hegon and one of his own men; and then he would bring such an answer as should please me. And after noon they came hither, and sent in to me to weten if they might speak with me, and they abode still without the gates. And I came out to them, and spake with them without, and prayed them that they would hold me excused that I brought them not into the place. I said, inasmuch as they were not well-willing to the goodman of the place, I would not take it upon me to bring them in to the gentlewoman. They said I did the best, and then we walk forth and desired an answer of them for that I had sent to them for. They said to me they had brought me such an answer as they hoped should please me, and told me how they had communed with all their fellowship of such matters as I had sent to them for, and that they durst undertake that there should no man be hurt of them that were rehearsed, nor no man that longeth to you, neither for them nor for none of their fellowship, and that they answered me by their troths. Nevertheless, I trust not to their promise, inasmuch as I find them untrue in other things.

I conceived well by them that they were weary of what they had done. Barrow swore to me by his troth that he had lever than eighty shillings that his lord had not commanded him to come to Gresham; and he said he was right sorry hitherward, inasmuch as he had knowledge of you before, he was right sorry of that that was done. I said to him that he should have compassion on you and others that were disseised of their livelode, inasmuch as he had been disseised himself; and he said he was so, told me that he had sued to my Lord of Suffolk divers times, and would do till he may get his good again. I said to him that ye had sued to my Lord Moleyns divers times for the manor of Gresham since ye were disseised, and ye could never get no reasonable answer of him; and therefore ye entered again, as ye hoped that was for the best. And he said he should never blame my Lord of Suffolk for the entry into his livelode, for he said my said Lord was set thereupon by the information of a false shrew; and I said to him, in likewise is the matter betwixt the Lord Moleyns and you. I told him I wost well he set never thereupon by no title of right that he had to the manor of Gresham, but only by the information of a false shrew.[1] I rehearsed no name, but methought by them that they wost who I meant. Much other language we had, which should take long leisure in writing. I rehearsed to them that it should be said that I should not long dwell so near them as I do; and they forswear it,

[1] John Heydon.

as they do other things more, that it was never said, and much things that I know verily was said.

I hear said that ye and John Damme be sore threatened alway, and said, though ye be at London ye shall be met with there as well as though ye were here. And therefore I pray you heartily beware how ye walk there, and have a good fellowship with you when ye shall walk out. The Lord Moleyns hath a company of brothel with him that reck not what they do, and such are most for to dread. They that be at Gresham say that they have not done so much hurt to you as they were commanded to do. Robert Lawrence is well amended, and I hope shall recover. He saith plainly he will complain of his hurt, and I suppose Beck will complain also, as he hath cause. Beck and Purry dare not abide at home till they hear other tidings. I would not John Damme should come home till the country be storied otherwise than it is. I pray God grant that it may soon be otherwise than it is. I pray you heartily that ye will send me word how ye do, and how ye speed in your matters; for by my troth I cannot be well at ease in my heart, nor nought shall be, till I hear tidings how ye do. The most part of your stuff that was at Gresham is sold and given away. Barrow and his fellow spake to me in the most pleasant wise, and meseemeth by them they would fain please me. They said they would do me service and pleasance, if it lay in their powers to do aught for me, save only in that that longeth to their lord's right. I said to them, as for such service as they had done to you and to me, I desire no more that they should do neither to you or to me. They said I might have had of them at Gresham what I had desired of them, and had as much as I desired. I said, nay; if I might have had my desire, I should neither have departed out of the place nor from the stuff that was therein. They said as for the stuff, it was but easy. I said ye would not have given the stuff that was in the place when they came in, not for £100. They said the stuff that they saw there was scarce worth £20. As for your mother and mine, she fareth well, blessed be God, and she had no tidings but good yet, blessed be God. The blessed Trinity have you in His keeping, and send you health, and good speed in all your matters. Written at Sustead [1] on the Saturday next after St Valentine's day.

Here dare no man say a good word for you in this country; God amend it!

Yours,

M. P.

[21st February 1450]

---

[1] John Damme's place, near Gresham.

## 33.    AGNES PASTON TO JOHN[1] PASTON

*To John Paston, dwelling in the Inner Inn of the Temple, at London, be this letter delivered in haste.*

Son, I greet you, and send you God's blessing and mine; and as for my daughter your wife, she fareth well, blessed be God, as a woman in her plight [1] may do, and all your sons and daughters.

And forasmuch as ye will send me no tidings, I send you such as be in this country. Richard Lynsted came this day from Paston and let me wit that on Saturday last past Dravell, half-brother to Warren Harman, was taken with enemies, walking by the seaside, and have him forth with them. And they took two pilgrims, a man and a woman, and they robbed the woman and let her go, and led the man to the sea; and when they knew he was a pilgrim they gave him money and set him again on the land. And they have this week taken four vessels off Winterton and Happisburgh and Eccles; men be sore afraid for taking of more, for there be ten great vessels of the enemy's. God give grace that the sea may be better kept than it is now, or else it shall be a perilous dwelling by the sea-coast.

I pray you greet well your brethren, and say them that I send them God's blessing and mine; and say William that if Janet Lauton be not paid for the crimson coat which Alson Crane [2] wrote to her for in her own name, that then he pay her, and see Alson Crane's name stricken out of her book, for she saith she will ask no man the money but Alson Crane. And I pray you that ye will remember the letter that I sent you last, and God be with you.

Written at Norwich, the Wednesday next before St Gregory.

By your mother,

AGNES PASTON.

[11th March 1450]


## 34.    MARGARET PASTON TO JOHN[1] PASTON

*To my right worshipful master, John Paston, be this delivered in haste.*

Right worshipful husband, I recommend me to you, desiring heartily to hear of your welfare, etc. . . .[3]

William Rutt, the which is with Sir John Heveningham,[4] came

---

[1] She was *enceinte*.
[2] This was probably a daughter of Robert Crane, of Stonham, in Suffolk.
[3] Here Fenn omitted a passage consisting of some business items.
[4] A kinsman of Sir John Fastolf.

home from London yesterday, and he said plainly to his master, and to many other folks, that the Duke of Suffolk is pardoned, and hath his men again waiting upon him, and is right well at ease and merry, and is in the King's good grace, and in the good conceit of all the lords, as well as ever he was.

There have been many enemies against Yarmouth and Cromer, and have done much harm, and taken many Englishmen, and put them in great distress, and greatly ransomed them. And the said enemies have been so bold that they come up to the land, and play them on Caister Sands and in other places, as homely as they were Englishmen. Folks be right sore afraid that they will do much harm this summer, but-if there be made right great purveyance against them.

Other tidings know I none at this time. The blissful Trinity have you in His keeping.

Written at Norwich on Saint Gregory's day.

Yours,

M. P.

[12th March 1450]


## 35.   THE DUKE OF SUFFOLK TO HIS SON

*The copy of a notable letter, written by the Duke of Suffolk [1] to his son,[2] giving him therein very good counsel.*

My dear and only well-beloved son, I beseech Our Lord in heaven, the maker of all the world, to bless you, and to send you ever grace to love Him and to dread Him; to the which, as far as a father may charge his child, I both charge you, and pray you to set all your spirits and wits to do, and to know His holy laws and commandments, by the which ye shall, with His great mercy, pass all the great tempests and troubles of this wretched world.

And that also, wittingly, ye do nothing for love nor dread of any earthly creature that should displease Him. And there as any frailty maketh you to fall, beseech His mercy soon to call you to Him again with repentance, satisfaction, and contrition of your heart, never more in will to offend Him.

[1] William de la Pole, Duke of Suffolk, succeeded his brother Michael (slain at the battle of Agincourt in 1415) as Earl of Suffolk.   Chief minister and favourite of Henry VI and Queen Margaret, he was created in 1444 Marquis, and in 1448 Duke of Suffolk.   He was banished by the King at the instigation of the Commons, and murdered at sea on 2nd May 1450. He married Alice, daughter and heiress of Thomas Chaucer, of Ewelme, in Oxfordshire, and grand-daughter of Geoffrey Chaucer.

[2] John de la Pole, son and heir of the above named, restored as Duke of Suffolk, in 1463.   He married Elizabeth, daughter of Richard Plantagenet, Duke of York, and sister of Edward IV.   He died in 1491, and was buried at Wingfield in Suffolk.

Secondly, next Him above all earthly things, to be true liegeman in heart, in will, in thought, in deed, unto the King our aldermost high and dread sovereign lord, to whom both ye and I be so much bound to; charging you, as father can and may, rather to die than to be the contrary, or to know anything that were against the welfare or prosperity of his most royal person, but that as far as your body and life may stretch ye live and die to defend it, and to let his Highness have knowledge thereof in all the haste ye can.

Thirdly, in the same wise, I charge you, my dear son, alway, as ye be bounden by the commandment of God to do, to love, to worship, your lady and mother; and also that ye obey alway her commandments, and to believe her counsels and advices in all your works, the which dread not but shall be best and truest to you. And if any other body would steer you to the contrary, to flee the counsel in any wise, for ye shall find it naught and evil.

Furthermore, as far as father may and can, I charge you in any wise to flee the company and counsel of proud men, of covetous men, and of flattering men, the more especially and mightily to withstand them, and not to draw nor to meddle with them, with all your might and power. And to draw to you and to your company good and virtuous men, and such as be of good conversation, and of truth, and by them shall ye never be deceived nor repent you of.

Moreover, never follow your own wit in no wise, but in all your works, of such folks as I write of above, ask your advice and counsel; and doing thus, with the mercy of God, ye shall do right well, and live in right much worship, and great heart's rest and ease.

And I will be to you as good lord and father as my heart can think.

And last of all, as heartily and as lovingly as ever father blessed his child in earth, I give you the blessing of Our Lord and of me, which of His infinite mercy increase you in all virtue and good living. And that your blood may by His grace from kindred to kindred multiply in this earth to His service, in such wise as after the departing from this wretched world here, ye and they may glorify Him eternally amongst His angels in heaven.

Written of mine hand,
   the day of my departing fro this land,
      Your true and loving father,
          SUFFOLK.

[30th April 1450]

36.          WILLIAM LOMNER TO JOHN[1] PASTON

*To the right worshipful John Paston, at Norwich.*

Right worshipful sir, I recommend me to you, and am right sorry
of that I shall say, and have so washed this little bill with
sorrowful tears, that unethe ye shall read it.

As on Monday next after May day [1] there came tidings to
London, that on Thursday before,[2] the Duke of Suffolk came
unto the coasts of Kent full near Dover with his two ships and
a little spinner; the which spinner he sent with certain letters,
by certain of his trusted men, unto Calais-ward, to know how he
should be received. And with him met a ship called Nicholas
of the Tower [3] with other ships waiting on him, and by them
that were in the spinner the master of the Nicholas had knowledge of the duke's coming. And when he spied the duke's
ships, he sent forth his boat to wit what they were, and the duke
himself spoke to them, and said he was by the King's commandment sent to Calais-ward, etc.

And they said he must speak with their master; and so he,
with two or three of his men, went forth with them in their boat
to the Nicholas. And when he came, the master bade him
'Welcome, traitor,' as men say; and further the master desired
to wit if the shipmen would hold with the duke, and they sent
word they would not in no wise; and so he was in the Nicholas
till Saturday [4] next following.

Some say he wrote much thing to be delivered to the King,
but that is not verily known. He had his confessor with him,
etc.

And some say he was arraigned in the ship on their manner
upon the impeachments,[5] and found guilty, etc.

Also he asked the name of the ship, and when he knew it, he
remembered Stacy that said, if he might escape the danger of the
Tower he should be safe; and then his heart failed him, for
he thought he was deceived.

And in the sight of all his men he was drawn out of the great
ship into the boat. And there was an axe and a stock, and one
of the lewdest of the ship bade him lay down his head, and he
should be fairly ferd with, and die on a sword; and took a rusty

---

[1] i.e. on 4th May.
[2] 30th April.
[3] This ship belonged to Bristol in 1442.   She was a great ship with forestages, and carried 150 men.
[4] 2nd May.
[5] Suffolk was impeached by the Commons on 7th February 1450 (Rolls
of Parliament, v. 177).

sword and smote off his head within half a dozen strokes, and took away his gown of russet and his doublet of velvet mailed, and laid his body on the sands of Dover. And some say his head was set on a pole by it, and his men set on the land by great circumstance and prey.

And the sheriff of Kent doth watch the body, and sent his under-sheriff to the judges to wete what to do, and also to the King what shall be done.

Further I wot not, but thus far is it that if the process be erroneous let his counsel reverse it, etc.

Also for all the other matters, they sleep, and the friar [1] also, etc. Sir Thomas Keriel [2] is taken prisoner and all the leg-harness, and about 3,000 Englishmen slain.

Matthew Gough,[3] with 1,500, fled, and saved himself and them. And Pierce Brusy was chief captain, and had 10,000 Frenchmen and more, etc.

I pray you let my mistress, your mother, know these tidings; and God have you all in His keeping.

I pray you this bill may recommend me to my mistresses, your mother and wife, etc.

James Gresham hath written to John Damme, and recommendeth him, etc.

Written in great haste at London, the 5th day of May, etc.

By your wife,

WILLIAM LOMNER.[4]

[1450]

37. JOHN CRANE TO JOHN(1) PASTON

*To my right worshipful cousin, John Paston, of Norwich, Esquire.*

Right worshipful sir, I recommend me unto you in the most goodly wise that I can; and forasmuch as ye desired of me to send you word of divers matters here, which have been opened in the Parliament openly, I send you of them such as I can.

First most especial, that for very truth upon Saturday that

---

[1] Hawteyn.

[2] He was taken prisoner at the battle of Fourmigni (15th April 1450) where he defended himself with great bravery. He was beheaded by Queen Margaret's order, after the second battle of St Albans, in 1460.

[3] Afterwards slain in Cade's rebellion, fighting with the citizens at the battle of the Bridge (July 1450).

[4] This curious subscription is explained by Fenn as due to the fact that William Lomner, who was frequently employed as amanuensis by Margaret Paston, here forgot in what capacity he was writing.

last was, the Duke of Suffolk was taken in the sea, and there he was beheaded, and his body with the appurtenance set at land at Dover; and all the folks that he had with him were set to land, and had none harm.

Also the King hath somewhat granted to have the resumption again, in some but not in all, etc.

Also, if ye purpose to come hither to put up your bills, ye may come now in a good time; for now every man that hath any, they put them in, and so may ye, if ye come with God's grace to your pleasure. . . .[1]

Furthermore, upon the 4th day of this month, the Earl of Devonshire[2] came hither with 300 men well beseen, etc., and upon the morrow after, my Lord of Warwick with 400 and more, etc.

Also, as it is noised here, Calais shall be besieged within this seven days, etc.

God save the King, and send us peace, etc.

Other tidings be there none here, but Almighty God have you in His keeping.

Written at Leicester, the 6th day of May.

Your cousin,<br>JOHN CRANE.[3]

[1450]

38.       THOMAS DENYS TO JOHN[(1)] PASTON

*To my Master Paston.*

I recommend me unto your good mastership. And as for tidings, Arblaster came home to my Lord[4] on Monday at supper time; and my master Daniel[5] is steward of the Duchy of Lancaster beyond Trent, and Arblaster saith he hath made me his under-steward.

And as for the chamberlainship of England, the Lord Beaumont[6] hath it, and the Lord Rivers[7] constable of England.

As for the Duchy on this side Trent, Sir Thomas Tuddenham

---

[1] Here follows some advice (omitted by Fenn) concerning private bills of John Paston to be presented to the Parliament.
[2] Thomas Courtney, Earl of Devon, was taken at the battle of Towton in 1461, and afterwards beheaded by order of Edward IV.
[3] Probably John Crane of Woodnorton.
[4] The Earl of Oxford.
[5] Thomas Daniel.
[6] John, Viscount Beaumont.
[7] Richard Woodville, created Baron Rivers in 1448.

had a joint patent with the Duke of Suffolk, which, if it be resumed, Sir Thomas Stanley hath a bill ready endorsed thereof.

My Lord will not to Leicester.[1] My master Daniel desireth you thither. I shall ride thitherward on Friday betimes.

Written in haste at Winch, the 13th day of May.

I pray you to think upon my matter to my mistress your wife for my mistress Anne; for in good faith I have fully conquered my lady since ye went, so that I have her promise to be my good lady, and that she shall help me by the faith of her body.

Your servant,

DENYS.

[1450]

## 39.　THE EARL OF OXFORD TO JOHN[(1)] PASTON

*To our right trusty and entirely well-beloved John Paston, Esquire.*

Right trusty and right entirely well-beloved, we greet you heartily well. And it is so, as ye know well yourself, we have, and long time have had, the service of Thomas Denys, by continuance whereof we weened to have had his attendance at our lust. And nevertheless, we have so strictly examined his demeaning that we feel and plainly conceive that the love and affection which he hath to a gentlewoman not far from you, and which ye be privy to, as we suppose, causeth him alway to desire towards your country rather than towards such occupation as is behoveful to us. We write therefore to you, praying you heartily as ye love us, that it like you to do that labour at our instance, by such mean as your wisdom can seem, to move that gentlewoman in our behalf for the weal of this matter, undertaking for us that we will show our bounty to them both, if it please her that this matter take effect, so that by reason she shall have cause to take it in gree. And if the coming thither of our person self should be to pleasure of her, we will not leave our labour in that. Wherefore we pray you that ye will do your part herein, as ye will we do for you in time coming, and that ye see us in haste. The Holy Trinity keep you. Written at Wivenhoe, the 17th day of May.

The Earl of Oxford,

OXENFORD.

[? 1449–51]

---

[1] Where Parliament was sitting.

## 40.     SIR JOHN FASTOLF TO THOMAS HOWES

*To my trusty and well-beloved friend, Sir Thomas Howes,*[1] *Parson of Castlecombe.*

Trusty and well-beloved friend, I greet you well. [*Here follow some orders respecting his affairs at Caister.*] And I pray you send me word who dare be so hardy to kick against you in my right; and say them on my behalf that they shall be quit as far as law and reason will. And if they will not dread nor obey that, then they shall be quit by Blackbeard of Whitebeard, that is to say, By God or the Devil. And therefore I charge you, send me, word whether such as have been mine adversaries before this time continue still in their wilfulness, etc.

Item, I hear ofttimes many strange reports of the governance of my place at Caister and other places, as in my chatell approving,[2] in my wines, the keeping of my wardrobe and clothes, the avail[3] of my conies at Hellesdon, etc., and approvement[2] of my lands; praying you heartily, as my full trust is in you, to help reform it. And that ye suffer no vicious man at my place of Caister abide, but well governed and diligent, as ye will answer to it.

Almighty God keep you. Written at London, the 27th day of May, in the 28th year of the reign of King Henry VI.

                                    JOHN FASTOLF, *Knight.*

[1450]


## 41.           J. PAYN TO JOHN[(1)] PASTON[4]

*To my right honourable master, John Paston.*

Right honourable and my right entirely beloved master, I recommend me unto you with all manner of due reverence, in the most lowly wise as me ought to do, evermore desiring to hear of your worshipful state, prosperity, and welfare; the which I beseech God, of His abundant grace, increase and maintain to His most pleasance and to your heart's desire.

Pleaseth it your good and gracious mastership tenderly to consider the great losses and hurts that your poor petitioner hath, and hath had, ever since the commons of Kent came to the

---

[1] Thomas Howes was Sir John Fastolf's agent in Norfolk. The prefix 'Sir' was commonly used at this date to denote a cleric, as we say 'the Reverend.' Howes was rector of Blofield from about 1460 to 1471.

[2] i.e. turning them to profit.

[3] Use or profit.

[4] This letter, though written in 1465, is placed here because it deals with events in 1450, notably with Cade's rebellion.

Blackheath,[1] and that is at fifteen years passed; whereas my master, Sir John Fastolf, knight, that is your testator, commanded your beseecher to take a man, and two of the best horses that were in his stable, with him, to ride to the commons of Kent to get the articles that they come for. And so I did; and all so soon as I came to the Blackheath, the captain [2] made the commons to take me. And for the salvation of my master's horses, I made my fellow to ride away with the two horses; and I was brought forthwith before the captain of Kent. And the captain demanded me, what was my cause of coming thither, and why that I made my fellow to steal away with the horses. And I said that I came thither to cheer with my wife's brethren, and others that were mine allies, and gossips of mine, that were present there. And then was there one there and said to the captain that I was one of Sir John Fastolf's men, and the two horses were Sir John Fastolf's. And then the captain let cry treason upon me throughout all the field, and brought me at four parts of the field, with a herald of the Duke of Exeter [3] before me, in the duke's coat-of-arms, making four 'oyez' at four parts of the field; proclaiming openly by the said herald, that I was sent thither for to espy their puissance and their habiliments of war, from the greatest traitor that was in England or in France, as the said captain made proclamation at that time, from one Sir John Fastolf, knight, the which minished all the garrisons of Normandy, le Mans, and Maine, the which was the cause of the losing of all the King's title and right of an inheritance that he had beyond sea. And moreover, he said that the said Sir John Fastolf had furnished his place [4] with the old soldiers of Normandy, and habiliments of war, to destroy the commons of Kent when that they came to Southwark; and therefore he said plainly that I should lose my head. And so forthwith I was taken, and led to the captain's tent, and one axe and one block was brought forth to have smitten off mine head. And then my master Poynyngs your brother,[5] with other of my friends came, and letted the captain, and said plainly that there should die an hundred or two that in case be that I died; and so by that mean my life was saved at that time.

And then I was sworn to the captain and to the commons, that I should go to Southwark and array me in the best wise that I

---

[1] For the second time (29th June–1st July).

[2] Jack Cade.

[3] His herald had probably been forced into the service of the rebels.

[4] Sir John Fastolf had a house in Southwark.

[5] Robert Poynyngs married Elizabeth, sister of John Paston, and was sword-bearer and carver to Cade.

could, and come again to them to help them; and so I got the articles, and brought them to my master, and that cost me more amongst the commons that day than 27s.

Whereupon I came to my master Fastolf, and brought him the articles, and informed him of all the matter, and counselled him to put away all his habiliments of war, and the old soldiers; and so he did, and went himself to the Tower, and all his meny with him but Betts and one Matthew Brayn. And had I not been, the commons would have burned his place and all his tenuries; where through it cost me of mine own proper goods at that time more than six marks in meat and drink; and notwithstanding the captain that same time let take me at the White Hart in South-wark, and there commanded Lovelace to despoil me out of mine array, and so he did. And there he took a fine gown of muster develers furred with fine beavers, and one pair [1] of brigandines covered with blue velvet and gilt nails, with leg-harness; the value of the gown and the brigandines £8.

Item, the captain sent certain of his meny to my chamber in your rents, and there broke up my chest, and took away one obligation of mine that was due unto me of £36 by a priest of Paul's, and one other obligation of one knight of £10, and my purse with five rings of gold, and 17s. 6d. of gold and silver; and one harness complete of the touch of Milan; and one gown of fine perse blue, furred with martens; and two gowns, one furred with bogey and one other lined with frieze; and there would have smitten off mine head when that they had despoiled me at White Hart. And there my master Poynyngs and my friends saved me, and so I was put up till at night that the battle was at London Bridge. And then at night the captain put me out into the battle at the bridge, and there I was wounded, and hurt near hand to death; and there I was six hours in the battle, and might never come out thereof; and four times before that time I was carried about throughout Kent and Sussex, and there they would have smitten off my head. And in Kent, thereas my wife dwelled, they took away all our goods moveable that we had, and there would have hanged my wife and five of my children, and left her no more goods but her kirtle and her smock. And anon after that hurling, the Bishop of Rochester impeached me to the Queen, and so I was arrested by the Queen's command-ment into the Marshalsea, and there was in right great duress, and fear of mine life, and was threatened to have been hanged, drawn, and quartered; and so would have made me to have impeached my master Fastolf of treason. And because that I would not, they had me up to Westminster, and there would

----

[1] i.e. the breast and back.

have sent me to the jail-house at Windsor, but my wife's and
one cousin of mine own, that were yeomen of the crown, they
went to the King, and got grace and one charter of pardon.

Per le vostre,

J. PAYN.

[1465]


## 42. JOHN[1] PASTON AND LORD MOLEYNS[1] [J. G.]

*Unto the Right Reverend Father in God and my right gracious lord,
the Cardinal Archbishop of York, Primate and Chancellor of
England.*

Beseecheth meekly John Paston that whereas Robert Hungerford, knight, Lord Moleyns, and Alianore[2] his wife, late with
force and strength, and great multitude of riotous people, to the
number of a thousand persons and more, gathered by the
excitation and procuring of John Heydon against the King's
peace, in riotous manner entered upon your said beseecher and
others enfeoffed to his use in the manor of Gresham with the
appurtenances in the shire of Norfolk; which riotous people
brake, despoiled, and drew down the place of your said beseecher
in the said town, and drove out his wife and servants there being,
and rifled, took, and bare away all the goods and chattels that
your said beseecher and his servants had there to the value of
£200 and more; and the said manor, after the said riotous entry,
kept with strong hand in manner of war, as well against your
said beseecher and his feoffees, as against one of the King's
justices of the peace in the said shire, that came thither to
execute the statutes ordained and provided against such forcible
entries and keeping of possessions with force, as it appeareth
by record of the said justice certified unto the Chancery; and
yet the said Lord Moleyns the same manor keepeth with force
and strength against the form of the said statutes: Please it your
reverend Fatherhood and gracious Lordship, these premisses
considered, to grant unto your said beseecher for his feoffees
by him to be named a special assize against the said Lord
Moleyns, Alianore, and John Heydon, and others to be named
by your said beseecher, and also an oyer and determiner against
the said Lord Moleyns, John Heydon, and others of the said
riotous people in like form to be named, to inquire, hear, and
determine all trespasses, extortions, riots, forcible entries,

---

[1] This document concerns Paston's second expulsion from Gresham.
[2] She was daughter and heiress of William, Lord de Moleyns (*d.* 1429),
by Anne, daughter and co-heiress of John Whalesborough.

maintenances,[1] champerties,[2] embraceries,[3] offences, and mis-
prisions [4] by them or by any of them done, as well at suit of our
sovereign lord the King, as of your said beseecher and his said
feoffees, and every of them, or of any other of the King's lieges:
at reverence of God, and in way of charity.

[1450]

## 43. Henry VI to John[(1)] Paston

*To our trusty and well-beloved John Paston, Esquire.*

### BY THE KING

Trusty and well-beloved, forasmuch as our right trusty and
well-beloved the Lord Moleyns is by our special desire and
commandment waiting upon us, and now for divers considera-
tions moving us, we purpose to send him into certain places for
to execute our commandments, for the which he ne may be
attendant to be in our counties of Norfolk and Suffolk at the
time of our commissioners sitting upon our commission of oyer
determiner within the same our counties: We therefore desire
and pray you, that considering his attendance upon us, and that
he must apply him to execute our commandment, ye will respite
as for anything attempting against him as for any matters that ye
have to do or say against him, or any other of his servants,
well-wishers, or tenants, because of him, unto time he shall
mowe be present to answer thereunto; wherein ye shall minister
unto us cause of pleasure, and over that deserve of us right
good thank. Given under our signet at our palace of Westminster, the 18th day of September.

[1450]

## 44. William Wayte[5] to John[(1)] Paston

*To my master, John Paston, in right great haste.*

Sir, and it please, I was in my Lord of York's house, and I
heard much thing more than my master writeth unto you of;
I heard much thing in Fleet-street. But, sir, my Lord was with
the King, and he visaged so the matter that all the King's
household was, and is, afraid right sore. And my said Lord

[1] Unlawful support given to a disputant by one not concerned in the cause.
[2] Bargains made with litigants for a share of what may be gained by the suit.
[3] Attempts to corrupt juries.
[4] Treason or felony committed by oversight or wilful neglect of duty.
[5] Justice Yelverton's clerk.

hath put a bill to the King, and desired much thing which is much after the Commons' desire, and all is upon justice, and to put all those that be indicted under arrest, without surety or mainprise, and to be tried by law as law will; insomuch that on Monday Sir William Oldhall was with the King at Westminster more than two hours, and had of the King good cheer. And the King desired of Sir William Oldhall that he should speak to his cousin York, that he would be good lord to John Penycock, and that my Lord of York should write unto his tenants that they should suffer Penycock's officers go and gather up his rent-farms within the said duke's lordships. And Sir William Oldhall answered again to the King, and prayed him to hold my Lord excused, for though my Lord wrote under his seal of his arms, his tenants will not obey it; insomuch when Sir Thomas Hoo met with my Lord of York beyond Saint Alban's, the western men fell upon him and would have slain him, had not Sir William Oldhall have been, and therefore would the western men have fallen upon the said Sir William and have killed him. And so he told the King.

Sir Borle Yonge and Josse labour sore for Heydon and Tuddenham to Sir William Oldhall, and proffer more than £2,000 for to have his good lordship; and therefore it is none other remedy but let Swaffham men be warned to meet with my said Lord on Friday next coming at Pickenham on horseback in the most goodly wise, and put some bill unto my Lord of Sir Thomas Tuddenham, Heydon, and Prentice, and cry out on them, and that all the women of the same town be there also, and cry out on them also, and call them extortioners, and pray my Lord that he will do sharp execution upon them. And my master counsels you that ye should move the mayor and all the aldermen with all their commoners to ride against my Lord, and that there be made bills, and put them up to my Lord, and let all the town cry out on Heydon, Tuddenham, Wyndham, and Prentice, and of all their false maintainers, and tell my Lord how much hurt they have done to the city, and let it be done in the most lamentable wise. For, sir, but-if my Lord hear some foul tales of them, and some hideous noise and cry, by my faith they are else like to come to grace. And therefore, sir, remember you of all these matters.

Sir, also I spake with William Norwich, and asked him after the Lord Moleyns how he stood to my Lord-ward; and he told me he was sore out of grace, and that my Lord of York loveth him nought. William Norwich told me that he durst undertake for to bring you unto my Lord, and make him your right good lord; and, sir, my master counselled you that ye should not spare, but get you his good lordship.

Sir, beware of Heydon, for he would destroy you by my faith. The Lord Scales and Sir William Oldhall are made friends.

Sir, labour ye for to be knight of the shire, and speak to my master Stapleton [1] also that he be it. Sir, all Swaffham, and they be warned, will give you their voices. Sir, speak with Thomas Denys and take his good advice therein. Sir, speak to Denys that he avoid his garrison at Reydon, for there is none other remedy but death for Daniel and for all those that are indicted. Sir, labour ye to the mayor that John Damme [2] or William Jenney be burgess for the city of Norwich; tell them that he may be it as well as Yonge is of Bristol, or the Recorder is of London, and as the Recorder of Coventry is for the city of Coventry, and it so in many places in England. Also, sir, think on Yarmouth, that ye ordain that John Jenney or Lomner or some good man be burgess for Yarmouth. Ordain ye that Jenney may be in the Parliament, for they can say well.

Sir, it were wisdom that my Lord of Oxford wait on my Lord of York. In good faith, good sir, think on all these matters; much more I had to write unto you, if I could have remembered me, but I had no leisure by my faith. Hold me excused of my lewd rude writing. Let John Damme beware for the Lord Moleyns; and, sir, let the city beware, for he will do them a villainy but-if he may have his men; and, sir, if he come to Norwich, look there be ready to wait upon the mayor a good fellowship, for it is said here that they are but beasts.

Sir, my master bade me write unto you that ye should stir the mayor and all the aldermen to cry on my Lord that they may have justice of these men that be indicted, and that my Lord will speak unto the King thereof. And, sir, in divers parts in the town where my Lord cometh, there would be ordained many portions of commoners to cry on my Lord for justice of these men that are indicted, and tell their names, in special Tuddenham, Heydon, Wyndham, Prentice. Sir, I send you a copy of the bill that my Lord of York put unto the King; and, sir, let copies go about the city enough, for the love of God, which have you in His keeping. Written on Saint Faith's day, in haste.

By your servant,

WILLIAM WAYTE.

[6th October 1450]

---

[1] Sir Miles Stapleton.
[2] Damme was in fact returned for Norwich in November 1450.

### 45. RICHARD, DUKE OF YORK, TO HENRY VI[1]

*Richard, Duke of York, his petition to King Henry for the punishment of traitors, etc.*

Please it your Highness tenderly to consider the great grouching and rumour that is universally in this your realm of that justice is not duly ministered to such as trespass and offend against your laws, and in special of them that be indicted of treason, and others being openly noised of the same; wherefore great inconveniences that have fallen, and great is like to fall hereafter in your said realm (which God defend), but-if by your Highness provision convenable be made for due reformation and punishment in this behalf. Wherefore I, your humble subject and liegeman, Richard, Duke of York, willingly and effectually as I can, and desiring surety and prosperity of your most royal person, and welfare of this your noble realm, counsel and advertise your excellency, for the conservation of good tranquillity and peaceable rule among all true subjects, for to ordain and provide that due justice be had against all such that be so indicted or openly so noised: wherein I offer, and will put me in devoir for to execute your commandments in these premises of such offenders, and redress of the said misrulers, to my might and power. And for the hasty execution hereof, like it your Highness to address your letters of privy seal and writs to your officers and ministers to do take and arrest all such persons so noised or indicted, of what estate, degree, or condition soever they be, and them to commit to your Tower of London, or to other your prisons, there to abide without bail or mainprise until the time that they be utterly tried and declared, after the course of your law.

[1450]

### 46. SIR JOHN FASTOLF TO THOMAS HOWES AND WILLIAM BARKER

*To my right trusty friend Sir Thomas Howes, parson of Castlecombe, being at Caister, and William Barker, in haste, at Caister Inn, by Yarmouth.*

Right trusty and well-beloved friend, I greet you well. And as for Heigham's place to be sold, as ye advise me to buy it at the sum of an hundred marks or within, and reserving in the said payment mine own duty, and pay the remnant in wool to the said Heigham's creditors, as your letter maketh mention; I have

---

[1] This is the 'copy of the bill' enclosed in Wayte's letter, No. 44, page 50.

understood that William Jenney shall be here this week, and I shall feel him how near it may be sold; for if the widow will sell it after fourteen year or fifteen year, that it may be let, send me utterly word, for I will not mell of it else thus advised. And send ye me word how much more in value in a stone shall I sell my wool, and how much another chapman will give me for the place when I have bought it; but after fourteen year I would buy the place.

Written at London, the 15th day of October, in the 29th year of King Henry VI.

JOHN FASTOLF.

[1450]

47.      MARGARET PASTON TO JOHN[1] PASTON

*To my right worshipful husband, John Paston, be this delivered in haste.*

Right worshipful husband, I recommend me to you, beseeching you that ye be not displeased with me, though my simpleness caused you for to be displeased with me.[1] By my troth, it is not my will neither to do nor say that should cause you for to be displeased; and if I have done, I am sorry thereof, and will amend it. Wherefore I beseech you to forgive me, and that ye bear none heaviness in your heart against me, for your dis-pleasance should be too heavy to me to endure with.

I send you the roll that ye sent for, ensealed, by the bringer hereof; it was found in your trussing coffer. As for herring, I have bought an horse-load for 4s. 6d.; I can get none eels yet.[2] As for bever, there is promised me some, but I might not get it yet. I sent to Joan Petche to have an answer for the windows, for she might not come to me. And she sent me word that she had spoke thereof to Thomas Ingham; and he said that he should speak with you himself, and he should accord with you well enough, and said to her it was not her part to desire of him to stop the lights; and also he said it was not his part to do it, because the place is his but for years.

And as for all other errands that ye have commanded for to be done, they shall be done as soon as they may be done. The Blessed Trinity have you in His keeping.

Written at Norwich, on the Monday next after Saint Edward.

Yours,

[22nd March ?1451]                    M. P.

[1] The cause of his displeasure does not appear; it was doubtless some-thing of trifling moment.
[2] These herrings and eels were for consumption during Lent.

### 48. DEBENHAM, TYMPERLEY, AND WHITE TO JOHN([1]) PASTON [J. G.]

Master Paston, we commend us to you, letting you wit that the sheriff[1] is not so whole as he was, for now he will show but a part of his friendship. And also there is great press of people, and few friends, as far as we can feel it. And therefore be ye sadly advised whether ye seem best to come yourself, or send, or, etc.; for we will assay as much as in us is to prevail to your intent. And yet, if it needed, we would have a man to give us information, or show evidence after the case requireth. Also the sheriff informed us that he hath writing from the King that he shall make such a panel to acquit the Lord Moleyns.[2] And also he told us, and as far as we can conceive and feel, the sheriff will panel gentlemen to acquit the Lord, and jurors to acquit his men; and we suppose that it is by the motion and means of the other party. And if any means of treaty be proffered, we know not what mean should be to your pleasure. And therefore we would fain have more knowledge, if ye think it were to do.

No more at this time, but the Holy Trinity have you in His keeping. Written at Walsingham, in haste, the second day of May. By your true and faithful friends,

DEBENHAM, TYMPERLEY, AND WHITE.

And also, sir, as we conceive, the Lord Moleyns shall not be quit before Thursday; inasmuch as he was indicted before the justice, we understand he shall not be quit but before the justice. Wherefore we advise you, if ye think it be to do, to send your friends in the meantime, and come yourself to your place at Sparham, and there abide unto time that we have knowledge how the said matter will draw, and till that we may have word from you, and ye from us, etc.

[1451, ? May]

### 49. WILLIAM LOMNER TO JOHN([1]) PASTON [J. G.]

Right worshipful sir, your good cousins and friends advise you to come to Walsingham, and that ye be there to-morrow betimes at six on the clock. For the Lord Moleyns offereth a treaty for the goods, and amends to be made, ere he goeth out of this country; and if it be not taken his men shall justify, whereupon

---

[1] John Jermyn.
[2] Paston had procured two indictments, one against Lord Moleyns, and the other against his men, because of their forcible entry at Gresham.

your title might be hurt. The Lord Scales, the justice, and other knights and squires marvel greatly ye come not, and though they that have not so true and evident matter as ye have counsel you to be absent; yet I would ye did as ye be desired by that fellowship, for many would you right well. When ye come, I shall tell you more.

The Lord Moleyns should not have been acquit of his commandment, had he not sworn on a book, such evidence was against him; and there is no gentleman would acquit his men for no good, etc.

W. Lomner.

50.        Sir John[1] Heveningham to
Margaret Paston

*To my right worshipful cousin, Margaret Paston, be this letter delivered.*

Right worshipful and well-beloved cousin, I commend me to you as heartily as I can, thanking you of your good cheer the last time I was with you.   And, worshipful cousin, please it you to call unto your remembrance, I wrote unto you for my cousin Agnes Loveday to have been in your service, and I received from you a letter that your will was good, but durst not to into the time ye had spoke with my cousin your husband.

Worshipful cousin, I have laboured for her in other places, but I cannot have my intent as yet.   Wherefore, if that it please you to have her with you to into the time that a mistress may be purveyed for her, I pray you thereof; and I shall content you for her board, that ye shall be well pleased.   For, cousin, an' I had a wife, I would not care for her.   And there as she is she is not well at her ease, for she is at Robert Lethum's; and therefore I pray you heartily that ye will tender this my writing, and I beseech you that in case be that ye will fulfil it, that ye will send my cousin William Staunton for her, and I shall keep you true promise as I have before written.   And I beseech Almighty Jesu preserve you.   Written at Heveningham on the 7th day of May, etc.

Your own cousin,

John Heveningham, *Knight.*

[? 1451]

51.    JOHN OSBERN TO JOHN[(1)] PASTON

*To my right reverend and worshipful master, John Paston, be this delivered.*

Please it your mastership to wete that I have spoken with the sheriff at his place, moving to him, as for that that was left with his under-sheriff,[1] it is your will he should send a man of his for it; for though it were more, ye would gladly he should take it. He thanked you, and said his under-sheriff was at London, and himself had none deserved; and if he had he would have taken it.    And when I departed from him, I desired him again to send therefore, and then he said it should abide till ye come home; whereby I conceive he would have it, and be glad to take it. Moreover, I remembered him of his promise made before to you at London, when he took his oath and charge, and that ye were with him when he took his oath, and other divers times; and for those promises made by him to you at that time, and other times at the oyer determiner at Lynn, ye proposed you by the trust that ye have in him for to attempt and rear actions that should be to the avail of him and of his office.    He would have known what the actions should be.    I said I could not tell him, and then he said he would do for you that he may, except for the acquittal of the Lord Moleyn's men, insomuch as the King hath written to him for to show favour to the Lord Moleyns and his men, and as he saith the indictment longeth to the King and not to you, and the Lord Moleyns a great lord.    Also, as he saith, now late the Lord Moleyns hath sent him a letter, and my Lord of Norfolk another, for to show favour in these indictments; he dare not abide the jeopardy of that that he should offend the King's commandment.    He know not how the King may be informed of him, and what shall be said to him.

And then I said, as for any jeopardy that he should abide in anything that he doth for you, or by your desire, ye have offered him, and will perform it, sufficient surety for to save him harmless; and therefore I supposed there would none reasonable man think but that he might do for you without any jeopardy.[2]    And then he said he might none surety take that passed an hundred pounds; and the Lord Moleyns is a great lord, he might soon cause him to lose that and much more.    Then I said, by that mean, in default of a sheriff, every man may be put from his livelode.    And then he said, if it were for the livelode, men would take them the nearer for to abide a jeopardy; but by his faith, as he swore, if the King write again to him he will no longer abide

---

[1] It was a sum of money intended as a bribe.

[2] This shows that the jeopardy of offending the King's commandment was merely legal and pecuniary.

the jeopardy of the King's writing, but he trusteth to God to impanel such men as should to his knowledge be indifferent, and none common jurors.

As meseemeth, it would do good and ye would get a commandment of the King to the sheriff for to show you favour, and to impanel gentlemen, and not for to favour none such riots, etc.; for he said that he sent you the letter that the King sent him, and ye said a man should get such one for a noble.[1]

Item, I remembered him of the promises that he made to Tymperley, and that if he would make you very true promise, ye would reward him as much as he would desire, or any other reasonable man for him, and as much and more than any adversary ye have would give him. Then he said he took never no money of none of them all. There was proffered him at Walsingham for the Lord Moleyns twenty nobles; he had not a penny. Moreover I proffered him, if he would make you promise that ye might verily trust upon him, ye would give him in hand as he would desire, or to leave a sum if he would have named it in a mean man's hand, and such as he hath trust to. And then he said, if he might do for you, or if he do anything for you, then he will take your money with a good will; and other promise I could not have of him, but that he would do for you all that he may, except for the indictments. I conceive verily he hath made promise to do his part that they shall be quit, but I suppose he hath made none other promise against you for the livelode. But he looketh after a great bribe; but it is not for to trust him verily without that he may not choose.

I suppose he had no writing from my Lord of Norfolk as he said.

I was at Framlingham for to have spoken with Tymperley, Debenham, or Berry, and they were all out. My Lord,[2] as he came from London, he was at Ipswich on Monday; and when he went without the town towards Framlingham, he had all his men ride forth afore a great pace, for he would follow softly. And when his men were out of sight, he rode with five men to a squire's place of his thereby, and on Tuesday rode my Lady to him; and so I did nought at Framlingham. No more at this time, but Almighty Jesu speed you, and have you in His keeping. Written at Norwich, the Thursday next after Saint Austin, etc.

By your servant,

JOHN OSBERN.

[27th May 1451]

---

[1] Another proof of the little importance of the King's interference, and of the one-sidedness of Paston's wishes. 'Non seche riotts' were to be favoured in Lord Moleyns, though the following letter from Agnes Paston evinces no disinclination to resort to the same means.
[2] The Duke of Norfolk.

52. AGNES PASTON TO JOHN[(1)] PASTON [J. G.][1]

*To . . .[2] Barker of St Clement's parish, in Norwich, to deliver to my master John Paston, in haste.*

On Thursday the wall was made yard high, and a good while before evening it rained so sore that they were fain to helle the wall and leave work. And the water is fallen so sore that it standeth under the wall a foot deep to Ball's-ward.[3] And on Friday, after sacring, one came from church-ward, and shove down all that was thereon, and trod on the wall and brake some, and went over; but I cannot yet wete who it was. And Warren King's wife, as she went over the style, she cursed Ball, and said that he had given away the way, and so it proved by John Paston's words. And after, King's folk and others came and cried on Agnes Ball, saying to her the same. Yestereven, when I shall go to my bed, the vicar [4] said that Warren King and Warren Harman, betwixt Mass and matins, took Sir Robert [5] in the vestry, and bade him say to me, verily the wall should down again. And when the vicar told me I wist thereof no word, nor yet do by Sir Robert, for he saith he were loth to make any strife. And when I came out of the church, Robert Edmunds showed me how I was amerced for suit of court the last year 6*d*., and said it was 12*d*. till Warren King and he gat it away 6*d*.

I send you word how John James was demeaned at Cromer, to send to James Gresham how he shall be demeaned. Geoffrey Benchard, Alexander Clover, haywards, took a distress of John James or the bond tenant of A. Paston, called Reynolds, in Cromer, the twenty-eighth year of this king, and W. Goodwin, bailiff of Cromer, with the said J. James, with force took away the distress, which was two horses and a plough. And God be with you.

By AGNES PASTON, your Mother.

[1451 or later]

---

[1] *See* footnote 4, page 9.
[2] The name 'Harry' is crossed out in the original, and a word which looks like 'Meye' is written over.
[3] i.e. towards the property of a neighbour called Ball.
[4] William Pope.
[5] Probably the vicar's curate

53.    Agnes Paston to John[(1)] Paston [J. G.][1]

*To John Paston be this bill delivered in haste.*

I spake this day with a man of Paston side, and he told me that
a man of Paston told him that Paston men would not go proces-
sion farther than the churchyard on St Mark's day; [2] for he said
the procession-way was stopped in, and said within short time
men hoped that the wall should be broke down again.    Item, he
said that I was amerced for stopping of the said way at the last
general court, but he could not tell how much the amercement
was.    And he that told it me asked the man that told it him if he
had the amercement in his estreat to distrain therefore; and he
said nay, but said he that should do it should better do take it
upon him than he should.    Item, the same man told me that he
met with a man of Blickling hight Barker, that came late from
London, and he told him that I had a suit at London against
Warren Harman of Paston, and said that Robert Branton was his
attorney, and said he saw him right busy at London.    And forget not your sister; and God have you in keeping.    Written at
Norwich the twelfth day of May,

By your mother,

A. Paston.

[1451 or later]

54.        Agnes Paston to John[(1)] Paston[3]

*To John Paston, dwelling in the Temple at London, be this letter
delivered in haste.*

I greet you well, and let you wete that on the Sunday before
St Edmund, after evensong, Agnes Ball came to me to my closet
and bade me good even, and Clement Spicer with her.    And I
asked him what he would.    And he asked me why I had stopped
in the King's way.    And I said to him I stopped no way but
mine own, and asked him why he had sold my land to John Ball.
And he swore he was never accorded with your father; and I told
him if his father had done as he did, he would have been ashamed
to have said as he said.    And all that time Warren Harman
leaned over the parclose and listened what we said, and said that
the change was a rewly change, for the town was undo thereby,
and is the worse by an £100.    And I told him it was no courtesy
to meddle him in a matter but-if he were called to counsel.
And proudly going forth with me in the church, he said the

---

[1] *See* footnote 4, page 9.          [2] 25th April, Rogation day.
[3] *See* footnote 4, page 9.

stopping of the way should cost me twenty nobles, and yet it should down again. And I let him wete he that put it down should pay therefor.

Also he said that it was well done that I set men to work to owl,[1] many, while I was here, but in the end I shall lose my cost. Then he asked me why I had away his hay at Walsham, saying to me he would he had wist it when it was carried, and he should have letted it. And I told him it was mine own ground, and for mine own I would hold it; and he bade me take four acres and go no farther. And thus curtly he departed from me in the church-yard. And since, I spake with a certain man and asked him if he heard aught said why the dinner was made at Norfolk's house; and he told me heard say that certain men had sent to London to get a commission out of the Chancery to put down again the wall and the dike. I received your letter by Robert Repps this day, after this letter written thus far. I have read it, but I can give you none answer more than I have written, save the wife of Harman hath the name of Our Lady,[2] whose blessing ye have and mine. Written at Paston, on the day after St Edmund.

By your mother,

AGNES PASTON.

[1451 or later]

## 55.   MARGARET PASTON TO JOHN[(1)] PASTON

*To my right worshipful husband, John Paston, be this delivered in haste.*

Right worshipful husband, I recommend me to you, desiring heartily to hear of your welfare, praying you to wete that I have spoken with my Lady Felbrigg[3] of that ye bade me speak to her of. And she said plainly to me that she would not, nor never was advised, neither to let the Lord Moleyns nor none other to have their intents as for that matter while yet she liveth; and she was right evil paid with Sauter, that he should report as it was told you that he should have reported. And she made right much of you, and said that she would not that no servant of hers should report nothing that should be against you, otherwise than she would that your servants should do or say against her; and if either your servants did against her, or

---

[1] The meaning here is uncertain, but it probably means to labour (in this case to build the wall) by night.
[2] i.e. her name was Mary.
[3] Catherine, widow of Sir Simon Felbrigg.

any of hers against you, she would that it should be reformed betwixt you and her, and that ye might be all one. For she said in good faith she desireth your friendship. And as for the report of Sauter, she said she supposed that he would not report so; and if she might know that he did, she would blame him therefore. I told her that it was told me since that ye yeden, and that it grieved me more that the said Sauter should report as he did than it had been reported of another, inasmuch as I had owed him good will before; and she prayed me that I should not believe such reports till I knew the truth.

I was at Topps's at dinner on St Peter's day. There my Lady Felbrigg and other gentlewomen desired to have had you there: they said they should all have been the merrier if ye had been there. My cousin Topps hath much care till she hears good tidings of her brother's matter. She told me that they should keep a day on Monday next coming betwixt her brother and Sir Andrew Ogard and Wyndham. I pray you send me word how they speed, and how ye speed in your own matters also.

Also, I pray you heartily that ye will send me a pot with treacle in haste; for I have been right evil at ease, and your daughter both, since that ye yeden hence. And one of the tallest young men of this parish lieth sick, and hath a great mur-rain; how he shall do God knoweth. I have sent my uncle Berney [1] the pot with treacle that ye did buy for him. Mine aunt recommendeth her to you, and prayeth you to do for her as the bill maketh mention of that I send you with this letter, and as ye think best for to do therein.

Sir Harry Inglose is passed to God this night, whose soul God assoil, and was carried forth this day at nine of the clock to St Faith's, and there shall be buried. If ye desire to buy any of his stuff, I pray you send me word thereof in haste, and I shall speak to Robert Inglose and to Wichingham thereof; I suppose they be executors. The Blessed Trinity have you in His keep-ing. Written at Norwich in haste on the Thursday next after St Peter.

I pray you trust not to the sheriff [2] for no fair language.

Yours,

MARGARET PASTON.

[1st July 1451]

---

[1] Philip Berney, third son of John Berney, Esq., of Reedham. This John Berney was Margaret Paston's maternal grandfather.
[2] John Clopton.

## 56.    SIR JOHN FASTOLF TO THOMAS HOWES

*To my trusty friend, Sir Thomas Howes, parson of Castlecombe, being at Caister.*

Right trusty friend, I greet you well.   Item, whereas the Bishop of Norwich [1] maketh but delays in my reasonable desire for an end to be had in the xxv marks of Hickling, I am upon an appointment and thorough with the heir of Clifford, that he shall enter in the whole manor that is chargeable with my xxv marks rent,[2] which the prior and convent have forfeited the said whole manor to the heirs under their convent seal of record, because of my non-payment of xxv marks.   And so then the prior shall lose for ever fourscore marks of rent, and that without any conscience, for they have been false both to the Cliffords and to me this seven year day.   And I trust to God to correct them so by spiritual law and temporal law, that all other religious shall take an example to break the covenant or will of any benefactor that advanceth them with lands, rents, or goods; and my confessors have exhorted me greatly thereto.   And Almighty God keep you.   Written at London the 23rd day of September, in the 30th year of King Henry VI.

JOHN FASTOLF, *Knight.*

There is one Walsham would desire acquittance of pardon for the widow of Heigham.   I have no cause; for her husband left her whereof to pay her debts sufficient, and for me he fare the better.   The widow noiseth you, Sir Thomas, that ye sold away salt but for 20*s.* that she might have had 40*s.* for every way; I pray you answer that for your acquittal.

Item, send me the value of Goold's tenement in Drayton with twenty acres land thereto, what it was worth yearly, when it stood whole; for Selling saith it was worth but one noble by the year.

[1451]

---

[1] Walter Lyhart.
[2] The estate out of which this rent-charge of twenty-five marks had been reserved was settled on the priory of Hickling by one of the Clifford family. William Clifford, in 1419, assigned this rent-charge to Henry Barton, who, in 1428, assigned it to Sir John Fastolf, who was now going to convey it to a Clifford again.   Hickling priory was first founded in 1185.

57. Agnes Paston to John[1] Paston [J. G.][1]

*To John Paston dwelling in the Temple at London be this letter delivered in haste.*

I greet you well and let you wete that Warren Harman, on the Sunday after Hallowmas day, after evensong, said openly in the churchyard that he wist well that, an' the wall were pulled down, though he were an hundred miles from Paston he wist well that I would say he did it and he should bear the blame; saying: 'Tell it here whoso will, though it should cost me twenty nobles it shall be pulled down again.' And the said Warren's wife with a loud voice said: 'All the devils of hell draw her soul to hell for the way that she hath made!' And at even a certain man supped with me and told me that the patent granted but to close but a perch on breadth, and that I had closed more than the grant of the patent is, as men said. And John Marshall told me that there was a thrifty woman come forby the watering, and found the way stopped, and asked him who had stopped the way; and he said, they that had power to give it, and asked her what was freer than gift, and he said she saw the day that Paston men would not have suffered that. And God be with you. Written at Paston on Monday after Hallowmas day. By your mother,

Agnes Paston.

58. Proclamation by the Duke of Norfolk

THE DUKE OF NORFOLK

Be it known to all the King's true liege people, the cause of our coming into this country [2] is, by the commandment of the King our sovereign lord, for to inquire of such great riots, extortions, horrible wrongs, and hurts, as his Highness is credibly informed be done in this country, and to know in certain, by you that know the truth, by what person or persons the said great riots, extortions, horrible wrongs, and hurts be done. Wherefore we charge you all, on the King's behalf, our sovereign lord, that ye spare neither for love, dread, nor fear that ye have to any person of what estate, degree, or condition he be, but that ye say the sooth by whom such offences be done, and that ye spare no man that ye know guilty; and, by the faith that we owe to our sovereign lord, they shall be chastised after their desert, and it reformed as law requireth.

---

[1] *See* footnote 4, page 9.　　　[2] The county of Norfolk.

Also it is openly published that certain servants of the Lord Scales should in his name menace and put men in fear and dread to complain to us at this time of the said hurts and griefs, saying that we would abide but a short time here, and after our departing he would have the rule and governance as he hath had aforetime. We let you wete that next the King our sovereign lord, by his good grace and licence, we will have the principal rule and governance through all this shire, of which we bear our name, while that we be living, as far as reason and law requireth, whosoever will grudge or say the contrary. For we will that the Lord Scales, Sir Thomas Tuddenham, Sir Miles Stapleton, and John Heydon [1] have in knowledge, though our person be not daily here, they shall find our power here at all times to do the King our sovereign lord service, and to support and maintain you all in your right that be the King's true liege men. For it may not be said nay, but that here hath been the greatest riots, horrible wrongs, and offences done in these parts by the said Lord Scales, Thomas Tuddenham, Miles Stapleton, John Heydon, and such as be confederated unto them, that ever was seen in our days; and most mischief through their malicious purpose like to have fallen among the King's true liege people now late at Norwich, nor had we better provided therefor. And also that God fortuned us to withstand their said malicious and evil-disposed purpose.

Wherefore, make bills of your grievance, and come to us; and we shall bring you to the King's presence ourself, whose presence will be here in all the haste with the mercy of God, and see the reformation there of his own person.

## 59. Sir John[(1)] Heveningham and Others to (?) The Sheriff of Norfolk [J. G.]

Right worshipful, we commend us to you. Please it you to wete that we and other gentlemen of Norfolk have been in purpose to have sued to the high and mighty prince and our right good lord the Duke of Norfolk to Framlingham, to have informed his Highness of divers assaults and riots made by Charles Nowell [2] and others against the King's law and peace, without any cause or occasion, upon John Paston and others of our kin, friends, and neighbours, nor had been that daily this ten days it hath

---

[1] These four men, especially Tuddenham and Heydon, were behind most of the disorders in Norfolk at this time.
[2] A servant of the Duke of Norfolk.

been done us to wete [1] that his Highness should come into Norwich or Claxton, we not being in certain yet whether he shall remove; praying you as we trust, that ye will tender the welfare of this shire and of the gentlemen therein, that ye will let our said lord have knowing of our intent in this, and after to send us answer whether it please his Highness we should come to his presence, and in what place, or to send our complaint to him if more information be thought behoveful, trusting to his good lordship of remedy in this matter; which done, seemeth us, shall be our said lord's honour and great rejoicing to all the gentlemen of the shire, and cause the peace to be kept hereafter by the grace of God, who have you in His blessed keeping. Written at Norwich on St George's day.

Sir John Heveningham. John Ferrers. Tho. Gurnay. John Groos. W. Rokewode. John Bacon, senior. John Bacon, junior. J. Palgrave. Robt. Mortimer. Nicholas Appleyard.

[23rd April 1452]

60.        John[1] Paston to (?) The
            Sheriff of Norfolk [J. G.]

Reverend and right worshipful sir, and my good master, I recommend me to you. Please you to wete that Charles Nowell with others hath in this country made many riots and assaults; and, among others, he and five of his fellowship set upon me and some of my servants at the Cathedral church of Norwich, he smiting at me, whilst one of his fellows held my arms at my back, as the bearer hereof shall more plainly inform you. Which was to me strange case, thinking in my conceit that I was my Lord's [2] man and his homager ere Charles knew his Lordship, that my Lord was my good lord, and that I had been with my Lord at London within eight days before Lent, at which time he granted me his good lordship so largely that it must cause me ever to be his true servant to my power. I thought also that I had never given cause to none of my Lord's house to owe me evil will, nor that there was none of the house but I would have done for as I could desire anyone to do for me, and yet will except my adversary. And thus I and my friends have mused on this and thought he was hard to do thus. And this notwithstanding, as

---

[1] Nor had been . . . wete: Unless we had been informed daily during the past ten days.
[2] The Duke of Norfolk's.

soon as knowledge was had of my Lord's coming to Framlingham, I never attempted to proceed against him [Nowell] as justice and law would, but to trust to my said Lord that his Highness would see this punished, and desired my master H . . . , my cousin Tymperley, the dean, and others to be ready with such gentlemen as dwell hereabout that can record the truth to have come complain to my Lord. But we have had continually tidings of my Lord's coming hither that caused us for to abide thereupon. Beseeching your good mastership that ye will let my Lord have knowledge of my complaint, and that ye will tender the good speed of the intent of the letters written to you from gentlemen of this shire. Praying you that ye will give credence to the bearer hereof, and be his good master in case any man make any quarrel to him. And what that I may do by your commandment shall be ready with the grace of God, who have you in His blessed keeping. Written at Norwich on St George's day.

[23rd April 1452]

### 61. ANONYMOUS: INFORMATION OF OUTRAGES [J. G.]

Charles Nowell, Otiwell Nowell, Robert Ledham, John the son of Hodge Ratcliff, Robert Dalling, Henry Bang, Roger Chirch, Nicholas Goldsmith, Robert Taylor, Christopher Grenesheve, . . . [1] Dunmow, Elis Duckworth, Christopher Bradley, John Cokkow, assembling and gathering to them great multitude of misruled people, keep a fronture and a forcelet at the house of the said Robert Ledham, and issue out at their pleasure, sometime six, sometime twelve, sometime thirty and more, armed, jacked, and saletted, with bows, arrows, spears, and bills, and override the country and oppress the people, and do many horrible and abominable deeds like to be destruction of the shire of Norfolk, without the King our sovereign lord seeth it redressed.

On Mid-Lent Sunday [2] certain of the said fellowship, in the church of Birlingham, made a fray upon two of the servants of the Reverend Father in God, Bishop of Norwich, the said servants at that time kneeling to see the using of the Mass. And there and then the said fellowship would have killed the said two servants at the priest's back, nor had they been letted, as it seemed.

Item, on the Monday [3] next before Easter day, six of the said

---

[1] Blank in the manuscript.    [2] 19th March.    [3] 3rd April.

persons made an assault upon John Paston and his two servants at the door of the Cathedral church of Norwich,[1] with swords, bucklers, and daggers drawn smote at the said Paston, one of them holding the said Paston by both arms at his back, as it seemeth purposing there to have murdered the said Paston, an' they had not been letted; and also smote one of the servants of the said Paston upon the naked head with a sword, and polluted the sanctuary.[2]

Item, on the Monday next before Easter day, ten of the said persons lay in wait in the highway under Thorpe Wood upon Philip Berney, Esquire, and his man, and shot at them and smote their horses with arrows, and then overrode him and brake a bow on the said Philip's head and took him prisoner, calling him traitor. And when they had kept him as long as they list, they led him to the said Bishop of Norwich and asked of him surety of the peace, and forthwith released their surety and went their way.

Item, three of the said fellowship lay in wait upon Edmund Brome, gentleman, and with naked swords fought with him by the space of a quarter of an hour and took him prisoner; and when they had kept him as long as they list, let him go.

Item, forty of the same fellowship came riding to Norwich jacked and saletted, with bows and arrows, bills, glaives, on Maunday Thursday,[3] and that day after noon, when service was done, they, in likewise arrayed, would have brake up the White-friars' doors, saying that they had come to hear evensong; how-beit that they made their avaunt in town they should have some men out of town, quick or dead; and there made a great rumour, where the mayor and the aldermen, with great multitude of people, assembled, and thereupon the said fellowship de-parted.

Item, divers times certain of the said fellowship have taken from John Wilton, without any cause, his neat, his sheep, and other cattle, and some thereof have salted and eaten, some thereof have eloined; so that the said Wilton wot not where for to seek his beasts. And on the morrow [4] next after Easter day last past, they took from him eleven beasts, and kept them two days without any cause.

Item, in likewise they have done to John Coke and Katherine Wilton.

Item, in likewise they have taken the goods and chattels of Thomas Barret and many others.

[1] *See* No. 60, page 64.
[2] The foregoing paragraph is crossed out in the original.
[3] 6th April.
[4] 10th April.

Item, certain of the said fellowship late made an assault upon John Wilton in Plumsted churchyard, and there beat him so that he was in doubt of his life.

Item, in like wise upon John Coke of Witton, breaking up his doors at eleven of the clock in the night, and with their swords maimed him and gave him seven great wounds. Item, smote the mother of the said Coke, a woman of fourscore years of age, upon the crown of the head with a sword, which wound was never healed to the day of her death.

Item, the said Dunmow, one of the said fellowship, now let beat the parson of Hasingham, and brake his head in his own chancel.

Item, threescore of the said fellowship, arrayed as men of war, now late entered with force upon Philip Berney and disseised him of the manor of Rockland Tofts, which dare not, for fear of murder, re-enter his own land; howbeit he and his ancestors have been peaceably possessed thereof many years.[1]

Item, Aelred's son of Earl Soham, fast by Framlingham, on the Saturday [2] next before Palm Sunday last past, was pulled out of a house and killed. Whether any of the said fellowship were there or not men cannot say; there be of them so many, of which many be unknown people.

Item, the said fellowship make such affrays in the country about the said Ledham's place, and so frighteth the people, that divers persons for fear of murder dare not abide in their houses, nor ride, nor walk about their occupations, without they take greater people about them than accordeth to their degree, which they will not do in evil example giving.

Item, the said fellowship, of afore-cast malice and purpose, now late took Roger Chirch, one of their own fellowship, by his own assent, which Roger Chirch by their assent had moved and stirred a rising in the Hundred of Blofield, and hath confessed himself to be at that arising, and hath embilled, as it is said, divers gentlemen and the most part of the trusty yeomen and husbands and men of good name and fame of the hundred about the said Ledham's place, where the said fellowship is abiding, and nameth them with other suspicious people for risers, to the intent to hide and cover their own guilt, and to hold them that be true men and innocent in that matter in a danger and fear that they should not gather people, nor attempt to resist their riotous governance of the said riotous fellowship.

Item, it is conceived that if the said riotous fellowship and they that draw to them were duly examined, it should be known

---

[1] The foregoing paragraph is crossed out in the original.
[2] 1st April.

that if there were any such rising, it was conjected, done, imagined, and laboured by the said riotous fellowship and by their means. For as well the said Chirch as divers of the most suspicious persons by the said Chirch embilled for risers, be and have been of long time daily in company with the said riotous fellowship.

Item, one of the said fellowship of late time, as it is said, to increase their malicious purpose, hath proffered rewards and goods to another person for him to take upon him to appeal certain persons, and affirm the saying of the said Roger Chirch.[1]

In witness of these premisses, divers knights and esquires and gentlemen, whose names follow, which know this matter by saying, hearing, or credible report, to this writing have set their seals, beseeching your Lordships to be means to the King our sovereign lord for remedy in this behalf. Written, etc.

[1452]                                                    [UNSIGEND.]


62.   MARGARET PASTON TO JOHN[(1)] PASTON

*To my right worshipful husband, John Paston, be this delivered in haste.*

Right worshipful husband, I commend me to you. I pray you that ye will do buy two dozen trenchers, for I can none get in this town. Also I pray you that ye will send me a book with chardeqweyns [2] that I may have of in the mornings, for the air be not wholesome in this town; therefore I pray you heartily let John Suffield bring it home with him.

No more, but the Blessed Trinity have you in His keeping, and send you good speed in all your matters. Written on St Leonard's even.

My Uncle Philip [3] commends him to you, and he hath been so sick since that I came to Reedham, that I weened he should never have escaped it, nor not is like to do but-if he have ready help; and therefore he shall into Suffolk this next week, to mine aunt, for there is a good physician, and he shall look to him.

My Lady Hastings [4] told me that Heydon hath spoken to Geoffrey Boleyn [5] of London, and is agreed with him that he

---

[1] The two foregoing paragraphs are crossed out in the original.
[2] A preserve made of quinces. 'Book,' here, means 1 lb.
[3] Philip Berney.
[4] Margery, widow of Sir Edward Hastings of Elsing.
[5] Mayor of London in 1457, an ancestor of Anne Boleyn.

should bargain with Sir John Fastolf to buy the manor of Blickling as it were for himself; and if Boleyn buy it, in truth Heydon
shall have it.

I came to Norwich on Soulmass day.[1]

Yours,

MARGARET PASTON.

[5th November 1452]

63.          AGNES PASTON TO JOHN[(1)] PASTON

*This letter be delivered to John Paston, being at London, in the
Inner Inn of the Temple.*

I greet you well, and send you God's blessing and mine. And
as touching the matter which ye desired my cousin Clere [2]
should write for, she hath done, and I send you the copy closed
in this letter. As for the inquiry, I have sent by Pynchemore to
inquire, and sent mine own man to William Bacton, and done
him inquire in divers places, and I can hear no word of none
such inquirance; I wot not what it meaneth. Robert Hill was
at Paston this week, and the man that dwelled in Bowers' place is
out thereof, and said to Robert he durst no longer abide therein,
for Warren Harman saith to him it is his place. As for Coket's
matter, my daughter your wife told me yestereven the man that
sueth him will now stand to your award.

Bartholomew White is condemned in Forncett court, in 40
marks as it is said.

Item, as for Talfas, the sheriffs have behest to do all the favour
they may. I sent the parson of St Edmund's to Gilbert; and he
said there was come a new writ for to have him up by the 15th
day of Saint Martin, and now Caley had been at them, and
desired to carry up Talfas on his own cost and give him good
wages.

Item, John Osbern said to me this day that he supposed they
will not have him up before Easter. And Margaret Talfas said
to me the same day that men told her that he should never have
end till he were at London, and asked me counsel whether she
might give the sheriffs silver or none; and I told her if she did, I
supposed she should find them the more friendly.

Item, as for Orwellbury, I send you a bill of all the receipts
since the death of your father, and a copy written on the back
how your father let it to farm to the said Gurney. I would ye
should write Gurney, and charge him to meet with you from
London-ward, and at the least way let him purvey £10; for he

---

[1] 2nd November.          [2] *See* footnote 1, page 22.

oweth, by my reckoning at Michaelmas last past, beside your father's debt, £18 14s. 8d. If ye would write to him to bring surety both for your father's debt and mine, and pay by days,[1] so that the man might live and pay us, I would forgive him of the old arrearages £10. And he might be made to pay 20 marks by year, on that condition I would forgive him £10;[2] and so thinketh me he should have cause to pray for your father and me, and was it let in my father's time. I feel by Robert, his wife is right loth to go thence; she said that she had lever I should have all her goods after her day than they should go out thereof.

Item, John Damme told me that the Lady Boys [3] will sell a place called Hales;[4] but he saith she speaketh it privily and saith it is not entailed, as John Damme knoweth, which will she hath said as largely of other things that hath not been so.

Item, he told me, as he heard said, Sir John Fastolf hath sold Hellesdon to Boleyn of London;[5] and if it be so, it seemeth he will sell more. Wherefore I pray you, as ye will have my love and my blessing, that ye will help and do your devoir that something were purchased for your two brethren. I suppose that Sir John Fastolf, and he were spoke to, would be gladder to let his kinsmen have part than strange men; assay him in my name of such places as ye suppose is most clear.

It is said in this country that my Lord of Norfolk saith Sir John Fastolf hath given him Caister, and he will have it plainly. I send you a bill of Osbern's hand, which was the answer of the sheriff and John of Damme.

John, bring me my letter home with you, and my cousin Clere's copy of her letter, and the copy of the receipt of Orwell-bury. And recommend me to Lomner, and tell him his best beloved fareth well; but she is not yet come to Norwich, for they die yet,[6] but not so sore as they did. And God be with you. Written at Norwich, in right great haste, the 16th day of November.

By your mother,

AGNES PASTON.

[? 1452]

[1] Fixed terms.
[2] That is, other £10 of her own debt.
[3] Sibilla, daughter and heiress of Sir Robert Ylley, and widow of Sir Roger Boys who died in December 1450. Sir Roger was cousin to Sir John Fastolf.
[4] Holm Hale.
[5] This was not true.
[6] There was plague in Norwich at this time.

## 64. INDENTURE BETWEEN RICHARD, DUKE OF YORK, AND SIR JOHN FASTOLF [J. G.]

This indenture witnesseth that whereas Richard, Duke of York, by his letter of sale bearing date the fifteenth day of the month of December, the thirty-first year of the reign of our sovereign lord King Henry the Sixth, hath bargained, aliened, sold, granted, and confirmed unto John Fastolf, knight, the jewels underwritten: That is to wit, a nowche with a great pointed diamond set upon a rose enamelled white; a nowche of gold in fashion of a ragged staff,[1] with two images of man and woman garnished with a ruby, a diamond, and a great pearl; and a flower of gold garnished with two rubies, a diamond, and three hanging pearls. To have, hold, and rejoice the same jewels to the same John, his executors and assignees, freely, quietly, and peaceably for evermore, like as in the said letter of sale more openly is contained. Nevertheless, the said John will and granteth hereby that if the said duke pay or do pay to the same John or to his attorney, his heirs, or to his executors, in the feast of the Nativity of St John Baptist next coming, £437 sterling without delay, that then the said letter of sale to be hold for nought; but he to deliver again unto the said duke, or to his attorney paying the said £437 sterling in the said feast, the said jewels. And if default be made in the payment of the said £437 in part or in all against the form aforesaid, then will and granteth the said Duke hereby that the foresaid letter of sale, by him as is abovesaid made, stand in full strength and virtue, this indenture notwithstanding. In witness whereof, to the part of this said indenture remaining towards the said John the said duke hath set his seal. Given at Fotheringay, the eighteenth day of the said month of December, the thirty-first year of the reign of our said sovereign lord King Henry the Sixth.

[1452]

R. YORK.

## 65. MARGARET PASTON TO JOHN[(1)] PASTON[2]

*To my right worshipful husband, John Paston, be this delivered in haste.*

Right worshipful husband, I recommend me to you, desiring to hear of your welfare; praying you to wete that Sir Thomas Howes hath purveyed four dormants for the draught-chamber, and the malthouse, and the brewery, whereof he hath bought

---

[1] The ragged staff was the badge of the earls of Warwick.
[2] This and the following letter refer to building operations at Caister Castle, for which John Paston seems to have been partly responsible.

three, and the fourth, that shall be the longest and greatest of all, he shall have from Hellesdon, which he saith my master Fastolf shall give me, because my chamber shall be made therewith. As for the laying of the said dormants, they shall be laid this next week because of the malthouse; and as for the remnant, I trow it shall abide till ye come home, because I can neither be purveyed of posts nor of boards not yet.

I have taken the measure in the draught-chamber, there as ye would your coffers and your countery [1] should be set for the while, and there is no space beside the bed (though the bed were removed to the door) for to set both your board and your coffers there, and to have space to go and sit beside. Wherefore I have purveyed that ye shall have the same draught-chamber that ye had before, thereas ye shall lie to yourself; and when your gear is removed out of your little house, the door shall be locked, and your bags laid in one of the great coffers, so that they shall be safe, I trust.

Richard Charles and John Dow have fetched home the child [2] from Rockland Tofts, and it is a pretty boy; and it is told me that Will is at Blickling with a poor man of the town. A young woman that was some time with Burton of this town sent me word thereof; I pray you send me word if ye will that anything that ye will be done to him ere ye come home. Richard Charles sendeth you word that Willes hath been at him here, and offered him to make him estate in all things according to their indenture; and if he do the contrary ye shall soon have word.

My mother prayeth you for to remember my sister, and to do your part faithfully ere ye come home to help to get her a good marriage. It seemeth by my mother's language that she would never so fain to have be delivered of her as she will now.

It was told here that Knivet, the heir, is for to marry. Both his wife and child be dead, as it was told here; wherefore she would that ye should inquire whether it be so or no, and what his livelode is, and, if ye think that it be for to do, to let him be spoken with thereof. [3]

I pray you that ye be not strange of writing of letters to me betwixt this and that ye come home. If I might I would have every day one from you. The Blessed Trinity have you in His keeping. Written at Norwich on the Tuesday next after the conversion Saint Paul.

By yours,

M. P.

[30th January 1453]

---

[1] Paston may have acted as paymaster when he visited Caister.
[2] The child now brought home seems to have been of the Berney family.
[3] With a view to the marriage of Paston's sister Elizabeth.

66. JOHN[(1)] PASTON TO JOHN NORWODE [J. G.]

*To John Norwode.*

I let you wete that Hache hath done no work of mine wherefor he ought to have received any money, saving only for the making of the little house above the hall windows, for the remnant was that fell down in his default. And as for the making of that little house, he took that in a covenant, with making of two chimneys of Sir Thomas Howes for 40s.; which covenant may not hold, because that I must have three chimneys and in another place.

Item, the said little house draweth not 5,000 tiles, which, after sixteen pence the thousand, should draw 6s. 8d. Notwithstanding, if Sir Thomas think that he should be allowed more, he shall be. And ye must remember how that he hath received 6s. 8d. of you, and of Robert Tolle before Hallowmas, as appeareth in his account, 8s. And he hath received of Tolle since Hallowmas 5s. 4d. And then by this reckoning he should be 13s. 4d. aforehand, which I would ye should gather up in this new work as well as ye might, for I am behold to do him but little favour.

Item, beware there leave no fires in the dike that ye repair, and that the wood be made of faggot and laid up forthwith as it is felled for taking away. I would ye were here on Saturday at even, though ye yed again on Monday.

JOHN PASTON.

[1453]

67. MARGARET PASTON TO JOHN[(1)] PASTON

*To my right worshipful master, John Paston, be this delivered in haste.*

Right worshipful husband, I recommend me to you, praying you to wete, etc. [*here follow some accounts of money received, etc.*].

As for tidings, the Queen [1] came into this town on Tuesday last past after noon, and abode here till it was Thursday three after noon. And she sent after my cousin Elizabeth Clere by Sharinborn, to come to her; and she durst not disobey her commandment, and came to her. And when she came in the Queen's presence, the Queen made right much of her, and desired her to have an husband, the which ye shall know of hereafter. But as for that, he is never nearer than he was before. The Queen was right well pleased with her answer, and reporteth of her in the best wise, and saith, by her troth, she saw no

[1] Margaret of Anjou.

gentlewoman since she came into Norfolk that she liked better than she doth her.

Blake, the bailiff of Swaffham, was here with the King's brother,[1] and he came to me, weening that ye had been at home, and said that the King's brother desired him that he should pray you in his name to come to him, for he would right fain that ye had come to him if ye had been at home; and he told me that he wist well that he should send for you when he came to London, both for Costessey and other things.

I pray you that ye will do your cost on me against Whitsuntide, that I may have something for my neck. When the Queen was here, I borrowed my cousin Elizabeth Clere's device; for I durst not for shame go with my beads amongst so many fresh gentlewomen as here were at that time.

The Blessed Trinity have you in His keeping.

Written at Norwich on the Friday next before St George.

By yours,

M. Paston.

[20th April 1453]

68.    Agnes Paston to John[1] Paston

*To my well-beloved son, John Paston.*

Son, I greet you well and send you God's blessing and mine, and let you wete that Robert Hill came homeward by Orwellbury, and Gurney telled him he had been at London for money and could not speed, and behested Robert that he should send me money by you. I pray forget it not as ye come homeward, and speak sadly for another farmer.

And as for tidings, Philip Berney[2] is passed to God on Monday last past[3] with the greatest pain that ever I saw man. And on Tuesday, Sir John Heveningham yed to his church and heard three Masses, and came home again never merrier, and said to his wife that he would go say a little devotion in his garden, and then he would dine; and forthwith he felt a fainting in his leg, and slid down. This was at nine of the clock, and he was dead ere noon.

My cousin Clere prays you that ye let no man see her letter, which is ensealed under my seal. I pray you that ye will pay your brother William for four ounces and an half of silk as he paid, which he sent me by William Tavener, and bring with you

---

[1] Either Edmund, afterwards Earl of Richmond, father to Henry VII, or Jasper, Earl of Pembroke. They were the half-brothers to Henry VI.
[2] *See* footnote 3, page 68.
[3] 2nd July.

a quarter of an ounce even like of the same that I send you closed in this letter; and say your brother William that his horse hath one farcy and great running sores in his legs. God have you in keeping. Written at Norwich on Saint Thomas's even, in great haste.

By your mother,

A. PASTON.

[6th July 1453]


69.   MARGARET PASTON TO JOHN[1] PASTON

*To my right worshipful master, John Paston, be this delivered in haste.*

Right worshipful husband, I recommend me to you, praying you to wete that I have spoke with Newman for his place, and I am thorough with him therefor; but he would not let it in no wise less than five marks.   I told him that surely ye should not know but that I hired it of him for £3.   I said as for the noble [1] I should pay it of mine own purse, that ye should no knowledge have thereof.   And this day I have had in two cartful of hay; and your stable shall be made, I hope, this next week.   I could not get no grant of him to have the warehouse; he saith if he may in any wise forbear it hereafter, ye shall have it, but he will not grant it in no covenant.   He hath granted me the house betwixt the vault and the warehouse, and that he said he granted not you.

And as for the chamber that ye assigned to mine uncle,[2] God hath purveyed for him as His will is: he passed to God on Monday last past, at eleven of the clock before noon; and Sir John Heveningham passed to God on Tuesday last past, whose souls both God assoil!   His [Heveningham's] sickness took him on Tuesday at nine of the clock before noon, and by two after noon he was dead.

I have begun your inventory that should have been made ere this time if I had been well at ease; I hope to make an end thereof and of other things by this next week, and be in that other place, if God send me health.   I must do purvey for much stuff ere I come there, for there is neither boards nor other stuff that must needs be had ere we come there.   And Richard hath

---

[1] One noble = 6s. 8d., one mark = 13s. 4d.   Therefore five marks = £3 6s. 8d.   But Margaret said she would pay the extra 6s. 8d. from her own purse and leave her husband in the belief that he had the place for £3.   Her purpose, no doubt, was to accept terms which she had told Newman her husband would never agree to.
[2] Philip Berney.

gathered but little money since he came from you. I have sent
John Norwode this day to Gresham, Besingham, and Matlaske,
to get as much money as he may. The Blessed Trinity have
you in His keeping. Written at Norwich, on the Utas [octave]
day of Peter and Paul.

Yours,

MARGARET PASTON.

[6th July 1453]

70. PETITION OF THE DUKE OF NORFOLK ( ? ) TO THE
PRIVY COUNCIL

My Lords, ye know well enough the great pains, labours, and
diligences that before this time I have done, to the intent that
the over-great dishonours and losses that be come to this full
noble realm of England, by the false means of some persons that
have taken on them over-great authority in this realm, should
be known, and that the persons living that have done them
should be corrected after the merits of their deserts. And to
that intent I have denounced and delivered to you in writing
certain articles against the Duke of Somerset, which is one of
them that is guilty thereof, whereto the Duke of Somerset hath
answered; and to that that he hath answered I have replied in
such wise that I trow to be sure enough that there shall be no
vailable thing be said to the contrary of my said replication, and
as much as he would say shall be but falseness and lesings, as
by the probations that shall be made thereupon shall more
appear. Howbeit that to all people of good intendment, knowing how justice ought to be ministered, it is full apparent that
the denunciations against him made be sufficiently proved by
deeds that have followed thereof. Whereupon I have required
to have overture of justice by you, which ye have not yet done
to me; whereof I am so heavy that I may no longer bear it,
specially since the matter by me pursued is so worshipful for all
the realm, and for you, and so agreeable to God, and to all the
subjects of this realm, that it may be no greater. And it is such
that for any favour of lineage, nor for any other cause there
should be no dissimulation, for doubt lest that other in time
coming take example thereof, and lest that the full noble virtue
of justice, that of God is so greatly recommended, be extinct or
quenched by the false opinions of some, that for the great bribes
that the said Duke of Somerset hath promised and given them,
have turned their hearts from the way of truth and of justice;
some, saying that the cases by him committed be but cases of
trespass, and others taking a colour to make an universal peace.

Whereof every man that is true to the said Crown hath greatly to marvel that any man would say that the loss of two so noble duchies as Normandy and Guienne, that be well worth a great realm, coming by successions of fathers and mothers to the said Crown, is but trespass; whereas it hath been seen in many realms and lordships that, for the loss of towns or castles without siege, the captains that have lost them have been dead and beheaded, and their goods lost: as in France one that lost Cherbourg; and also a knight that fled for dread of battle should be beheaded, so that all these things may be found in the laws written, and also in the book cleped *L'arbre de Bataille*.    Wherefore, for to abridge my language, I require you that, forasmuch as the more part of the deeds committed by the said Duke of Somerset be committed in the realm of France, that by the laws of France process be made thereupon; and that all things that I have delivered and shall deliver be seen and understood by people having know-ledge thereof, and that the deeds committed by him in this realm be in like wise seen and understood by people learned in the laws of this land; and for proof thereof to grant commissions to inquire thereof, as by reason and of custom it ought to be done, calling God and you all, my Lords, to witness of the devoirs by me done in this said matter; and requiring you that this my bill, and all other my devoirs may be enacted before you.    And that I may have it exemplified under the King's great seal for my discharge and acquittal of my troth, making protestation that in case ye make not to me overture of justice upon the said case, I shall for my discharge do my pain that my said devoirs and the said lack of justice shall be known through all the realm.

*Ainsi Signé,*

J. M. NORFF.

[1453]

71.   WILLIAM REYNOLDS TO AGNES PASTON [J. G.]

Right reverend and worshipful mistress, with most humble and lowly service in most goodly wise I commend me to your con-tinual supportation.    Please it your good grace to have notition that I have let a place of yours in which John Richman dwelled; for it stood at a great disrepair and I have let it for 15*s.*    But up your good grace, for the locks of the doors are pulled off and borne away, and the windows be broken and gone, and other boards be nailed on in the stead of the said windows.    Also, the swine-stye is down, and all the timber and the thatch born away; also the hedge is broken or borne away, which closed the garden; wherethrough the place is evil appeyred to the tenant.    On St

Mark's day I entered the said place and let it to your behove; and on the day after came Henry Goneld and said my letting should not stand, and went and sealed the doors. Wherefore I beseech your gracious favour that my letting may stand, for I have let all your lands [1] everyone. I know not one rood unlet, but all occupied to your profit. The tenant which by your licence should have your place to farm by my letting is greatly behated with one Joan (the wife of Robert Ichingham, chapman), which is voiced for a misgoverned woman of her body by the most part of our town well recordeth the same, and she dwelleth all by your said place. And because this said tenant is greatly against her for her ungodly governance, therefore she made means to one Abraham Whale, which is one of her supporters, and he hath spoke to the said Henry Goneld that he might seek a remedy to cause this said tenant to be voided and kept out your said place and not come therein.

He that is bringer of this bill is the man to which I have let to farm by the licence of you; therefore I beseech your gracious favour to be showed unto him. Meekly I beseech your continual supportation that ye would send me writing under your seal how I shall be demeaned. No more, etc. Written at Cromer the next day after St Mark. By your servant at all times,

WILLIAM REYNOLDS *of Cromer.*

[26th April 1453]

## 72. MARGARET PASTON TO JOHN[(1)] PASTON

*To my right worshipful husband, John Paston, be this delivered in haste.*

Right worshipful husband, I recommend me to you, praying you to wete that I spake yesterday with my sister; [2] and she told me that she was sorry that she might not speak with you ere ye yed. And she desireth, if it pleased you, that ye should give the gentleman that ye know of such language as he might feel by you that ye will be well willing to the matter that ye know of. For she told me that he hath said before this time that he conceived that ye have set but little thereby; wherefore she prayeth you that ye will be her good brother, and that ye might have a full answer at this time whether it shall be yea or nay. For her mother hath said to her, since that ye ridden hence, that she hath no fantasy therein, but that it shall come to a jape; and saith to her that there is good craft in daubing; and hath such language

---

[1] i.e. at Cromer and in the neighbourhood.
[2] Elizabeth Paston, her sister-in-law.

to her that she thinketh right strange, and so that she is right weary thereof. Wherefore she desireth the rather to have a full conclusion therein. She saith her full trust is in you, and as ye do therein she will agree her thereto.

Master Brackley [1] was here yesterday to have spoken with you; I spake with him, but he would not tell me what his errand was.

It is said here that the sessions shall be at Thetford on Saturday next coming; and there shall be my Lord of Norfolk and others with great people, as it is said. Other tidings have we none yet.

The blissful Trinity have you in His keeping. Written at Norwich on the Tuesday next before Candlemas.

I pray you that ye will vouchsafe to remember to purvey a thing for my neck,[2] and to do make my girdle.

Yours,

M. P.

My cousin Crane recommendeth her to you, and prayeth you to remember her matter, etc., for she may not sleep on nights for him.

[29th January ? 1454]

73.    AGNES PASTON TO JOHN[1] PASTON

*This letter be delivered to John Paston, dwelling in the Inner Inn of the Temple, at London, in haste.*

I greet you well, and let you wete that this day I was with my daughter your wife, and was in good health at the making of this letter, thanked be God! And she let your sister and me wete of a letter which ye sent her, that ye have been laboured to for Sir William Oldhall to have your sister, and desiring in the said letter to have an answer in short time how she will be demeaned in this matter.

Your sister recommendeth her to you, and thanketh you heartily that ye will remember her, and let her have knowledge thereof, and prayeth you that ye will do your endeavour to bring it to a good conclusion; for she saith to me that she trusteth that ye will do so, that it shall be both for her worship and profit. And, as for me, if ye can think that his land standeth clear, inasmuch as I feel your sister well-willed thereto, I hold me well content.

And as for the obligation of the parson of Marlingford, which

---

[1] John Brackley was a member of the Order of Friars Minor at Norwich.
[2] Probably a repetition of the request made in No. 67, page 74.

I sent you by John Newman, I pray you let it be sued; and as for the parson and Lyndesey, they be accorded. And God have you in keeping, and send you His blessing and mine. Written at Norwich on Pulver Wednesday.[1]

By your mother,

AGNES PASTON.

[*Circa* 1454]


74. WALTER INGHAM'S PETITION TO THE KING IN
PARLIAMENT [J. G.]

Full meekly beseecheth your humble liegeman, Walter Ingham of your shire of Norfolk, gentleman, that whereas the said Walter was in God's peace and yours at Dunston in the said shire the eleventh day of the month of January, the year of your reign the thirty-second, one Thomas Denys, of full great malice prepensed, ungodly sore against good faith and conscience, imagining utterly to destroy your said beseecher, contrived a letter in the name of my Lord of Oxenford, he not knowing of any such letter, commanding your said beseecher to be with the said Lord at Wivenhoe, in your shire of Essex, the thirteenth day of the said month of January, for divers great matters touching my said Lord. The said Thomas, thinking in his conceit that your said beseecher would in nowise disobey the said writing, but that he would put him in his devoir to fulfil my said Lord's desire, laid divers folks arrayed in manner of war with jacks, saletts, langedebiefs, and boar-spears in two bushments for your said beseecher in two places, knowing well that your said beseecher must come one of these two ways, for there were no more, to that intent that they might murder your said beseecher because he had laboured for his father in a writ *subpoena* against the said Thomas Denys and Agnes his wife for a notable sum of money that the said Agnes should have paid to the father of your said beseecher; the said Thomas commanding the said misdoers in anywise which of them that met first with your said beseecher should slay him and they shall be notably rewarded for their labour, and the said Thomas should keep and save them harmless. Because of which commandment one of the said bushments met with the foresaid beseecher the twelfth day of the said month, as he came toward my said Lord of Oxenford, according to his letter, at Dunston aforesaid; and him then and there grievously beat and wounded, as well as upon his head as upon his legs, and other full grievous strokes and many

[1] Ash Wednesday.

gave him upon his back, so that your said beseecher is maimed upon his right leg, and fain to go on crutches, and so must do all days of his life to his utter undoing.   Notwithstanding, the said misdoers and riotous people in this conceit left your said beseecher for dead.   Upon the which riot it was complained to my Lord Chancellor [1] by the friends of your beseecher, desiring of him because of the great riot done by the said Thomas, and also for the safeguard of your said beseecher, that one of your sergeants of arms might by commandment go and arrest the said Thomas to appear before you in your Chancery for the said riot, because the said Thomas was at that time in London; by force of which commandment one of your sergeants of arms went to Lincoln's Inn to arrest the said Thomas.   The which arrest the said Thomas utterly disobeyed in great contempt of your Highness; nevertheless he is now in the ward of the warden of the Fleet by the commandment of my Lord Chancellor.   Wherefore, please it your Highness of your most noble and abundant grace, by the assent of your Lords Spiritual and Temporal, and of your Commons, in this your present Parliament assembled, and by the authority of the same, to ordain and establish that the said Thomas Denys may abide in the said prison of the Fleet, and not to be admitted to bail or mainprise in no wise until such time that the said Thomas have answered to such action or actions as your said beseecher shall take against him for the said maiming and beating, and also until such time as the same actions be fully discussed and determined between your said beseecher and the said Thomas Denys, considering that if the same Thomas should go at large, he would never answer your said beseecher but him delay by protections and other ways, so that the same beseecher should never be content nor agreed for the exorbitant offence done to him; and also until the time the said Thomas find sufficient surety of his good bearing from this time forth.   And he shall pray to God for your most noble estate.

[1454]

75.     THOMAS DENYS TO JOHN[(1)] PASTON

*To my right worshipful master, John Paston.*

Right worshipful and mine especial good master, I recommend me to you with all service and prayer to my power.   And like it you to wete that, how be a full strange act is passed against me in the Higher House before the Lords, whereof I send you a

---

[1] John Cardinal Kemp, Archbishop of Canterbury.

*D 752

copy, nevertheless I hope to God that it shall not pass in the
Common House. But me is befallen the most sorrowful infor-
tune that ever poor man had, standing in such case as I do, for
my Lords the Cardinal and of Oxford have imprisoned my wife
in the Counter, and how they shall guide her forth God knoweth.
Which standeth too nigh mine heart, if God's will were; but well
I know that by these vengeable malices done to her and me they
will not be content, for Ingham lieth beside that to take away my
wife's daughter out of Westminster, to make an end of my wife
if he can, and also to arrest my servants, that I dread that she nor
I shall have no creature to attend us nor help us; and such malice
have I never heard of herebefore. And it is told me that, beside
that, they will despoil, if any goods they can find of mine in
Norwich or Norfolk, and imprison my servants there. Wherefore I lowly beseech your mastership, for Our Lord's mercy,
that ye vouchsafe to succour them in this necessity; and if any
entry be made or should be made upon my wife's place in
Norwich, that ye vouchsafe to succour my servants, and
do therein after your wisdom for Christ's love and Saint
Charity.

Beside this, a friend and kinsman of mine, one Robert Clement
of Beetley, hath written to me that he is arrested and like to be
imprisoned by a writ of debt, taken against him upon an obligation of £100, in which he and I and others were bound to my
Lord of Oxenford fourteen years ago, whereof I have many
acquittances. Wherefore I pray your good mastership to send
to the sheriff that my said kinsman may be eased, and no return
made against him, but that he may answer the next time by
attorney; for truly that writ was taken out in the end of the term
after I was arrested, and after it was appeared to.

I pray your mastership, for God's sake, to be not displeased
nor weary to do for me in these matters of your charity; for I
had lever give the said Robert such good, little if it be, as I have,
than he were undone for me, or any man else that ever did for
me. And I hope, if God vouchsafe that the matter may come
to reason, to save him harmless, and all other with God's mercy,
ever praying you of your mastership and succour for God's love,
who ever keep you for His mercy.

Written in Fleet, the Wednesday, the second week of Lent.

Moreover, in augmenting of my sorrow, I weened my wife
should have died since; for after she was arrested she laboured
of her child that she is withal, waiting either to die or be delivered, and she hath not gone eight weeks quick. What
shall befall, Almighty God knoweth and shall dispose merci-
fully.

Afterward my wife was some deal eased by the labour of the

warden of Fleet; for the cursed Cardinal had sent her to Newgate, God forgive his soul! Now she is taken to bail till
Tuesday. The Cardinal is dead, and the King is relieved.[1]

[ UNSIGNED. ]

[20th March 1454]


76. JOHN[(1)] PASTON TO THE EARL OF OXFORD [J. G.]

Right worshipful and my right especial Lord, I recommend me
to your good Lordship, beseeching your Lordship that ye take
not to displeasance though I write to you; as I say here that
Agnes Denys, by the means of your Lordship and of my Lord
the Cardinal, whose soul God assoil and forgive, was set in
prison, being with child—which, and the sorrow and shame
thereof, was nigh her death—and yet daily is vexed and troubled,
and her servants in like wise, to the uttermost destruction of her
person and goods. In which, my Lord, at the reverence of
God, remember she was married by you and by my means, by
your commandment and writing,[2] and drawn thereto full sore
against her intent in the beginning; and was worth 500 marks and
better, and should have had a gentleman of this country of 100
marks of land and well born, nor had by your good Lordship and
writing[3] to her and me. And this considered in your wise
discretion, I trust, my Lord, though her prisoning were of
others' labour, ye would help her; and if she be destroyed by
this marriage, my conscience thinketh I am bound to recompense her after my poor and simple power. My Lord, ye know
I had little cause to do for Thomas Denys, saving only for your
good Lordship. Also, my Lord, I know well that Walter Ingham
was beat, the matter hanging in mine award, right foul and
shamefully; and also how the said Thomas Denys hath, this last
term, against your noble estate, right unwisely demeaned him to
his shame and greatest rebuke that ever he had in his life.
Wherefore it is right well do his person be punished as it
pleaseth you. But this notwithstanding, for God's love, my
Lord, remember how the gentlewoman is accombered only for
your sake, and help her; and if aught lieth in my power to do that
that might please your Lordship, or could find any way for

---

[1] Wednesday in the second week of Lent, 1454, fell on 20th March.
Cardinal Kemp died on 22nd March in that year. Therefore the final
sentence must have been written a few days after the remainder of the letter.
The King's relief refers to Henry VI's recovery from his first attack of
insanity.

[2] See No. 39, page 43.

[3] *Nor had . . . writing:* Had it not been for your good Lordship writing.

Walter Ingham's avail and worship, I will do it to my power; and the rather if your Lordship support the gentlewoman, for I know the matter and that long plea is of little avail, and everything must have an end. I have told my brother Matthew Drury more to inform your Lordship than I may have leisure to write for his hasty departing. Right worshipful and my right especial Lord, I beseech Almighty God send you as much joy and worship as ever had any of my Lords your ancestors, and keep you and all yours. Written at Norwich the fourth Sunday of Lent.

Your servant to his power,

JOHN PASTON.

[31st March 1454]

77.     THOMAS DENYS TO JOHN[(1)] PASTON [J. G.]

*To my Master Paston.*

Right reverend and worshipful sir, mine especial good master, I recommend me to you. And for as much as adversity and prosperity both lie in the disposition of one Man above, I thank God, and let you wete that I stand yet in as great trouble as ever I did or greater; praying you ever to be my good master and to continue your benevolence, as I am ever bound to you. My heaviness is somewhat increased; for a false harlot, save your reverence, one James Cook, a servant of mine, falsely and traitorously is hired by Walter Ingham and hath accused and defamed me and my wife of setting up bills against lords, that, Almighty God I take to record, I not am nor never was guilty thereof. But the same thief and Ashcote have made an appointment to come and rob me of such little goods of mine as they can get in Norfolk and Norwich. Wherefore I beseech your mastership for charity of your help and succour to my servants if such case fall. For I trow this is a trouble that never man suffered none like in such case; and therefore, gentle sir, as God hath endued you of might and power to succour such troubles, show your bounty to me in this need, and that for God's love, who Almighty preserve. Written in Fleet the eighth day of April. Your woeful servant,

DENYS.

The said Ashcote can counterfeit my hand, and therefore I dread he will steal by some false letters such as he might get. I have written my servants thereafter.

[1454]

78.     JOHN CLOPTON TO JOHN[(1)] PASTON[1]

*Unto right reverend sir, and my good master, John Paston.*

Right worthy and worshipful sir, and my right good master, I
·recommend me unto you, thanking you evermore of your great
gentleness and good masterhood showed unto me at all times,
and specially now to my heart's ease, which on my part cannot be
rewarded, but my simple service is ever ready at your commandment.    Furthermore, as for the matter that ye wete of, I have
laboured so to my father that your intent as for the jointure shall
be fulfilled.    And, sir, I beseech you since that I do my part to
fulfil your will, that ye will show me your good masterhood in her
chamber [2] as my full trust is, insomuch that it shall not hurt you
nor none of yours, and the profit thereof shall be unto the avail of
my mistress your sister, and to me, and to none other creature.

And also my mistress your mother shall not be charged with
her board after the day of the marriage, but I to discharge her
of her person, and to ease me that hath her chamber may be
none contradiction.

And, sir, I am ready, and alway will to perform that I have
said unto you, etc.

Furthermore, like it you to wete I was on Thursday last past at
Cavendish, to deliver an estate to Wentworth in the land that
was my brother Cavendish's, as I told you when I was last with
you.    And there I spake with Crane; and he besought me that I
would send over to my mistress your mother for his excuse, for
he might not be with her at this time, but on the Saturday in
Easter week he will not fail to be with her.    So he counselled
me that I and my brother Denston [3] should meet with him there;
and so, without your better advice, I and my brother purpose us
to be with you there at that time.    For the sooner the lever me;
for, as to my conceit, the days be waxing wonderly long in a
short time.    Wherefore I beseech you send me your advice how
ye will have me ruled, etc.

No more I write to you at this present time, but beseeching
you to recommend in the lowliest wise.    And the Trinity
preserve you body and soul.

Written with my chancery hand, in right great haste, on the
Friday before Palm Sunday.

Your

[*Circa* 1454]                                JOHN CLOPTON.

---

[1] John Clopton was sheriff of Norfolk and Suffolk in 1452.    Soon after
this letter was written, articles of marriage were drafted, but the union never
took place.

[2] i.e. in the furnishing of her chamber.

[3] John Denston who married Clopton's sister Catherine.

## 79.  WILLIAM BOTONER TO JOHN[1] PASTON

### To my Master Paston.

Worshipful sir, and my good master, after due recommendation, with all my due service preceding, like you to wete that as to novelties, etc., the Prince shall be created at Windsor, upon Pentecost Sunday;[1] the Chancellor,[2] the Duke of Buckingham, and many other lords of estate, present with the Queen.

As to my Lord of York, he abideth about York till Corpus Christi Feast be passed,[3] and with great worship is there received.

And certain justices (Prisot,[4] Bingham,[5] Portington,[6] and etc.) be thither for execution of justice upon such as have offended in cause criminal.

It is said the Duke of Exeter [7] is here covertly.  God send him good counsel hereafter.

And the Privy Seal [8] is examined how, and in what manner, and by what authority privy seals were passed forth in that behalf; which is full innocent and right clear in that matter, as it is well known.

The Frenchmen have been afore the isles of Jersey and Guernsey, and a great navy of them; and five hundred be taken and slain of them by men of the said true isles, etc.

Sir Edmund Mulso is come from the Duke of Burgundy; and he saith, by his servants' report, that he will not discharge the goods of the merchants of this land, but so be that justice be done upon the Lord Bonvile, or else that he be sent to him to do justice by himself, as he hath deserved, or satisfaction be made to the value.[9]

Your matter is ensealed as of the thing ye wot of.[10]

[1] 9th June.
[2] Richard Neville, Earl of Salisbury.
[3] i.e. until after 20th June.
[4] John Prisot, Chief Justice of the Common Pleas.
[5] Richard Bingham, Justice of the King's Bench.
[6] John Portington, Justice of the Common Pleas.
[7] Henry Holland, Duke of Exeter.
[8] Thomas Lyseux.
[9] According to Egerton MS. 914, in the British Museum, 'the Mayor and merchants of the staple of Calais were with the Chancellor on Monday last past [14th January] at Lambeth, and complained on the Lord Bonvile for taking of the ships and goods of the Flemings and others of the Duke of Burgundy. . . .'
[10] Probably the grant of the wardship of Thomas Fastolf of Cowhaw. (*See* No. 80, page 87.)

I can no more for haste and lack of leisure, but Our Lord keep you. Writ hastily 8th of June.

I send a letter to Master Berney to let you see for the govern-ance in Yorkshire.

BOTO—H. R.—NER.[1]

[1454]

80.          R. DOLLAY TO JOHN[(1)] PASTON[2]

*Unto my right worshipful master Paston be this bill delivered in haste.*

Right trusty and well-beloved master, I recommend me unto you, desiring to hear of your good prosperity and welfare. And as touching for Sir Philip Wentworth, he rode unto London-ward upon Saint John's day;[3] and on the evening afore he sent to my master for to have some of his men for to ride with him to Colchester. And, for-because he should not have no suspicion to me, I rode myself and a fellow with me; and he rode with an hundred horse with jackets and saletts, and rusty haubergeons. And there rode with him Guybon of Debenham, and Tymperley, and all the fellowship that they could make. And Guybon said that he would indict as many as he could understand that were of the other party. And long Bernard was there also; and he made Sir Philip Wentworth to turn again, and made every man to bend their bows and alight down off their horse for to wete any man would come against them; and he said how he should not let his way neither for Sir John Fastolf nor for Paston, nor for none of them all.

And as for the ward, he was not there. But there was had another child like him, and he rode next him; and when that he was two miles beyond Colchester he sent him home again with a certain. And Sir Philip Wentworth, and Guybon of Debenham, and Tymperley, and Bernard, they took a man of Stratford, a sowter, and his name is Pearson; and they inquired him of every man's name of the other party, and he told them as many as he could. And they bade him inquire further for to know all, for they desired of him for to inquire as far as he could, and he should have well for his labour. No more to you

---

[1] William Worcester, or Botoner as he often called himself, often intro-duced the letters H. R. into or above his signature.
[2] On 6th June 1454, the wardship of Thomas, son of John Fastolf, Esq., of Cowhaw in Suffolk was granted to John Paston and Thomas Howes, apparently as agents for Sir John Fastolf. This letter tells of proceedings taken to secure the person of young Thomas in opposition to their claims. (*See also* Nos. 89, 90, pages 94–5.)
[3] 24th June.

at this time, but the Holy Ghost have you in His keeping.
Written at Hadley, the Saturday after Saint John's day. And I
beseech you heartily recommend me to my master Arblaster.

By your man,

R. Dollay.
[29th June 1454]


81.    Edmund, Lord Grey of Hastings, to John[1]
Paston

*To my trusty and well-beloved John Paston, Esquire, be this letter
delivered.*

Trusty and well-beloved friend, I commend me to you, certifying you that, and your sister be not yet married, I trust to God
I know that where she may be married to a gentleman of 300
marks of livelode; the which is a great gentleman born, and of
good blood. And if ye think that I shall labour any farther
therein, I pray you send me word by the bringer of this letter,
for I have spoke with the parties, and they have granted me that
they will proceed no farther therein till I speak with them again.
And therefore I pray you send me word in haste how that ye will
be disposed therein, and God have you in His keeping. Written
at Ampthill, the 11th day of July last past.

By Edmund Grey,
*Lord of Hastings, Weysford, and Ruthyn.*
[1454]


82.     John[1] Paston to Lord Grey

*Dominus de Grey.*

Right worshipful and my right good Lord, I recommend me to
your good Lordship. And whereas it pleased your Lordship to
direct your letter to me for a marriage for my poor sister to a
gentleman of your knowledge of 300 marks livelode in case she
were not married, wherefore I am bound to do your Lordship
service. Forsooth, my Lord, she is not married, nor insured to
no man. There is and hath been, divers times and late, communications of such marriages with divers gentlemen not
determined as yet; and whether the gentleman that your Lordship meaneth of be one of them or nay I doubt. And whereas
your said letter specifieth that I should send you word whether
I thought ye should labour farther in the matter of nay, in that,
my Lord, I dare not presume to write so to you without I knew

the gentleman's name. Notwithstanding, my Lord, I shall take upon me, with the advice of other of her friends, that she shall neither be married nor insured to no creature, nor farther proceed in no such matter, before the feast of the Assumption of our Lady [1] next coming; during which time your Lordship may send me, if it please you, certain information of the said gentleman's name, and of the place and country where his livelode lieth, and whether he hath any children. And after, I shall demean me in the matter as your Lordship shall be pleased; for in good faith, my Lord, it were to me great joy that my said poor sister were, according to her poor degree, married by your advice, trusting then that ye would be her good lord.

Right worshipful and my right good Lord, I beseech Almighty God to have you in His keeping. Writ at Norwich, the 15th day of July.

[UNSIGNED.]

[1454]

## 83.   WILLIAM[(1)] PASTON TO JOHN[(1)] PASTON

*To his worshipful brother, John Paston.*

Right worshipful brother, I recommend me to you; and as for tidings, my Lord of York hath taken my Lord of Exeter into his award. The Duke of Somerset [2] is still in prison, in worse case than he was. Sir John Fastolf recommends him to you, etc. He will ride into Norfolk-ward as on Thursday, and he will dwell at Caister, and Scrope [3] with him. He saith ye are the heartiest kinsman and friend that he knoweth. He would have you at Mauteby dwelling.

I had great cheer of Billing [4] by the way, and he told me in counsel what he said to Ledham.

Ledham would have done his wise to have made a complaint to Prisot in the shire house of you. And Billing counselled him to leave, and told Ledham ye and he were no fellows, and said to Ledham: ‘That is the guise of your countrymen, to spend all the goods they have on men and livery gowns, and horse and harness, and so bear it out for a while, and at the last they are but beggars; and so will ye do. I would ye should do well,

---

[1] 15th August.
[2] Edmund Beaufort, Duke of Somerset. He was committed to the Tower at the end of 1453.
[3] Stephen Scrope, Sir John Fastolf's stepson and ward.
[4] Thomas Billing was made a serjeant in 1453, and about 1469 was appointed chief justice of the King's Bench.

because ye are a fellow of Gray's Inn, where I was a fellow. As for Paston, he is a squire of worship, and of great livelode, and I wot he will not spend all his goods at once, but he spareth yearly an hundred marks or £100; he may do his enemy a shrewd turn and never fare the worse in his household, nor the less men about him. Ye may not do so, but-if it be for one season. I counsel you not to continue long as ye do. I will counsel you to seek rest with Paston.'

And I thanked Billing on your behalf. God have you in His keeping.

By your poor brother,

WILLIAM PASTON.

Much other thing I can tell you, an' I had leisure. Recommend me to my sister Margaret, and my cousin Elizabeth Clere, I pray you.

[July 1454]

84.    THE DUKE OF YORK TO JOHN[1] PASTON

*To our right trusty and well-beloved John Paston, Esquire.*

THE DUKE OF YORK

Right trusty and well-beloved, we greet you heartily well. And of your benevolence, aid, and tender love by you, at the instance and at the reverence of us, to our right trusty and well-beloved in God, the prior and convent of the house of Our Lady of Walsingham, of our patronage, in such matters as they had ado for certain livelode by them claimed to belong unto the said house, favourably and tenderly showed—as heartily as we can we thank you, and desire and pray you of your good continuance; and as far as right, law, and good conscience will, to have in favourable recommendation such persons as be or shall be committed to take possession and seisin, in the name and to the use of our full worshipful nephew, the Earl of Warwick,[1] in and of the manors and lordships of Boles and Walcotes, with the appurtenances in Little Snoring in the county of Norfolk, as our great trust is unto you. And God have you in His keeping.

Given under our signet, at our castle of Sandal, the 19th day of August.

[1454]

---

[1] Richard Neville, 'the Kingmaker,' Earl of Warwick.

## 85.   THE EARL OF WARWICK TO JOHN[1] PASTON

*To the worshipful and my right trusty friend, John Paston, Esquire.*

Worshipful and my right trusty and well-beloved friend, I greet
you well.   And forasmuch as I have purchased of the worshipful
and my well-beloved friend, prior of Walsingham,[1] two manors
in Little Snoring, with the appurtenances, in the county of
Norfolk, which manors be cleped Boles and Walcotes—I desire
and heartily pray you that ye will show to me, and my feoffees
in my name, your good will and favour, so that I may be your
friendship the more peaceably rejoy my foresaid purchase.

And moreover, I pray you to give credence in this matter to
my well-beloved chaplain, Sir [2] John Southwell, bearer of this
my letter, and in the same matter to be my faithful friend, as
my great trust is in you; wherein ye shall do to me a singular
pleasure, and cause me to be to you right good lord, which some
time shall be to you available by the grace of God, who preserve
you and send you welfare.

Given under my signet at Middleham, the 23rd day of August.

Richard Earl of  }
Warwick,          }

                                    R. WARWICK.

[1454]


## 86.   WILLIAM WORCESTER TO JOHN[1] PASTON[3]

*To my Master Paston.   H.R.*

After due recommendation with my simple service preceding,
please your mastership to wete that, as to such remembrance
that ye desire me to continue forth to the uttermost, I shall with
good will, so as my master will license me, as oft as I can, the
officer to have leisure to be with me, for ye know well I cannot
do it alone, etc.

And whereas ye of your pleasure write me or call me ‘Master
Worcester,’ I pray and require you forget that name of mastership; for I am not amended by my master of a farthing in certainty, but of wages of household in common *entant comme nous
plaira.*   By Worcester or Botoner I have five shillings yearly, all
costs borne, to help to pay for bonnets that I lose.   I told so my

---

[1] Thomas Hunt was prior from 1437 to 1474.
[2] For the honorific ‘Sir,’ *see* footnote 1, page 44.
[3] This letter appears to be written between jest and earnest.   Fastolf had
just taken up residence in his newly built castle at Caister; his secretary,
Worcester, had expected an increase of salary; while Paston had evidently
written in a tone suggesting that Worcester's new importance might prove
useful to himself.

master this week, and he said me yesterday he wished me to have been a priest, so I had been disposed, to have given me a living by reason of a benefice, that another must give it, as the bishop, but he would; and so I ensure *inter egenos ut servus ad aratrum.*

Forgive me, I write to make you laugh; and Our Lord bring my master into a better mood for others as for me.   At Caister, the 2nd day of September.

I pray you displeasure not your servant by so long, for my master letted him.

Your

W. WORCESTER.

[? 1454]

87.        THOMAS HOWES TO JOHN[1] PASTON

*To my master, John Paston, Esquire, be this delivered.*

Right worshipful sir, I recommend me to you; and my master heartily thanketh you for the venison that ye sent him from my Lord of Oxford, and prayeth you that he may be recommended to his noble Lordship.   And God thank you for your special remembrance of my matter, that ye have it so tenderly to heart; for ye may know well the good speed of that is my welfare, and the contrary is my utter undoing.

I have sent to John Porter to wete verily how it standeth with him, as ye shall wete the certainty this week.   As for the matter writ to John Bocking, he hath read his letter and will remember your desire, and also of William Jenney's coming, in case he know of it rather than ye.

And my master heard the substance of your letter read, and liked it right well.   And as for the matter of Worcester's remembrance, he shall give his attendance thereto in that he can.   And where ye call him 'master,' he is displeased with that name, for he may spend 5s. yearly more by the name of Worcester or Botoner, and by his master not a farthing in certainty. He prayeth you forget it.

I pray God keep you.   Writ at Caister, hastily, the 2nd day of September.

Your own

T. HOWES.

Item, in case Jankyn [1] be whole, my Lord of Norfolk hath granted him by mean of Robert Wingfield to be in my said Lord's household, as my master hath it by letter from Wingfield.

[? 1454]

---

[1] Probably Jankyn or John Porter mentioned above.

88.      WILLIAM[1] PASTON TO JOHN[1] PASTON

*To my right worshipful brother, John Paston, be this delivered.*

Right worshipful brother, I recommend me to you, desiring to hear of your welfare. Billing,[1] the serjeant, hath been in his country, and he came to London this week. He sent for me and asked me how I fared; I told him here is pestilence, and said I fared the better he was in good health, for it was noised that he was dead. He took me to him and asked how my sister did, and I answered well, never better. He said he was with the Lord Grey,[2] and they talked of a gentleman which is ward to my Lord. I remember he said it was Harry Grey that they talked of, and my Lord said: 'I was busy within this few days to have married him to a gentlewoman in Norfolk that shall have 400 marks to her marriage, and now he will not by me, for 400 marks would do me ease; and now he would have his marriage money himself, and therefore,' quoth he, 'he shall marry himself for me.'

These words had my Lord to Billing; as he told me, he understood that my Lord laboured for his own avail, and counselled to bid her be wise. And I thanked him for his good counsel.

I sent you an answer of your letter of Sir John Fastolf's coming home [3] as he told me himself; nevertheless he bode longer than he said himself he should ado.

He told me he should make an end betwixt Scrope [4] and my sister while he is in Norfolk. Many would it should not prove, for they say it is an unlikely marriage.

In case Cressener be talked of any more, he is counted a gentlemanly man and a worship. Ye know he is most worshipful better than I. At the reverence of God, draw to some conclusion; it is time.

My Lord Chancellor [5] came not here since I came to London, neither my Lord of York.[6]

My Lord of Canterbury [7] hath received his cross, and I was with him in the King's chamber when he made his homage. I told Harry Wilton the demeaning betwixt the King and him; it were too long to write.

---

[1] *See* footnote 4, page 89.
[2] Edmund, Lord Grey of Hastings. (*See* Nos. 81, 82, page 88.)
[3] i.e. coming to take up residence at Caister. (*See* footnote 3, page 91.)
[4] Stephen Scrope.
[5] Richard Neville, Earl of Salisbury, who died in 1460.
[6] Richard, Duke of York, at this time Protector.
[7] Thomas Bourchier.

As for the priest that did arrest me, I cannot understand that it is the priest that ye mean.

Here is great pestilence. I purpose to flee into the country. My Lord of Oxford is come again from the sea, and he hath got him little thank in this country. Much more thing I would write to you, but I lack leisure.

Harry Wilton saw the King. My Lord of Ely [1] hath done his fealty. God have you in His blessed keeping.

Written at London, on the Friday before Our Lady's-day the Nativity, in great haste. I pray recommend me to my sister and to my cousin Clere.

By your brother,

WILLIAM PASTON.

[5th September 1454]

89. THOMAS HOWES TO (?) JOHN[1] PASTON [J. G.][2]

Please your mastership to wete, for as much as the writ directed to the escheator came not till in the vigil of Simon and Jude,[3] at eight of the clock at even, which could in no wise profit us that day; notwithstanding we had a yeoman of my Lord's chamber, and were at Cowhaw, having Bartholomew Ellis with us, and there was Long Bernard sitting to keep a court. And we at the first noy came in the court, and Bartholomew having these terms to Bernard, saying: 'Sir, for as much as the King hath granted by his letters patent the wardship with the profits of the lands of T. Fastolf during his nonage to you [4] and T. H., wherefore I am come in as their steward, by their command-ment, upon their possession to keep court and leet, which is of old custom used upon this day; wherefore I charge you, by the virtue hereof, to cease and keep neither court nor leet, for ye have no authority.' Quoth Bernard: 'I will keep both court and leet, and ye shall none keep here; for there is no man hath so great authority.' Then quoth Bartholomew: 'I shall sit by you and take a recognizance as ye do.' 'Nay,' quoth Bernard, 'I will suffer you to sit, but not to write.' 'Well,' quoth Bartholomew, 'then forcibly ye put us from our possession, which I doubt not but shall be remembered you another day,' etc. 'But, sirs,' quoth he, 'ye that be tenants to this manor, we charge you that ye do neither suit nor service, nor pay any rents

[1] William Grey.
[2] This letter concerns the dispute as to the wardship of Thomas Fastolf of Cowhaw. (See footnote 2, page 87.)
[3] 27th October.
[4] The writer here confuses direct and indirect speech.

or farms but to the use of John Paston and T.; for an' ye do,
ye shall pay it again; and as for one year past, we have surety of
Skilly, which hath received it of you to their use.' And thus
we departed, and Bernard kept court and leet.

And there was Sir P. Wentworth and his brother, young
Hopton, young Brewse, young Calthorp, with twenty-four
horses; and we spoke with none of them, nor they with none of
us, for we would not seek upon them. And we have entered in
all other places under this form. I would we had had the writ
betimes lever than twenty shillings of mine own, but it fareth
thus in many other matters, God amend them.

Memorandum. To send home wine and two quart bottles.

[October or November 1454]


90.    SIR JOHN FASTOLF TO JOHN[1] PASTON[1]

*To the worshipful and my right well-beloved cousin, John Paston.*

Worshipful and right well-beloved cousin, I commend me to
you. Like you to wete that I have received a letter at this time
from John Bocking, with a copy of the patent concerning the
wardship that ye wot of; by which I understand that ye have
both wrought and holpen by your great wisdom to bring this
matter about which I desired your friendship and good advice
for the surety of the said ward; and for expedition of which I
thank you right heartily, and pray you to continue forth your
good labours in the same in such wise as it may be made sure in
all wise, though it cost me the more of my goods.

And whereas it is remembered me by the said letters that I
should labour to get the said ward into my governance, truly I
cannot see how I could do it to be done, for I have none acquaintance in that country that I could trust to, without the sheriff
might be my tender friend in this cause, or other such as ye
think best. Wherefore I pray you heartily to take this matter
tenderly to heart, and that ye like seek a mean of such friends as
ye can best advise, and may verily trust upon, to guide this
matter in such wise as mine intent might be sped for the
possession of it; for now that I have gone so far in the matter,
I would not it failed for no good,[2] but it proved well and took to
a good conclusion.

And whereas I have understood lately, by certain well-willers

---

[1] This number, like the last, is concerned with the wardship of Thomas
Fastolf. (*See* footnote 2, page 87.)
[2] i.e. I would not have it fail at any cost.

to you-ward, which have moved me, that in case the said ward might be had, that ye desire an alliance should take atwixt a daughter of yours and the said ward, of which motion I was right glad to hear of, and will be right well willing and helping that your blood and mine might increase in alliances. And if it please you that by your wisdom and good conduct that ye would help bear out this matter substantially against my party contrary and evil-willers, that I might have mine intent, I ensure you ye and I should appoint and accord in such wise as ye should hold you right well pleased both for the increasing of your lineage and also of mine. And I pray you beware whom ye make of your counsel and mine in this matter, and that it may be well bore out ere ye come thence, and in a sure way. And if I had known rather of your intent,[1] it should have cost me more of my good before this, to have come to a good conclusion; which I promise yet shall be, and the matter take, by the faith of my body.

Worshipful and right well-beloved cousin, I pray God speed you in this matter, and send you your good desires. Written at Caister, the 11th day of November, in the 33rd year of King Henry VI.

Your cousin,

JOHN FASTOLF.

Item, cousin, I pray you, when ye see time, that my Lord of Canterbury, and my Lord Cromwell [2] may be spoken with for the goods of my Lord Bedford,[3] being in divers men's hands, be compelled to be brought in, as ye shall see more along of this matter, with the writings that I have made mention and left with John Bocking and William Barker.

[1454]

91. THOMAS HOWES TO JOHN[1] PASTON

*To the worshipful sir, and my good master, John Paston, at London, in haste.*

Worshipful and reverend sir, and my good master, I recommend me to you in as diligent wise as on my part appertaineth. And please you to wete that my master was right well pleased with

---

[1] i.e. If I had known earlier of your intention.

[2] Ralph, Lord Cromwell.

[3] John, Duke of Bedford, had died in 1435 in possession of the ransom money paid in 1427 for the Duke of Alençon. Part of this sum was due to Sir John Fastolf, and its recovery caused the wealthy knight agonies of suspense over a number of years.

your faithful labour in fulfilling the patent for the ward of A.B.C., and he will faithfully labour as ye have advised him by writing to John Bocking. And to put my master in more courage, I moved to him upon mine head that in case be the child were wise, that then it were a good marriage between my wife your daughter [1] and him; and, sir, my master was glad when he heard that mean, considering that your daughter is descended of [2] him by the mother's side. And, sir, I have inquired after the said child, and no doubt of but he is likely and of great wit, as I hear by report of sundry persons. And it is so, as I am credibly informed, that Geoffrey Boleyn maketh great labour for marriage of the said child to one of his daughters. I would well to him, but better to you. Wherefore that ye diligently labour for expedition of this matter, that in case ye can find any mean there to have the said child, and we shall do faithfully our diligence in like wise here, as ye advise us, etc.

And, sir, as ye think with advice of my master Yelverton, Jenney, and others my masters' counsel therein, that the sheriff may be rewarded, and if my said masters' counsel think it be to done, that then ye like to take an action upon an atteint,[3] which ye must with them take upon you at this time in my master's absence; for as ye do in that matter he will hold him content, for William Barker hath an instruction of my master's intent upon the same. And I send John Bocking a copy of the panel, which I showed you at Caister, etc.

Almighty Jesu have you eternally in His merciful governance. Written at Caister the Wednesday next after Saint Martin, anno 33 [H. VI]

THOMAS HOWES.

[13th November 1454]


92.     EDMUND CLERE TO JOHN[(1)] PASTON

*To my well-beloved cousin, John Paston, be this delivered.*

Right well-beloved cousin, I recommend me to you, letting you wit such tidings as we have.

Blessed be God, the King is well amended, and hath been since Christmas day; and on Saint John's day [4] commanded his

---

[1] Anne or Margery, the eldest of whom was no more than ten years old. 'Wife' here has the sense of 'lady.'

[2] i.e. is related to.

[3] An action against a jury that has given a false verdict.

[4] 27th December.

almoner to ride to Canterbury with his offering, and commanded the secretary to offer at Saint Edward's.

And on the Monday afternoon the Queen came to him, and brought my Lord Prince [1] with her. And then he asked what the prince's name was, and the Queen told him Edward; and then he held up his hands, and thanked God thereof.

And he said he never knew him till that time, nor wist not what was said to him, nor wist not where he had been whilst he hath been sick till now. And he asked who were godfathers, and the Queen told him, and he was well apaid.

And she told him that the cardinal [2] was dead, and he said, he knew never thereof till that time; and he said one of the wisest lords in this land was dead.

And my Lord of Winchester [3] and my lord of Saint John's [4] were with him on the morrow after Twelfth day, and he spake to them as well as ever he did; and when they came out they wept for joy.

And he saith he is in charity with all the world, and so he would all the lords were.

And now he saith matins of Our Lady, and evensong, and heareth his Mass devoutly.

And Richard shall tell you more tidings by mouth.

I pray you recommend me to my Lady Morley, and to Master Prior,[5] and to my Lady Felbrigg, and to my Lady Heveningham, and to my cousin your mother, and to my cousin your wife.

Written at Greenwich, on Thursday after Twelfth day.

> By your cousin,
>
> EDMUND CLERE.

[9th January 1455]

93.    SIR JOHN FASTOLF TO JOHN[(1)] PASTON

*To my right trusty and well-beloved cousin, John Paston, in goodly haste.*

Right trusty and well-beloved cousin, I commend me to you. And please you to wete that I am advertised that at a dinner in Norwich, whereas ye and other gentlemen were present, that

---

[1] Prince Edward was born at Westminster, in October 1453.
[2] John Kemp, Archbishop of Canterbury, Cardinal, etc., died on the 22nd March 1453.
[3] William Waynflete, Bishop of Winchester.
[4] Robert Botill, Prior of the Order of St John of Jerusalem.
[5] Probably the Prior of Bromholm.

there were certain persons, gentlemen, which uttered scornful language of me, as in this wise with more, saying: 'Ware thee cousin, ware, an' go we to dinner; go we where? to Sir John Fastolf's and there we shall well pay therefore.' What their meaning was, I know well to no good intent to me-ward; wherefore, cousin, I pray you, as my trust is in you, that ye give me knowledge by writing what gentlemen they be that had this report with more, and what more gentlemen were present, as ye would I should and were my duty to do for you in semblable wise. And I shall keep your information in this matter secret, and with God's grace so purvey for them as they shall not all be well pleased. At such a time a man may know his friends and his foes asunder, etc. Jesu preserve and keep you.

Written at Caister, the 7th day of February, in the 33rd year of King Henry VI.

JOHN FASTOLF, Knight.

[1455]

## 94. THOMAS HOWES TO JOHN[(1)] PASTON [J. G.]

*To the right worshipful sir, my good Master John Paston.*

Right worshipful sir, and my good master, I recommend me lowly unto you, thanking your good mastership for your good remembrance for the church of Stokesby, whereupon I have desired my trusty friend William Worcester to come by the abbot[1] homeward, beseeching you to advertise him your good advice how he may behave him best in this matter to the said abbot, etc. And, sir, in case ye might be at a leisure to be with my master upon Thursday next coming, forasmuch as Master Yelverton and Jenney shall be here, ye should do my master right great pleasure. And I beseech you the rather for my sake, for at that time the conveyance of all matters shall be communed of; and I know verily your advice shall peyse deeper in my master's conceit than both theirs shall do. Ye have daily great labour for me, God reward you, and my poor prayer ye shall have, etc. I beseech Almighty Jesu have you in His merciful governance, and grant you ever that may be to your most heart's pleasance, etc.

Your chaplain and beadsman,

THOMAS HOWES.

[1455]

[1] John Martin, Abbot of St Benet's Hulme.

95. THE ABBOT OF ST BENET'S TO JOHN[1] PASTON

*To my right well-beloved John Paston, Esquire, be this delivered.*

Worshipful sir, and right well beloved, I greet you well, desiring to hear of your welfare, praying you entirely to be with me at dinner on St Benedict's day,[1] the which shall be on Friday next coming, or else in brief time convenable to your ease, to the intent that I may commune with you of divers matters, the which I purpose to have a do in by your good advice, and in one especial as for the church of Stokesby, which I understand shall much be ruled after your advice and content. Trusting our communication had in the said matters shall cause peace and pleasure to all parties by leave of Our Lord, the which Lord preserve you in all good.

Written in my monastery the 17th day of March.

By your good friend,

THE ABBOT OF ST BENET'S.

[1455]

96. MEMORIAL TO HENRY VI[2]

*Tradatur, J. P.*

Most Christian King, right high and mighty Prince, and our most redoubted sovereign lord, we recommend us as humbly as we suffice unto your high excellence. Whereunto please it to wete that for so much as we hear and understand to our greatest sorrow earthly that our enemies of approved experience, such as abide and keep themselves under the wing of your majesty royal, have thrown unto the same right studiously and right fraudulently many ambiguities and doubts of the faith-liegance and duty, that, God knoweth, we bear unto your Highness, and have put them in as great devoir as they could to estrange us from your most noble presence and from the favour of your good grace; which good grace to us is and ought to be our singular and most desired joy and consolation: We at this time be coming with grace as your true and humble liege men, toward your said high excellence to declare and show thereto at large our said faith and legiance, intending, with the mercy of Jesu in the said coming, to put us in as diligent and hearty devoir and duty as any your liege men alive to that that may advance or prefer the

[1] 21st March.
[2] This is the memorial (or rather a copy sent to John Paston) addressed by the Duke of York and other lords to their sovereign immediately before the first battle of St Albans. The Duke of Somerset prevented its reaching Henry.

honour and welfare of the said majesty royal and the surety of the said most notable person; the which we beseech our blessed Creator to prosper in as great honour, joy, and felicity as ever had any prince earthly, and to your said Highness so to take, accept, and repute us, and not to please to give trust or confidence unto the sinister, malicious, and fraudulent labours and reports of our said enemies unto our coming to your said most noble presence; whereunto we beseech humbly that we may be admitted as your liege men, to the intent to show us the same; whereof yesterday we wrote our letters of our intent, to the right reverend father in God, the Archbishop of Canterbury, your Chancellor of England, to be showed to your said Highness, whereof, for so much as we be not ascertained whether our said intent be by his fatherhood showed unto your said good grace or not, we send thereof under this closed a copy of our said letters of our disposition towards your said high excellence, and the honour and weal of the land, wherein we will persevere with the grace of Our Lord.

[21st May 1455]

## 97.    JOHN CRANE TO JOHN[(1)] PASTON[1]

*Unto my worshipful and well-beloved cousin, John Paston, be this letter delivered in haste.*

Right worshipful and entirely well-beloved sir, I recommend me unto you, desiring heartily to hear of your welfare.

Furthermore letting you wete, as for such tidings as we have here, such three lords be dead: the Duke of Somerset,[2] the Earl of Northumberland,[3] and the Lord Clifford.[4] And as for any other men of name, I know none, save only Quotton[5] of Cambridgeshire.

As for any other lords, many of them be hurt; and as for Filongley he liveth and fareth well, as far as I can inquire, etc.

And as for any great multitude of people that there was, as we can tell, there was at most slain six score. And as for the lords that were with the King, they and their men were pilled and spoiled out of all their harness and horses; and as for what

---

[1] This letter refers to the first battle of St Albans.

[2] Edmund Beaufort, Duke of Somerset, etc.; he was some years Regent of Normandy, and in this battle commanded the royal army.

[3] Henry Percy, Earl of Northumberland, had been a favourite with Henry V, and continued a loyal and faithful subject to his son Henry VI: when slain he was about sixty years of age.

[4] Thomas, Lord Clifford.

[5] William Quotton or Cotton, of Landwade, in Cambridgeshire, was vice-chamberlain to Henry VI.

rule we shall have yet I wot not, save only there be made new certain officers.

My Lord of York [1] Constable of England; my Lord of Warwick [2] is made Captain of Calais; my Lord Bourchier [3] is made Treasurer of England; and as yet other tidings have I none.

And as for our sovereign lord, thanked be God he hath no great harm.

No more to you at this time, but I pray you send this letter to my Mistress Paston, when ye have seen it; praying you to remember my sister Margaret against the time that she shall be made a nun.

Written at Lambeth on Whitsunday, etc.

By your cousin,

JOHN CRANE.

[25th May 1455]

## 98.   WILLIAM BARKER TO WILLIAM WORCESTER

### To William Worcester be this letter delivered in haste.

Sir, I recommend me to you.   And as for tidings, ye may inform mine master there is none but that he hath knowledge of, but that the King, the Queen and the Prince remove to Hertford tomorrow without fault; my Lord of York to the Friars at Ware; my Lord of Warwick to Hunsdon; the Earl of Salisbury to Rye; and there they shall abide to the time the Parliament begins.[4]

The Duke of Buckingham is come in, and sworn that he shall be ruled, and draw the line with them; and thereto he and his brethren be bound by recognizance in notable sums to abide the same.

The Earl of Wiltshire sent to the lords, from a place of his called Petersfield, a letter desiring to know if he should come and abide about the King's person as he did before; and if he should not, then that they would license him to go into Ireland, and live there upon his lands, etc.   And before this done, the lords were advised to have made him to do as the Duke of Buckingham hath done, and no more; but what that will fall now thereof, no man can tell as yet.

The Baron of Dudley [5] is in the Tower; what shall come of him, God wot.

[1] Richard Plantagenet, Duke of York.
[2] Richard Neville, Earl of Warwick.
[3] Henry Bourchier, Viscount Bourchier.
[4] The Parliament was summoned to meet on Wednesday, 9th July 1455.
[5] John Sutton, fourth Baron Dudley.

The Earl of Dorset [1] is in ward with the Earl of Warwick.

It was said, forsooth, that Harper and two other of the King's chamber [2] were confederated to have sticked the Duke of York in the King's chamber; but it was not so, for they have cleared them thereof. But London upon the same tale arisen, and every man to harness on Corpus Christi even, and much ado there was.

Sir William Oldhall abideth no longer in sanctuary than the Chief Justice come, for that time he shall go at large and sue all his matters himself, etc.

The Baron Dudley hath impeached many men; but what they be, as yet we cannot wete.

Sir Philip Wentworth was in the field, and bare the King's standard, and cast it down and fled. My Lord of Norfolk saith he shall be hanged therefore, and so is he worthy. He is in Suffolk now. He dare not come about the King.

Edmund Stendale was with Wenlock there in the field, and foully hurt.

Filongley is at home at his own place with his wife, and shall do right well; but we have a great loss of his absence this term, for it will be long ere he come this term, I am afraid.

All the lords that died at the journey are buried at St Alban's.

Other things be none here, but ye shall see by Thomas Scales' letter the rule of the Frenchmen, etc.

God speed us well in our matters this term, I pray to God, who have you in His keeping, etc.

W. B.

[June 1455]

## 99. The Duchess of Norfolk to John [1] Paston [3]

*To our right trusty and well-beloved John Paston, Esquire.*

### THE DUCHESS OF NORFOLK

Right trusty and well-beloved, we greet you heartily well. And forasmuch as it is thought right necessary for divers causes that my Lord [4] have at this time in the Parliament such persons as belong unto him, and be of his menial servants, wherein we

---

[1] Henry Beaufort, Earl of Dorset, son and heir of the late Duke of Somerset. He is here styled only Earl of Dorset, though, by the death of his father at the battle of St Albans, he was now Duke of Somerset, etc.

[2] Grooms of the King's chamber.

[3] This and the three following letters refer to the Parliamentary elections in June 1455.

[4] Her husband, John Mowbray, third Duke of Norfolk.

conceive your goodwill and diligence shall be right expedient, we heartily desire and pray you that, at the contemplation of these our letters, as our special trust is in you, ye will give and apply your voice unto our right well-beloved cousin and servants, John Howard and Sir Roger Chamberlain,[1] to be knights of the shire, exhorting all such others as by your wisdom shall now be behoveful, to the good exploit and conclusion of the same.

And in your faithful attendance and true devoir in this part ye shall do unto my Lord and us a singular pleasure, and cause us hereafter to thank you therefore, as ye shall hold you right well content and agreed with the grace of God, who have you ever in His keeping.

Written at Framlingham Castle, the 8th day of June.

[1455]

100. WILLIAM PRYCE TO JOHN[1] PASTON

*The copy of a letter sent to John Paston, by the under-sheriff of Norfolk.*

Right worshipful sir, I recommend me unto you, etc. And, sir, as for the election of the knights of the shire here in Norfolk, in good faith here hath been much to do. Nevertheless, to let you have knowledge of the demeaning, my master Berney, my master Grey, and ye had greatest voice, and I purpose me, as I will answer God, to return the due election, that is after the sufficient, you and Master Grey, nevertheless I have a master. Written at Hethersett, the Thursday next before Midsummer.

By WILLIAM PRYCE.

[19th June 1455]

101. JOHN JENNEY TO JOHN[1] PASTON

*To my worshipful master John Paston, Esquire.*

My master Paston, I recommend me to you. And where ye should be informed that I should say to Howard that ye laboured to be knight of the shire, I said never so to him. I told my Lord of Norfolk at London that I laboured divers men for Sir Roger Chamberlain, and they said to me they would have him, but not Howard, inasmuch as he had no livelode in the shire nor

---

[1] These two were duly elected on 23rd July. John (afterwards Sir John) Howard was created Baron Howard in 1470 and Duke of Norfolk in 1483. He was killed at Bosworth.

conversement; and I asked them whom they would have, and they said they would have you, and thus I told him. And he said unadvisedly, as he can do full well, I might not say ye laboured there, for I heard never say ye laboured therefore by the faith I vow to God.

As for this writ of the Parliament of Norwich, I thank you that ye will labour therein; as for my friends there, I trust right well all the aldermen except Brown [1] and such as be in his danger.[2] I pray you speak to Walter Jeffery [3] and Harry Wilton,[4] and make them to labour to your intent. I pray you that if ye think that it will not be, that it like you to say that you move it of yourself, and not by my desire. Some men hold it right strange to be in this Parliament, and methinketh they be wise men that so do. Written at Intwood,[5] on St John's day, in haste.

Your servant,

JOHN JENNEY.

[24th June 1455]


102.    ·    JOHN JENNEY TO JOHN[(1)] PASTON

*To my worshipful master, John Paston, Esquire.*

My worshipful master, I recommend me to you; and I thank you that it pleaseth you to take such labour for me as ye do. My servant told me ye desired to know what my Lord of Norfolk said to me when I spake of you; and he said inasmuch as Howard might not be, he would write a letter to the under-sheriff that the shire should have free election, so that Sir Thomas Tuddenham were not, nor none that was toward the Duke of Suffolk; he said he knew ye were never to him-ward. Ye may send to the under-sheriff, and see my Lord's letter. Howard was as wode as a wild bullock; God send him such worship as he deserveth. It is an evil precedent for the shire that a strange man should be chosen, and no worship to my Lord of York, nor to my Lord of Norfolk, to write for him; for if the gentlemen of the shire will

---

[1] Richard Brown was mayor of Norwich in 1454, and M.P. for that city in 1460.

[2] i.e. *in his debt*, and therefore under his influence.

[3] Walter Jeffery was under-sheriff of Norwich in 1451, 1452, and 1459.

[4] Henry Wilton was returned, with John Jenney, in 1477.

[5] This estate came afterwards by purchase to the Greshams, and here it was that, in 1549, Sir Thomas Gresham, Kt, founder of the Royal Exchange, entertained John Dudley, Earl of Warwick, when he marched against Kett, the rebel tanner.

suffer such inconvenience, in good faith the shire shall not be called of such worship as it hath been.

Written at Intwood, the Wednesday next after Saint John, in haste.

Your servant,

[25th June 1455]                                    JOHN JENNEY.

103.          ALICE CRANE TO MARGARET PASTON

*To my cousin, Margaret Paston, be this letter delivered.*

Right worshipful cousin, I recommend me unto you, desiring to hear of your welfare; and if it like you to hear of my welfare, at the making of this letter I was in good health, loved be God. The cause of my writing to you at this time is this, praying you to send me word of your welfare, and how ye do of your sickness, and if the medicine do you any good that I sent you writing of last; thanking you of the great friendship that ye have done to my mother with all my heart.

Also I pray you that ye will be good mean to my cousin your husband, that he will see that my father be well ruled in his livelode for his worship and his profit.

Also praying you to hold me excused that I have written no oftener to you, for, in good faith, I had no leisure. For my Lady hath been sick at London near hand this quarter of this year, and that hath been great heaviness to me; but now, blessed be God, she is amended and is in the country again.

Also thanking you of the great cheer that I had of you when I was with you last with all my heart, praying you of good continuance, for I had never greater need than I have now, and if I had leisure and space I would write to you the cause.

No more at this time, but the Holy Trinity have you in His keeping. Written at Windsor, the 29th day of June.

By your poor beadswoman and cousin,

ALICE CRANE.

Also, cousin, I pray you to send me some Norfolk thread to do about my neck, to ride with.

[? about 1455]

104.          WILLIAM WORCESTER TO JOHN⁽¹⁾ PASTON

*To my Master Paston.*

Please your good mastership to wete that as yesterday came letters from London that the parson ¹ must needs up to London

¹ Thomas Howes.

to save the next amercement; and so is forth to appear, if he needs must, xv Johannis,[1] as ye shall see by Barker's letter, and shall be to-morrow at London, and with God's grace he shall be relieved by the mean of the Parliament; by Sunday ye shall have weting.

As for my master,[2] he departeth not to London till the next week after this, an' he ride.

As for tidings, be none couth, but Poynyngs[3] is quit and delivered of all treasons; and Sir William Oldhall's process in the King's Bench reversed; and the priest that accused Lords Cromwell,[4] Grey,[5] and my master will confess who caused him to do it, so that he may have his life, etc.

As soon as ye goodly may to see my master, it shall be to him a singular pleasure. Sir, a bailiff of my master's is in Drayton. John Edmond brought a letter to you, and he sent me weting he was shent upon some matter, as he supposeth, contained in the letter. I pray you in right be his good master, and that I may wete the cause, for I doubt he shall and must obey if he hath offended.

At Caister the noneday,[6] 7th day July

Your,

WILLIAM WORCESTER.

[1455]

*On the top of this letter, in a different hand, is written :*

Prove untruth in the undersheriff, or that he did otherwise than your counsel advised him, and Paston shall demean him according.


105. HENRY WINDSOR TO JOHN BOCKING AND
WILLIAM WORCESTER

*Unto my most faithful brethren, John Bocking and William Worcester, and to either of them.*

Worshipful sir, and my most heartily and best-beloved brother, I recommend me unto you in more lowly wise than I can either think or write; and with all my service and true heart thank you of your gentle letters, full brotherly, written unto me at many

[1] *Quindena Johannis*, i.e. 8th July, fifteenth day from St John the Baptist's day.
[2] Sir John Fastolf.
[3] Robert Poynyngs, for raising disturbances in 1453 and 1454.
[4] Ralph, Lord Cromwell. He and the others named here were accused of treason by a priest named Colynson. (*Privy Council Proceedings*, vi. 198.)
[5] Probably Edmund, Lord Grey de Ruthyn.
[6] The day of the nones.

times of old, and especial of late time passed. And truly, brother, I thank Almighty God of your welfare, of the which the bearer of this my poor letter certified me of, etc.

And, sir, as touching all manner of new tidings, I know well ye are avarous; truly the day of making of this letter there were none new, but such I heard of ye shall be served withal.

As for the first, the King, our sovereign lord, and all his true lords, stand in health of their bodies, but not all at hearts' ease as we.

Amongst other marvel, two days afore the writing of this letter, there was a language between my Lords of Warwick and Cromwell afore the King, insomuch as the Lord Cromwell would have excused himself of all the stirring or moving of the male journey of St Alban's; of the which excuse making my Lord Warwick had knowledge, and in haste was with the King, and swore by his oath that the Lord Cromwell said not truth, but that he was beginner of all that journey at St Alban's. And so between my said two Lords of Warwick and Cromwell there is at this day great grudging, insomuch as the Earl of Shrewsbury [1] hath lodged him at the hospital of St James [2] beside the Mews,[3] by the Lord Cromwell's desire, for his safeguard.

And also all my Lord of Warwick's men, my Lord of York's men, and also my Lord of Salisbury's men, go with harness, and in harness with strange weapons, and have stuffed their lords' barges full of weapons daily unto Westminster. And the day of making of this letter there was a proclamation made in the Chancery on the King's behalf, that no man should neither bear weapon nor wear harness defensible, etc.

Also, the day afore the making of this letter, there passed a bill both by the King, Lords, and Commons, putting Thorp, Joseph, and my Lord of Somerset in all the default; by the which bill, all manner of actions that should grow to any person or persons for any offences at that journey done, in any manner of wise, should be extinct and void, affirming all things done there well done, and nothing done there never after this time to be spoken of; to the which bill many a man grudged full sore now it is passed.

And if I might be recommended unto my special master and yours, with all lowliness and true service, I beseech you heartily as I can.

<hr>

[1] John Talbot, second Earl of Shrewsbury, was Lord Treasurer in 1456, and fell in the battle of Northampton, in 1460, fighting for the House of Lancaster.
[2] Now St James's Palace.
[3] A place for the keeping of hawks, afterwards the royal stables.

And also to my brethren Th. Upton, Lodowick of Pole, William Lincoln, and John Marshall.

No more, but Our Lord have you both in His perpetual keeping.

Written at London on St Margaret's even in haste; and after this is read and understood, I pray you burn or break it, for I am loth to write anything of any lord, but I must needs; there is nothing else to write.   Amen.

Your own<br>HENRY WINDSOR.

[20th July 1455]

106.      JAMES GLOYS TO JOHN[1] PASTON

*To the right worshipful sir and my good master, my master, John Paston, be this delivered.*

Reverend and right worshipful sir, and my good master, I recommend me to you, praying you to wete that there is raised a slanderous noise in this country upon my master Yelverton and you and my master Alington, which I suppose is done to bring you out of the conceit of the people, for at this day ye stand greatly in the country's conceit.

It is said by Heydon and his disciples that my master Yelverton and ye and my master Alington should have do one Sir Thomas Tattersall (parson of the east church of Warham [1] and chaplain to the Prior of Walsingham [2]) to put into the Parliament a bill of divers treasons done by my Lord of Norwich,[3] Sir Thomas Tuddenham, and John Heydon, and ye should have set to your seals; and if that Heydon had been six hours from the Parliament longer than he was, there had been granted an oyer determiner to have inquired of them, etc.   This was told yesterday in right worshipful audience, and among the thriftiest men of this country; and they said right shrewdly, for my Lord of Norwich hath so flattered the lay people, as he hath ridden about his visitation, that he hath their hearts.   Wherefore, and it please you to let me have knowledge what ye would I should say to it, where as I hear any such language, I will do my part, and have done hitherward as I have thought in my conceits best, etc.   And if there be any other service that ye will command me,

---

[1] There were three churches in the parish of Warham.

[2] Thomas Hunt became prior in 1437.

[3] Walter Lyhart, Bishop of Norwich, 1446–72.

I am and will be ready at your commandment with the grace of God, who ever have you in His blessed keeping. Written at Wighton in haste, on Saint James's day.

By your servant,

JAMES GLOYS.

[25th July 1455]

## 107.     JAMES GRESHAM TO JOHN[1] PASTON

*To my right worshipful master, John Paston, at Norwich, be this delivered.*

Please it your mastership to wete [*here follows an account of some law business*, etc.]

Here be many marvellous tales of things that shall fall this next month, as it is said. For it is talked that one Doctor Green, a priest, hath calked, and reporteth that before St Andrew's day next coming shall be the greatest battle that was since the battle of Shrewsbury,[1] and it shall fall between the Bishop's Inn of Salisbury and Westminster Bars,[2] and there shall die seven lords, whereof three should be bishops. All this and much more is talked and reported. I trust to God it shall not fall so.

Also there is great variance between the Earl of Devonshire[3] and the Lord Bonvile,[4] as hath been many day, and much debate is like to grow thereby. For on Thursday[5] at night last passed, the Earl of Devonshire's son and heir[6] came with sixty men of arms to Radford's place[7] in Devonshire, which was of counsel with my Lord Bonvile; and they set an house on fire at Radford's gate, and cried and made a noise as though they had been sorry

---

[1] The battle of Shrewsbury was fought on the 22nd July 1403, the Percys being the leaders of the malcontents who were routed by the King's army.

[2] The Bishop of Salisbury's Inn was situated in the Strand. Westminster Bars was probably the City of London gates towards Westminster, as Westminster itself was never walled.

[3] Thomas Courtney, Earl of Devon, was beheaded by order of Edward IV immediately after the battle of Towton, in 1461.

[4] William Bonvile was created Lord Bonvile in 1449, and was beheaded, by order of Queen Margaret, after the battle of Barnard's Heath, near St Albans, in February 1461, though he had stayed with Henry VI on a promise of safety.

[5] 23rd October.

[6] Thomas Courtney, son and heir of the Earl of Devon, was beheaded very soon after his father, in 1461.

[7] Nicholas Radford was an eminent lawyer, who resided at Poghill, near Kyrton.

for the fire; and by that cause Radford's men set open the gates and yed out to see the fire. And forthwith the Earl's son aforesaid entered into the place, and entreated Radford to come down of his chamber to speak with them, promising him that he should no bodily harm have; upon which promise he came down, and spake with the said Earl's son. In the meantime his meny rob his chamber, and rifled his hutches, and trussed such as they could get together, and carried it away on his own horses. Then the Earl's son said: 'Radford, thou must come to my Lord, my father.' He said he would, and bade one of his men make ready his horse to ride with them, which answered him that all his horses were taken away. Then he said to the Earl's son: 'Sir, your men have robbed my chamber, and they have mine horses, that I may not ride with you to my Lord your father, wherefore I pray you let me ride, for I am old, and may not go.'

It was answered him again that he should walk forth with them on his feet; and so he did till he was a flight-[1]shot or more from his place, and then he was [2] . . . softly, for cause he might not go fast. And when they were thus departed, he turned . . . one; forthwith came nine men again upon him and smote him in the head and felled . . . of them cut his throat.

This was told to my Lord Chancellor [3] this forenoon . . . messengers as came of purpose out of the same country. This matter is taken greatly . . . passed at two after midnight rode out of London, as it is said, more than . . . the best wise. Some say it was to ride toward my Lord of York, and some . . . so much rumour is here; what it meaneth I wot not, God turn it . . . at Hertford,[4] and some men are afraid that he is sick again. I pray God . . . my Lords of York, Warwick, Salisbury, and others are in purpose to convey him . . . etc.

The said Nicholas Crome, bearer hereof, shall tell you such tidings . . . in haste at London on Saint Simon's day and Jude.

Your poor<br>JAMES GR.

[28th October 1455]

---

[1] A flight was a light arrow.
[2] Dots here and in the following lines indicate mutilations of the manuscript.
[3] Archbishop Bourchier.
[4] The King was at Hertford in August and September 1455.

108.     MARGARET PASTON TO JOHN[1] PASTON

*To my right worshipful husband, John Paston, be this delivered in
haste.*

Right worshipful husband, I recommend me unto you. Pleaseth
you to wete that mine aunt Mundeford [1] hath desired me to write
to you, beseeching you that ye will vouchsafe to chevise for her
at London twenty marks for to be paid to Master Poynyngs,
either on Saturday or Sunday, which shall be St Andrew's day,
in discharging of them that be bounden to Master Poynyngs of
the said twenty marks for the wardship of her daughter; the
which twenty marks she hath delivered to me in gold for you to
have at your coming home, for she dare not adventure her money
to be brought up to London for fear of robbing. For it is said
here that there goeth many thieves betwixt this and London,
which causeth her to beseech you to content the said money in
discharging of the matter and of them that be bounden, for she
would for no good that the day were broken. And she thanketh
you heartily for the great labour and business that ye have had
in that matter, and in all others touching her and hers, wherefore she saith she is ever bounden to be your beadswoman, and
ever will be while she liveth.

My cousin, her son, and his wife recommendeth them unto
you, beseeching you that ye will vouchsafe to be their good
master, as ye have been aforetime; for they be informed that
Daniel is come to Rising Castle, and his men make their boast
that their master shall be again at Brayston within short
time.[2]

Furthermore, as for the matter that my son wrote to me for,
the box whereon written *False Carte Sproute*, that I should
inquire of William Worcester where it were, the said William
was not at home since that I had his letter; but as soon as
he cometh home, I shall inquire of him and send you an
answer.

As touching for your liveries, there can none be got here of
that colour that ye would have of, neither murrey nor blue nor
good russet, underneath 3s. the yard at the lowest price; and yet
is there not enough of one cloth and colour to serve you. And
as for to be purveyed in Suffolk, it will not be purveyed not now
against the time, without they had had warning at Michaelmas,

[1] Osbert Mundeford, Esq., of Hockwold, married Elizabeth, daughter
of John Berney, Esq.
[2] Thomas Daniel had occupied Brayston the previous year but was soon
afterwards dispossessed.

as I am informed. And the Blessed Trinity have you in His keeping. Written at Norwich, on St Katherine's day.

By your

MARGARET PASTON.

[25th November 1455]

109.     LORD CROMWELL TO JOHN[1] PASTON

*To my right trusty friend, John Paston, Esquire.*

Trusty and well-beloved friend, I greet you well. And forasmuch as it is done me to understand that there is a great strangeness betwixt my right trusty friend John Radcliff[1] and you, without any matter or cause of substance as I am learned; wherefore, inasmuch as I love you well both, I am not content it should so be.

Praying you heartily to forbear the said strangeness on your part to such time as I speak with you next myself, letting you wit I have written to him to do the same. And that ye fail not hereof, as I may do anything for you hereafter.

And Our Lord have you in His keeping. Written at London the 10th day of February.

CROMWELL.[2]

[Before 1456]

110.     WILLIAM BOTONER TO JOHN[1] PASTON

*To my master, John Paston.*

Please your mastership to wete that I had sent you word of the good cheer that the persons ye wot of had here upon New Year's day, and how well they took it, but W. Barker could plainly inform you. And John Sadler of Acle told me how they avaunted of it when of Lynn came by him at night lying, that he had never better cheer, etc.

My master demandeth me sundry times when ye shall be here. I could not say till this day be passed. William Jenney shall be here to-morrow, so would Jesus ye were here then. I asked licence to ride into my country, and my master did not grant it; he said his will was for to make, etc. I answered it fit not me to know it. God give him grace of wholesome counsel, and of a good disposition; *non est opus unius diei, nec unius septimanae.*

[1] John Radcliff, married Elizabeth, daughter and heiress of Walter, Lord Fitzwalter. He was later in her right called Lord Fitzwalter, and was killed at Ferrybridge in 1461, the day before Towton.
[2] Ralph, Lord Cromwell, died 4th January 1456.

My Lord Bedford's will was made in so brief and general terms, that unto this day by the space of twenty year [1] can neither have end, but alway new to construe and opinionable; so a generalty shall never be so good as a particular declaration.

I write bluntly. I had forgot to have told you Master Filongley moved me to inform my master to have a general peace, so it might be worshipful. I have said no word, for I cannot meddle in high matters that pass my wit; and therefore if ye and W. Jenney meet together, ye know and can devise best what is to be done. Our Lord be with you. Writ hastily, 6th day January.

W. BOTONER, H.R.

[1456]

111.   SIR JOHN FASTOLF TO JOHN[1] PASTON

*To the worshipful sir, and my right well-beloved cousin, John Paston, and in his absence to John Bocking and William Barker.*

Worshipful sir and cousin, I recommend me to you. And like you to wete that I have a tally [2] with my cousin Fenn [3] of 500 marks and more, for to be changed upon such places as a man might have most speedy payment. And I pray you heartily to commune with the said Fenn, that I might be ensured of the said tally to be exchanged; and for what reward competent to be given upon the same, I will agree it.

Item, I desire to know who be the residue, the remnant, of the co-executors of the Lord Willoughby,[4] now the Lord Cromwell [5] is deceased; for this cause. It was so, that there was due to the Lord Willoughby and to me 10,000 marks for a reward to be paid of my Lord Bedford's [6] goods, for the taking of the Duke of Alençon.[7]

And the said Lord Willoughby had but 1,000 marks paid, and

[1] Bedford died at Rouen on 14th September 1435.

[2] A taille or tally was a cleft stick, both parts of which were notched according to the sum of money advanced, and of which one part was given to the creditor, whilst the other remained with the debtor.

[3] Hugh Fenn, ancestor of Sir John Fenn, the original editor of these letters.

[4] Robert, Lord Willoughby of Eresby.

[5] *See* footnote 2, page 113.

[6] *See* footnote 3, page 96.

[7] John II, Duke of Alençon, son of him slain at Agincourt, was born in 1409, and taken prisoner at the battle of Verneuil, in 1424. He was detained a prisoner three years, but released at the intercession of the Duke of Burgundy, on paying a ransom of 200,000 crowns. He afterwards was convicted of treason towards his own sovereign, and died in prison in 1476.

I 1,000 marks, so 8,000 leaveth yet to pay; of which sum, 4,000 must grow to the executors of the said Lord Willoughby to dispose.

And therefore I desire that the executors, and such as most have interest in the Lord Willoughby's goods, may be communed with; that they make pursuit for payment of the said 4,000 marks, for his part to be had, and I shall make for my part.

And Master Neville,[1] the which hath wedded my Lady Willoughby, have power or interest to receive the Lord of Willoughby's debts, then he to be laboured unto. And my Lord of Salisbury will be a great helper in this cause.

The King, which is supervisor of my Lord Bedford's testament, hath written and commanded by sundry letters that the said Lord Willoughby should be content for his part. And so much the matter is the furtherer.

And there is one Young, a servant of the Lord Willoughby, which pursued this matter; if he were in London, he could give good information upon this matter.

I pray you write to me how my masters do, and of such novelties as ye have there. And Our Lord have you in His keeping.

Written at Caister hastily, 5th day of February, in the 34th year of King Henry VIth.

Your cousin,

JOHN FASTOLF.

[1456]


## 112. ARCHBISHOP BOURCHIER TO SIR JOHN FASTOLF

*To the right worshipful, and my right entirely well-beloved Sir John Fastolf, knight.*

Right worshipful, and my right entirely well-beloved, I greet you right heartily well, thanking you specially, and in full hearty wise, for the very gentle goodness that ye have showed unto me at all times, praying you of good continuance.

And as touching such matters as ye sent unto me for, I trust to God verily, insomuch as the rule is amended here, and the weather waxeth seasonable and pleasant, to see you in these parts within short time, at which time I shall commune and demean unto you in such wise that ye shall be right well pleased.

---

[1] Sir Thomas Neville, a younger son of Richard, Earl of Salisbury, married Maud, the widow of Robert, Lord Willoughby.

And as for the matter concerning my Lord of Bedford, think it not contrary, but that ye shall find me heartily well-willed to do that I can or may for the accomplishment of your desire, as well in that matter as in other, like as your servant John Bocking, bearer hereof, can clearlier report unto you on my behalf; to whom like it you to give faith and credence in this part. And the Blessed Trinity have you everlastingly in His keeping.

Written in my manor of Lambeth the 27th day of March.

Your faithful and true,

TH. CANT.

[1456]

113. DAME ALICE OGARD TO JOHN[1] PASTON

*To my right worshipful cousin, John Paston, Esquire.*

Right worshipful and entirely well-beloved cousin, I commend me to you heartily; letting you wete that there is a controversy moved betwixt my cousin John Radcliff,[1] of Attleborough and me for the advowson of the church of Attleborough, the which is now void, whereof the title is mine verily as God knoweth, the which shall be opened unto you. And upon Thursday next, at Wymondham, there shall be taken an inquiry *de jure patronatus* afore Master Robert Popy and Master Simon Thornham,[2] at which day I may not be myself as God knoweth, and though I might it were not convenient. And, therefore, right trusty cousin, considering that I am a widow impotent as of body, tenderly and heartily I pray you, if it like you to be there assisting my counsel in my right as reason and law will upon Thursday next by eight of the clock; and Fincham,[3] Spelman, and other of my counsel shall be then there waiting upon you.[4] And, gentle cousin, have me excused though I write thus briefly and homely to you; for in truth I do it of a singular trust and affection, the which I have in you, considering the good name and fame of truth, wisdom, and good conduct, the which I hear of you. And therefore, and ye may to your weal, I beseech you heartily to be there, and ye shall not lose thereby, with the grace

[1] *See* footnote 1, page 113.

[2] These were civilians and officers belonging to the bishop's court.

[3] Simeon Fincham (*d.* 1458), whose son John married Agnes, daughter of John Spelman of Beckerton.

[4] It appears that Lady Ogard's cousin and counsel assisted her to good purpose, for on 2nd August 1456 we find that Master Thomas Fairclowe, D.D., was presented by her to the church of Attleborough.

of Almighty Jesu, the which ever preserve and promote you, gentle cousin, in much worship to your heart's ease. At Buckenham Castle, on Tuesday in Pasch Week, in haste.

Dame ALICE OGARD.[1]

[30th March 1456]

114.     JOHN BOCKING TO JOHN[(1)] PASTON

*To my Master Paston.*

Worshipful sir and my good master, I recommend me to you. This day I came home; and as to our matters, I shall be with you on Monday and Tuesday next by my master's advice, and inform you of all, and of such as I will not write. Your coffer is at the Prince inn; send for it when ye like, by the token I had of Margaret Goche, a book of law that Wigge brought me.

As for tidings, my masters your brethren fare well, and recommend them to my mistress their mother, to you, and to all, etc. As for tidings else, the King is at Sheen, the Queen and Prince at Tutbury, but-if it be the latter removing. Tidings were that the Lord Beaumont was slain, and my Lord Warwick sore hurt, 1,000 men slain, and six score knights and squires hurt; and nothing true, blessed by God. As for the Lombards,[2] two of the trespassers were hanged on Monday, and there are by this time proclamations made, or shall be, through London, the peace to be kept upon great pains; and the Lombards to occupy the merchandises as they did, till the Council and Parliament have otherwise determined. And no more as yet.

The atteint abideth unruled till the next term, as I shall tell you, and it shall do well with God's grace, who have you in keeping and all yours. Written at Caister *vigilia Pentecosten*.

Your own

JOHN BOCKING.

[15th May 1456]

115.     HENRY WINDSOR TO JOHN[(1)] PASTON

After humble and due recommendation, please it your good mastership to understand that at making of this my poor letter there were no novelties with us, but such as ye understood full well afore your departing, except the King will into Scotland

---

[1] She was the widow of Sir Andrew Ogard, whose first wife was Margaret, daughter of Sir John Clifton, of Buckenham Castle. He died in 1454; she in 1460.

[2] The foreign merchants. A riot took place about this time in London, in which the houses of foreigners were attacked.

in all manner wise of war, and that my Lord of Wiltshire shall
be made Chancellor, I suppose the better is but a slander, and
therefore be ye advised how ye deliver them as tidings.[1]

Also I wot full well where I left you in such matters as it
pleased you to make me of your counsel, as touching one matter
specially; and how that ye said unto me, when I desired your
good mastership to show favour in such as ye best might, if anything should be showed *ad lumen*, my master F[astolf] except;
and how that ye answered and said as it pleased you that I was
conquered, in truth, that should prove but a full great unstable-
ness in me, with more, etc. But, sir, I pray you, howsomever
my master reckoneth with any of his servants, bring not the
matter in revolution in the open court; for an' it were once
opened afore the judges how that any letters patent should be
purchased of an ante-date,[2] and the default found in me, ye
would be a thousand times advised, and my master F. both, ere
that ye would amend me so much as I should be appeyred
thereby. And therefore I beseech you be well advised how that
matter be opened for my ease.

I was not desired to write unto you of no one person, so God
be my help, yourself except; but I would ye would take advice
and counsel of the priest that had you so long under hands on
Shoe Thursday,[3] when I and my fellowship, God thank you,
had of you right great cheer to our great comfort and your great
cost, how that the same priest understandeth this letter of the
gospel underwritten, ' Jesus dixit Simoni Petro, si peccaverit in
te frater tuus, vade et corripe eum inter te et ipsum solum; si
te audierit lucratus es fratrem tuum. Si autem te non audierit
adhibe tecum adhuc unum vel duos, ut in ore duorum vel trium
testium stet omne verbum. Quod si non audierit, dic ecclesiae,
si autem ecclesiam non audierit sit tibi sicut ethnicus et publi-
canus,' etc. And in another place 'Tunc accedens Petrus ad
Jesum dixit. Domine, quotiens peccavit in me frater meus, et
dimittam ei? usque septies? Dicit illi Jesus, non dico tibi
usque septies, sed usque septuagesies septies.' [4]

My master can do nothing the which shall come in open
audience at these days, but it shall be called your deed; and it
is not unknown that cruel and vengible he hath been ever, and
for the most part without pity and mercy. I can no more, but

[1] Both pieces of intelligence were false rumours.
[2] A law was passed in the eighteenth year of Henry VI to stop the abuse
of persons having interest about the Court procuring ante-dated letters
patent whereby they were enabled to claim the emoluments of lands or
offices granted to them from a date anterior to the actual passing of the
grant.
[3] Maundy Thursday.
[4] Matthew xviii. 15–17; 21, 22.

*vade et corripe eum*, for truly he cannot bring about his matters in this world, for the word is not for him. I suppose it will not change yet by likeliness; but I beseech you, sir, help not to amend him only, but every other man if ye know any more misdisposed.

I can no more, but as I can or may, shall be his servant and yours unto such time as ye will command me to surcease and leave off, if it please him.

Sir, I pray you take this copy[1] of your statute, it is not examined by me, for I found it these five years passed.

Written in my sleeping time at afternoon, on Whitsunday. Also, sir, if I have rehearsed wittingly the text of the gospel singularly unto your mastership, I beseech you to be had excused.

Your own

H. W.

[16th May ? 1456]

## 116.   JOHN BOCKING TO JOHN[(1)] PASTON

*To my right good master, John Paston, Esquire, at Norwich, in haste.*

Sir, please it your mastership to wit, I have my attachments granted in open court with help of Lyttleton and Hugh Fenn, and was bid to make ready the names, etc., before the Barons, of which Haltoft[2] was one. . . .[3]

As for tidings, the King is at Sheen, the Queen at Chester; the Duke of Buckingham was, as I came hitherward, at Writell, the Earl of Warwick at Warwick, and the Lords Chancellor,[4] Treasurer,[5] and the Earl of Salisbury in London, and no more lords at the beginning this day of the great council. Many men say that there should be, but they wot not what. The siege shall, as men say, come to Calais and Guisnes; for much people come over the water of Somme, and great navies on the sea.

The Earl of Pembroke[6] is with the King, and no more lords.

---

[1] This relates to papers sent with this letter, and accounts for there being no direction, as the whole was enclosed in a parcel.

[2] Gilbert Haltoft.

[3] Here, in the original, followed various passages relating to legal business, which Fenn did not print.

[4] Archbishop Bourchier.

[5] Henry, Viscount Bourchier, appointed Lord Treasurer, 29th May 1455.

[6] Jasper Tudor, the King's half-brother.

The Earl of Richmond [1] and Griffith Suoh [*sic in MS.*] are at war greatly in Wales. The commons of Kent, as they were wont, are not all well disposed, for there is in doing amongst them whatever it be. Of Scots is here but little talking. My Lord of York is at Sandal still, and waiteth upon the Queen and she upon him. [2]

I did my mistress your mother's errands, as ye have heard of, for Master William hath written his intent, and he and Clement fare well.

Written at Horsleydown, 7th day of June.

Rokewode and Crane fare well, and they and I recommend them to my mistress your wife.

And, as I understand, the Clerk of the Rolls is out of charity with Master Yelverton, and my Lord Chancellor a little moved, etc.

Your own,

J. B.

[? 1456]

117. HENRY FILONGLEY TO SIR JOHN FASTOLF

*To my right worshipful uncle, and my right good master, Sir John Fastolf, knight.*

Right worshipful uncle, and my right good master, I recommend me to you with all my service.

And, sir, my brother Paston and I have communed together as touching to your college [3] that ye would have made. And, sir, it is too great a good that is asked of you for your licence; for they ask, for every 100 marks that ye would amortise, 500 marks, and will give it no better cheap.

And, sir, I told my brother Paston, that my Lady Abergavenny [4] hath in divers abbeys in Leicestershire seven or eight priests singing for her perpetually, by my brother Darcy's and my uncle Brokesby's means, for they were her executors; and they accorded for money, and gave a 200 or 300 marks, as they might accord, for a priest.

And for the surety that he should sing in the same abbey for ever, they had manors of good value bounden to such persons

[1] Edmund Tudor, the King's half-brother.
[2] i.e. they were keeping watch upon one another
[3] This is the college which Sir John Fastolf intended to have founded at Caister.
[4] Elizabeth, daughter and heiress of Richard Beauchamp, Earl of Worcester (son and heir of William Beauchamp, Lord Bergavenny), and wife of Sir Edward Neville, a younger son of Ralph, first Earl of Westmorland, who by this marriage was summoned to Parliament as Lord Bergavenny in 1450.

as pleased the said brethren, Brokesby and my brother Darcy, that the said service should be kept.

And for little more than the King asked them for a licence, they went through with the said abbots.

And I hold this way as sure as that other; ye may commune with your counsel thereof.

And if there be any service that I may do for you, it shall be ready at all times, with the grace of God, who have you in His keeping.

Written at London, the 17th day of July.

Your nephew and servant,

HENRY FILONGLEY.

[? 1456]


118. THOMAS, LORD SCALES, TO JOHN[(1)]PASTON

*To my right trusty and entirely well-beloved friend, John Paston, Esquire.*

Right trusty and entirely well-beloved friend, I greet you well, and will ye wit that Daniel hath required me to write unto you, praying you that ye will keep the day upon Thursday seven days next coming, which shall be for the best, as I trust; notwithstanding I suppose learned men will not be easy for to get because of this busy time of harvest. Almighty God have you in His governance,

Written at Middleton, the 10th day of August.

Your friend,

SCALES.

[1456]


119.        JAMES GRESHAM TO JOHN[(1)]PASTON

*To the right worshipful and mine especial master, John Paston, Esquire, in haste be this delivered.*

After all due recommendation, . . . [1]  As for tidings, my Lord Chancellor [2] is discharged.  In his stead is my Lord of Winchester.[3]  And my Lord of Shrewsbury [4] is Treasurer, and Brown [5] of your Inn is Under-Treasurer.  If ye would send to him to grant you the naming of the escheatorship of Norfolk,

[1] Here follow three short paragraphs concerning legal business.
[2] Thomas Bourchier, Archbishop of Canterbury.
[3] William Waynflete, Bishop of Winchester.
[4] John Talbot, second Earl.
[5] John Brown, of the Inner Temple.

etc., it were well done, for it is told me he would do much for you.

Master Laurence Booth [1] is Privy Seal. And it is said that my Lord of York [2] hath been with the King, and is departed again in right good conceit with the King, but not in great conceit with the Queen; and some men say, had not my Lord of Bucks [3] not have letted it, my Lord of York had been distressed in his departing.

On Monday last passed was a great affray at Coventry between the Duke of Somerset's men and the watchmen of the town; and two or three men of the town were killed there, to great disturbance of all the lords there. For the alarm bell was rung, and the town arose, and would have jeoparded to have distressed the Duke of Somerset, etc., had not the Duke of Bucks taken a direction therein.

Also it is said the Duke of Bucks taketh right strangely that both his brethren [4] are so suddenly discharged from their offices of Chancellery and Treasurership; and that among other causeth him that his opinion is contrary to the Queen's intent, and many other also, as it is talked. Item, some men say the Council is dissolved, and that the King is forth to Chester,[5] etc. Also some say that many of the lords shall resort hither to London against Allhallowtide.

And as touching the election of sheriffs, men ween that my Lord of Canterbury shall have a great rule, and special in our country. I can no more, but Almighty God send us as His most pleasure is. Written all in haste, the Saturday next after St Edward's day.

Your servant,

JAMES GRESHAM.

[16th October 1456]

120.    SIR JOHN FASTOLF TO JOHN[(1)] PASTON

*To the worshipful, and my right well-beloved cousin, John Paston, at the Temple, or to William Barker, at Southwark, be this delivered.*

Worshipful cousin, I commend me to you. And whereas I late wrote unto you in a letter by Henry Hansson for the foundation

---

[1] Afterwards Bishop of Durham, and finally Archbishop of York.
[2] Richard, Duke of York.
[3] Humphrey Stafford, Duke of Buckingham.
[4] The two Bourchiers, Thomas, Archbishop of Canterbury, and Henry, Viscount Bourchier, who had been Treasurer. They were Buckingham's half-brothers.
[5] The Court had been in residence at Coventry.

of my college, I am sore set thereupon; and that is the cause I write now, to remember you again to move my Lords of Canterbury and Winchester for the licence to be obtained, that I might have the amortising without any great fine, in recompense of my long service continued and done unto the King and to his noble father, whom God assoil, and never yet guerdoned or rewarded.

And now since I have ordained to make the King founder, and ever to be prayed for, and for his right noble progenitors, his father, and uncles, methinketh I should not be denied of my desire, but the rather to be remembered and sped.

Wherefore, as I wrote unto you, I pray you acquaint me and you, for the rather speed hereof, with a chaplain of my Lord of Canterbury, that in your absence may remember me, and in likewise with my Lord Chancellor;[1] for seeing the King's disposition, and also his, unto the edifying of God's service, it might in no better time be moved, etc.

My Lord of Norfolk is removed from Framlingham on foot to go to Walsingham,[2] and daily I wait that he would come hither.

Your cousin,

J. FASTOLF.

[18th November 1456]

121.    WILLIAM BOTONER TO JOHN[(1)] PASTON

*To my Master Paston.*

Please you to wete that, after due recommendation, it is so that my master sendeth me to London for the matter of Rochester, as for divers of his own particular matters which concern not the law, etc.; and I am like to tarry there till ye come, in case ye come within three weeks.

Sir, at reverence of God, sith my master is fully in will to renew his feoffment, that it may be done betimes by the surest ground that may be had, for, be it never so surely done, it shall be thought little enough to keep his land out of trouble; and to spare for no counsel nor cost to make it sure, for a penny in season spent will save a pound.

I communed with my brother Spyrling, which saith he will do his attendance, and to keep it right close of the names.[3] Tarrying draweth peril.

And ye moved a good matter to the parson [Howes] and to me

---

[1] William Waynflete, Bishop of Winchester.
[2] On pilgrimage to the shrine of Our Lady of Walsingham.
[3] Of the trustees named in the feoffment.

at your last being at Caister, that my master should be learned what his household standeth upon yearly, since he kept it wholly together at one place; and that done, then to see by the revenues of his yearly livelode what may be laid and assigned out for that cause to maintain his said household, and over that, what may be assigned to bear out his pleas,[1] and also do pay for his foreign charges [2] and deeds of alms to a convenient sum.

And since the greatest ordinary charge must be his household keeping, it were most expedient that ye would note well to remember specially my master to do his auditors cast up and make rolls of his accounts concerning the said household since he came into Norfolk these two years and half, which was never so long to do these forty winters, as ye know. And it is pity that his audit is none otherwise in that intended; ye must needs, if ye will my master know how it stand with him yearly of his charges, that this be done first, as it was alway accustomed. My master will accord it to be done, but it is forgotten through negligence of men given to sensuality, as Thomas Upton, me, and others. My master cannot know whether he go backward or forward till this be done.

I can nought else, but ye will not forget this, that the auditors go verily about it to an end. And Hellesdon accounts be behindhand for two years, too great pity is, and it were yours or in any wise man's governance. At Norwich, hastily, the Wednesday in Easter week.

Boto—H.R.—ner.

[20th April 1457]

## 122.   William Botoner to John[1] Paston

*To the right worshipful sir, John Paston, Esquire, being in Norwich, in haste.*

Right worshipful sir, after due recommendation, please you to wete that I wrote a remembrance to you the day that I departed out of Norwich, by Richard, the parson's servant of Blofield, concerning certain matters to be remembered by your wisdom for my master's avail, which your great wisdom can well understand is right needful, as one thing in especial, that Shipdam and Spyrling ought to labour, first of anything that belongeth, to audit the accounts of the receipts and dispenses of my master's household in Caister since he came last into Norfolk, which as well for the provisions that is had of his own growing as in money

[1] His law business.
[2] Charges not connected with his household accounts.

paid. For till the said accounts be made ordinately, which be of a great charge yearly, wete ye for certain my master shall never know whether he goeth backward or forward. And many other accountants that make livery of provisions of corns and cattle to the household by the receiver and by the bailiffs cannot approve their liberates just till the said household books be make up. And since it hath been kept ordinarily since my master began to keep house this fifty year almost, and when he hath been absent beyond sea, etc., it ought to be more readilier done and made up while he is present, and well the rather that his household meny were not so whole together this forty year as be now at Caister. Also his minustres of accounts of his chief manor of Hellesdon for three years to make up and to examine; and I assure you full simply approved his wools and his farm.

And the third is, that, so would Jesus, my master's auditors would faithfully and plainly inform my master of the truth of the yearly great damage he beareth in disbursing his money about shipping and boats, keeping an house up at Yarmouth to his great harm, and receiveth but chaffer and ware for his corns and wools, etc., and then must abide a long day to make money. Of such chaffer taking he shall never be monied nor be answered clearly of his revenues yearly, but those things abovesaid be amended betimes. In Lewis's days twelve years together my master was wont to lay up money yearly at London and Caister, and now the contary—*de malo in pejus.*

I dare not be known of this bill, but ye may question and feel of the disposition of these matters of others, and then understand if I write justly or no; and ye, as of your motion for my master's worship and profit, exhorting him, the steward, Shipdam, and Spyrling to take a labour and a pain that this be reformed.

I pray you and require you keep this matter to yourself.

Your

BOTONER.

As for novelties, none couth; but it is said the siege shall come to Calais. The Earl of Warwick is yet at Canterbury with the archbishop, and the earl's younger brother [1] is married to Sir Edmund Inglethorpe's daughter upon Saint Mark's day. The Earl of Worcester [2] brought about the marriage. The Queen and the King at Hereford, the Lords Buckingham, Shrewsbury, and others there. And now it is said Herbert [3] shall come in,

---

[1] John Neville, afterwards Marquis Montague, married Isabel, daughter and heiress of Sir Edmund Ingoldesthorpe, of Burgh Green in Cambridgeshire, by his wife Jane, sister and at length co-heiress of John Lord Tiptoft, first Earl of Worcester. He was slain in the battle of Barnet in 1471.

[2] John Tiptoft.

[3] Sir William Herbert, afterwards Earl of Pembroke.

and appear at Leicester before the King and the lords, his life granted and goods, so he make amends to them he hath offended. Many be indicted, some causelessly, which maketh Herbert's party strong; and the burgesses and gentlemen about Hereford will go with the King's wife and child, but a peace be made ere the King part thence, for else Herbert and his affinity will acquit them, as it is said.

The Earl of Warwick hath had the folks of Canterbury and Sandwich before him, and thanked them of their good hearts and victualling of Calais, and prayeth them of continuance.

I send a bill of the names indicted, to my master and you, to see and laugh at their Welsh names descended of old pedigrees. Our Lord be with you.   Written hastily at London, the 1st day of May.

BOTONER.

[1457]

## 123.   Sir John Fastolf to Stephen Scrope

### To Stephen Scrope.

Worshipful and my right well-beloved son, I commend me to you, and heartily thank you for your good advertisements, and right well advised letters to me sent from time to time, and so pray you of your good continuance.

Please it you to wete that, forasmuch as the parson Sir Thomas Howes cometh up at this time by the grievous pursuit of John Andrews and Heydon to appear before the right worshipful sir, my right well-beloved brother, your father,[1] and other the King's judges of the King's Bench, I pray you heartily that ye will have in remembrance for to recommend me to him when ye speak with him, and for to thank him for his rightful favour showed in Sir Thomas's matter, and in all other matters that toucheth me, which he attained in that high court; and so it like you, pray him of his good continuance, and I shall do serve it unto him to my simple power for his good will to me showed, and to mine; and I trust to God that he shall hold him pleased. And that it like you to give credence to the said Sir Thomas of that he shall say to you for my worship and profit, and that this letter may recommend me to my daughter your wife, beseeching the Blessed Trinity to send you the accomplishment of your good desire.

Written at Caister, the 30th day of October.

[1457]                                         J. F.

¹ Sir Richard Bingham whose daughter Joan Stephen Scrope had married.

### 124. RICHARD, EARL OF SALISBURY, TO VISCOUNT BEAUMONT

*To the right worshipful, and, with all mine heart, right entirely well-beloved brother, the Viscount Beaumont.*

Right worshipful, and, with all mine heart, right entirely well-beloved brother, I recommend me unto you. And for so much as by the King's most noblest letters brought me late by Hagerston, one of the grooms of his chamber, I am desired to come unto his Highness to London; whereunto for such grievous disease and infirmities as it hath liked Our Lord to visit me with, whereof Robert Danby can at large declare unto you, I cannot nor may dispose me, without feigning, by the troth I owe unto the King, but that thereby I doubt not I should not recover all the days of my life from such hurt as, by the reason of the said disease, would grow unto me, the which hath right fervently and sore holden me in many divers behalves, so that since my last coming from London I had not by the space of six days together my health.

Wherefore, brother, I pray you with all mine whole heart that it like you to call tofore you the said Robert Danby, and to take of him the very truth in the premises, and thereupon to be my good and tender means, as by your wisdom can best be thought convenable, unto the King's good grace, for the excuse of my non-coming; praying you heartily to certify me, by comersbetween, such tidings as ye shall have in those parts, with other your good pleasure to be performed at my power, as knoweth Our Lord, to whom I beseech to ever have you in His blessed protection and keeping.

Written at Sheriff Hutton, the 24th day of January.

Your true brother, which prayeth you heartily to excuse me to the King's Highness,

R. SALISBURY.

[1458]

### 125. AGNES PASTON

*Errands to London of Agnes Paston, the 28th day of January 1457, the year of King Henry VI the 36th.*

To pray Greenfield to send me faithfully word, by writing, how Clement Paston hath done his devoir in learning.

And if he hath not done well, nor will not amend, pray him that he will truly belash him, till he will amend; and so did the last master, and the best that ever he had, at Cambridge.

And say Greenfield that if he will take upon him to bring him into good rule and learning, that I may verily know he doth his devoir, I will give him 10 marks for his labour, for I had lever he were fairly buried than lost for default.

Item, to see how many gowns Clement hath, and they that be bare, let them be raised.[1]

He hath a short green gown, and a short musterdevelers gown, were never raised.

And a short blue gown, that was raised, and made of a side gown [2] when I was last at London.

And a side russet gown, furred with beaver, was made this time two years.

And a side murrey gown was made this time twelvemonth.

Item, to do make me six spoons of eight ounces of troy weight, well fashioned and double gilt.

And say Elizabeth Paston that she must use herself to work readily, as other gentlewomen do, and somewhat to help herself therewith.

Item, to pay the Lady Pole 26s. and 8d. for her board.

And if Greenfield have done well his devoir to Clement, or will do his devoir, give him the noble.

Agnes Paston.

[1458]

126. Agnes Paston to John[1] Paston

*To my well-beloved son, John Paston, be this delivered in haste.*

Son, I greet you well, and let you wete that forasmuch as your brother Clement letteth me wete that ye desire faithfully my blessing—that blessing that I prayed your father to give you the last day that ever he spake—and the blessing of all saints under heaven, and mine, may come to you all days and times. And think verily none other but that ye have it, and shall have it, with that that I find you kind and willing to the weal of your father's soul, and to the welfare of your brethren.

By my counsel, dispose yourself as much as ye may to have less to do in the world; your father said: 'In little business lieth much rest.' This world is but a thoroughfare, and full of woe; and when we depart therefrom, right nought bear with us but our good deeds and ill. And there knoweth no man how soon God will clepe him, and therefore it is good for every creature to be ready. Whom God visiteth, him He loveth.

[1] i.e. let them be given a new nap.
[2] A side gown may mean a long one; for in Laneham's account of Queen Elizabeth's entertainment at Kenilworth Castle, 1575, the minstrel's 'gown had side (i.e. long) sleeves down to the mid-leg.'

And as for your brethren, they will, I know, certainly labour all that in them lieth for you. Our Lord have you in His blessed keeping, body and soul. Written at Norwich, the 29th day of October.

By your mother,

A. P.

[1458]


### 127.  WILLIAM BOTONER TO SIR JOHN FASTOLF[1]

*To my right worshipful master, Sir John Fastolf.*

Right worshipful sir, and my right good master, I recommend me to you in my full humble wise. Please you to wete as to novelties here, both Christopher Barker writeth to you more along.

The King came the last week to Westminster, and the Duke of York came to London with his own household only to the number of 140 horse, as it is said; the Earl of Salisbury with 400 horse in his company, fourscore knights and squires.

The Duke of Somerset came to London last day of January with 200 horse, and lodgeth without Temple Bar, and the Duke of Exeter shall be here this week with a great fellowship and strong, as it is said.

The Earl of Warwick is not yet come, because the wind is not yet for him.

And the Duke of Exeter [2] taketh a great displeasure that my Lord Warwick occupieth his office, and taketh the charge of the keeping of the sea upon him.

Item, as for tidings of beyond sea, I hear none certain, but that the French king [3] should have married his daughter to the King of Hungary [4] which had the discomfiture upon the Turks, and the said king is deceased within this six weeks, ere the spousal was made; but he ordained ere he died that the French king's daughter should be named Queen of Hungary during her life.

Right worshipful sir, I beseech the Blessed Trinity have you in His governance.

---

[1] The first part of this letter is omitted; it refers to legal business of no present interest.

[2] Henry Holland, Duke of Exeter. Warwick was at this time governor of Calais.

[3] Charles VII.

[4] Ladislaus V, who died on 23rd November 1457, when on the point of marriage with Magdalen, daughter of Charles VII of France. He is believed to have been poisoned.

Writ at London, the 1st day of February in the 36th year of King Henry VI.

Moreover, please you to wete that William Canyngs the merchant writeth an answer of your letter. I trust it shall be the better for your writing.

My brother promitted me a certain sum when I married, and I shall have it of my sister if I may.

Your humble servant,

W. BOTONER, dit WORCESTER.

[1458]

128. JOHN BOCKING TO SIR JOHN FASTOLF[1]

*To my Master Fastolf, at Caister, in haste.*

Like it your mastership to wit that, as for tidings, the Council is, the forenoon, at the Black Friars, for the ease of resorting of the lords that are within the town; and at afternoon at the White Friars in Fleet-street, for the lords without the town. And all things shall come to a good conclusion with God's grace; for the King shall come hither this week, and the Queen also, as some men say, and my Lords Buckingham and Stafford with her, and much people.

My Lord of Canterbury taketh great pain upon him daily, and will write unto you the certainty of such tidings as fall; and should have done ere this time, save for that he would know an end of the matter.

Other tidings here are none, save my Lord of Exeter is displeased that the Earl of Warwick shall keep the sea, and hath therefore received this week £1,000 of the Hanaper.[2]

The messenger was on horseback when I wrote you this bill, and therefore it was done in haste; and our Lord Jesu keep you. Written at London the Wednesday after Mid-lent.

And my Lord of Canterbury told me that the Frenchmen have been before you,[3] and that ye shot many guns, and so he told all the lords. I have desired him to move the Council for refreshing of the town of Yarmouth with stuff of ordnance and guns and gunpowder, and he said he would.

Your humble servant,

JOHN BOCKING.

[15th March 1458]

---

[1] This letter refers to the temporary reconciliation of the Lancastrian and Yorkist lords in the spring of 1458.
[2] The Hanaper of Chancery.
[3] French ships had appeared off Caister.

## 129. John Jerningham to Margaret Paston

*Unto my right worshipful cousin, Margaret Paston, this letter be*
*delivered in haste.*

Right worshipful, and my most best-beloved mistress and cousin, I recommend me unto you as lowly as I may, evermore desiring to hear of your good welfare; the which I beseech Almighty Jesu to preserve you, and keep you to His pleasure, and to your gracious heart's desire.

And if it please you to hear of my welfare, I was in good health at the making of this letter, blessed be God.   Praying you, that it please you for to send me word if my father were at Norwich with you at this Trinity-mass or no, and how the matter doth between my mistress Blanche Witchingham and me; and if ye suppose that it shall be brought about or no, and how ye feel my father, if he be well willing thereto or no; praying you lowly that I may be recommended lowly unto my mistress, Arblaster's wife, and unto my mistress Blanche her daughter specially.

Right worshipful cousin, if it please you for to hear of such tidings as we have here, the basset of Burgundy shall come to Calais the Saturday after Corpus Christi day, as men say five hundred horse of them.

Moreover, on Trinity Sunday, in the morning, came tidings unto my Lord of Warwick that there were 28 sail of Spaniards on the sea, and whereof there was sixteen great ships of fore-castle.[1]   And then my lord went, and manned five ships of forecastle and three carvels [2] and four spinnes; [3] and on the Monday, on the morning after Trinity Sunday, we met together afore Calais at four at the clock in the morning, and fought together till ten at the clock.   And there we took six of their ships, and they slew of our men about fourscore, and hurt a 200 of us right sore; and there were slain on their part about twelve score, and hurt a 500 of them.

And happed me, at the first aboarding of us, we took a ship of 300 ton, and I was left therein, and twenty-three men with me; and they fought so sore that our men were fain to leave them, and then came they and aboarded the ship that I was in, and there I was taken, and was prisoner with them six hours, and was delivered again for their men that were taken before.   And, as men say, there was not so great a battle upon the sea this forty

---

[1] Ships of forecastle were ships with forestages, and carried about 150 men each; they were the largest ships then in use.   A barge carried about eighty men, and a balinger about forty.

[2] Carvels were ships of a middle size.

[3] Spinnes, or pinnaces, carried about twenty-five men each.

winter. And forsooth we were well and truly beat; and my Lord hath sent for more ships, and like to fight together again in haste.

No more I write unto you at this time, but that it please you for to recommend me unto my right reverend and worshipful cousin your husband, and mine uncle Gurney, and to mine aunt his wife, and to all good masters and friends where it shall please you; and after the writing I have from you I shall be at you in all haste.

Written on Corpus Christi day in great haste.

By your own humble servant and cousin,

JOHN JERNINGHAM.

[Thursday, 1st June 1458]

130.     HENRY WINDSOR TO JOHN[1] PASTON

*To my full special good master, John Paston.*

Worshipful sir, and my full special good master, after humble recommendation, please it you to understand that such service as I can do to your pleasure, as to mine understanding, I have showed my diligence now this short season since your departing; and in especial about such a copy of a foundation [1] as your mastership commanded me to get you a copy of, of the which I send unto you at this time by my brother William Worcester, three copies written by Luket, because I had no leisure, but so much business in setting forth of my Master of the Rolls.[2]    At this time, and in all this King's days, ye can have none other according anything to your intent.

And as for the names of the Poles,[3] William hath more writing than ye and I could find, found by labour made by him and me.

And also, sir, he hath caused me to examine old and many records written by some Frenchman concerning the manor of Dedham; that was a cumbrous labour, for these copies were full defective, as it appeareth by the correcting of them.

Item, sir, I may say to you that William [Botoner] hath gone to school to a Lombard called Carol Giles, to learn and to be read in poetry, or else in French; for he hath been with the same Carol every day two times or three, and hath bought divers books of him, for the which as I suppose he hath put himself in danger to the same Carol.

---

[1] For Sir John Fastolf's proposed college at Caister.
[2] Thomas de Kirkeby.
[3] Worcester appears to have been investigating the pedigree of the Duke of Suffolk's ancestors. (*See* vol. ii, No. 251, page 21.)

I made a motion to William to have known part of his business, and he answered and said that he would be as glad and as fain of a good book of French, or of poetry, as my master Fastolf would be to purchase a fair manor; and thereby I understand he list not to be communed withal in such matters.

Item, sir, as for any tidings, William can tell you here at London are but full few; but Henry Bourchier is dead suddenly at Ludlow; my Lord of Canterbury and my Lord Bourchier shall be this week at Hunsdon, and hunt and sport them with Sir William Oldhall.

At this time nothing else to your mastership; but an' it please you to remember my master at your best leisure, whether his old promise shall stand as touching my preferring to the Boar's Head in Southwark.   Sir, I would have been at another place, and of my master's own motion he said that I should set up in the Boar's Head, in the which matter I report me to William Worcester, Bocking, and William Barker, and most specially to my master's own remembrance.   I know full well there can no conclusion be taken to mine avail without help of your mastership, unto the which I utterly submit me in this and in all other. And our Lord Jesu preserve you and all yours, and send you your heart's desire with right.

Written at London on Sunday next after Saint Bartholomew's day in haste.

By your servant,

HENRY WINDSOR.

[27th August ? 1458]

131.    ELIZABETH POYNINGS[1] TO AGNES PASTON

*To my right worshipful mother, Agnes Paston.*

Right worshipful and my most entirely beloved Mother, in the most lowly manner I recommend me unto your good motherhood, beseeching you daily and nightly of your motherly blessing, evermore desiring to hear of your welfare and prosperity, the which I pray God to continue and increase to your heart's desire.   And if it liked your good motherhood to hear of me and how I do, at the making of this letter I was in good health of body, thanked be Jesu.   And as for my master, my best beloved that ye call, and I must needs call him so now, for I find none other cause, and as I trust to Jesu none shall; for he is full kind unto me, and is as busy as he can to make me sure of my jointure, whereto he is bound in a bond of £1,000 to you,

[1] Agnes Paston's daughter Elizabeth had recently been married to Robert oynings.

Mother, and to my brother John, and to my brother William, and to Edmund Clere,[1] the which needed no such bond. Wherefore I beseech you, good mother, as our most singular trust is in your good motherhood, that my master, my best beloved, fail not of the hundred marks at the beginning of this term, the which ye promised him to his marriage, with the remnant of the money of Father's will. For I have promitted faithfully to a gentleman called Bain, that was one of my best beloved's sureties, and was bound for him in £200, of which he rehearseth for to receive at the beginning of this term, £120, and if he fail thereof at this time he will claim the whole of us, the which were to us too great an hurt; and he cannot make an end with none of his other sureties without this said silver, and that can my brother John tell you well enough and it lusteth him to do so, and in all other things. As to my Lady Pole, with whom I sojourned, that ye will be my tender and good mother that she may be paid for all the costs done to me before my marriage; and to Christopher Hansson, as ye wrote unto my brother John that it should have been so; and that it please your good motherhood to give credence to William Worcester. And Jesu for His great mercy save you. Written at London, the Wednesday the 3rd day of January.

By your humble daughter,

ELIZABETH POYNINGS.

[1459]

## 132. JOHN[2] PASTON TO JOHN[1] PASTON

*To my right worshipful father, John Paston, Esquire, be this letter delivered in hasty wise.*

Right worshipful sir, in the most lowly wise I commend me to your good fatherhood, beseeching you of your blessing. Might it please your fatherhood to remember and consider the pain and heaviness that it hath been to me since your departing out of this country, here abiding till the time it please you to show me grace, and till the time that by report my demeaning be to your pleasing; beseeching you to consider that I may not nor have no mean to seek you as I ought to do, saving under this form, which I beseech you be not taken to no displeasure, nor am not of power to do anything in this country for worship or profit of you, nor ease of your tenants, which might and should be to your pleasing. Wherefore I beseech you of your fatherly pity to tender the more this simple writing, as I shall out of doubt

[1] Edmund Clere was the second son of John Clere of Ormesby, and died in 1463.

hereafter do that shall please you to the uttermost of my power and labour; and if there be any service that I may do, if it please you to command me, or if I may understand it, I will be as glad to do it as anything earthly, if it were anything that might be to your pleasing.    And no more, but Almighty God have you in keeping.

Written at Norwich, the 5th day of March.

By your older son,

JOHN PASTON.

[1459]

### 133.    MARGARET PASTON TO JOHN[(1)] PASTON

*To my right worshipful husband, John Paston, in haste.*

Right worshipful husband, I recommend me unto you.    Pleaseth you to wete that on Thursday last was there were brought unto this town many privy seals, and one of them was endorsed to you, and to Hastings, and to five or six other gentlemen.    And another was sent unto your son, and endorsed to himself alone, and assigned within with the King's own hand, and so were but few that were sent as it was told me; and also there were more special terms in his than were in others.    I saw a copy of those that were sent unto other gentlemen.    The intent of the writing was, that they should be with the King at Leicester the 10th day of May, with as many persons defensibly arrayed as they might, according to their degree, and that they should bring with them for their expenses for two months.

As for the letter that was endorsed to you and to others, it was delivered to William Yelverton, for there appeared no more of the remnant.

Hastings is forth into Yorkshire.    I pray you that ye vouchsafe to send word in haste how ye will that your son be demeaned herein.    Men think here, that be your well-willers, that ye may no less do than to send him forth.

As for his demeaning since ye departed, in good faith it hath been right good and lowly and diligent in oversight of your servants and other things; the which I hope ye would have been pleased with, an' ye had been at home.    I hope he will be well demeaned to please you hereafterward.

He desired Arblaster to be mean to you for him, and was right heavy of his demeaning to you, as I sent you word also by Arblaster, how I did to him after that ye were gone; and I beseech you heartily that ye vouchsafe to be his good father, for I hope he is chastised, and will be the worthier hereafter.

As for all other things at home, I hope that I and others shall do our part therein as well as we may; but as for money, it cometh but slowly. And God have you in His keeping, and send you good speed in all your matters.

Written in haste at Norwich on the Sunday next before the Ascension day.

Sir, I would be right glad to hear some good tidings from you.

By yours,

M. P.

[29th April 1459

134. John, Lord Lovel,[1] to Viscount Beaumont

*To my right worshipful, and my most best-beloved lord father, my Lord Beaumont.*

Right worshipful, and my most best-beloved lord father, I recommend me unto your good Lordship. Please it you to wit, I have conceived your writing right well; and forasmuch as ye desire the stewardship of Baggeworth for your well-beloved Thomas Everingham, which I trow verily be right a good and a faithful gentleman. Howbeit, my Lord, your desire shall be had in all that is in me; and at the instance of your Lordship, I, by the advice of my counsel, shall give it him in writing, under such form as shall please you, wherein I would be glad to do that that might please your good Lordship, praying you right heartily ye would be mine especial good lord and father in all such as ye can think should grow to my worship or profit in any wise, as my singular trust is most in you. And I alway ready to do you service with God's grace, who have you, my right worshipful and my most best-beloved lord father, ever in His blessed keeping.

Written at Rotherfield Grey, the 24th day of July, etc.

Furthermore, my Lord, and it like you, my Lady my mother recommended her unto your good Lordship, in whom her most faith and trust is in, praying you ye will be good brother unto her, for she hath taken you for her chief counsel, etc.

John, Lord Lovell.

[1454-9]

---

[1] He succeeded to the barony of Lovel in 1454, and married Jane, daughter of John, first Viscount Beaumont. The latter was killed at the battle of Northampton on 10th July 1460.

## 135. Eleanor, Duchess of Norfolk, to John, Viscount Beaumont

*To my right worshipful and right entirely well-beloved cousin, the Viscount Beaumont.*

Right worshipful, and right entirely well-beloved cousin, I commend me to you with all my heart, desiring to hear and verily to know of your worshipful estate, profit, health, and good prosperity, the which I beseech our Lord Jesu ever to maintain and preserve in all worship, to His pleasance and to your heart's ease.

Please it you, cousin, to wit that your well-beloved servant Roger Hunt, and a servant of my most dread Lord my husband, one William, yeoman of his ewry,[1] have communed together, and been fully thorough and agreed, that the said William shall have his office,[2] if it may please your good Lordship.

Wherefore, cousin, I pray you, as my special trust is in you, that ye will, at the instance of my prayer and writing, grant by your letters patent to the said William the foresaid office, with such wages and fees as Roger your said servant hath it of you; trusting verily that ye shall find the said William a faithful servant to you, and can and may do you right good service in that office.

And, cousin, in the accomplishment of my desire in this matter ye may do me a right good pleasure, as God knoweth, whom I beseech for His mercy to have you ever in His blessed governance, and send you good life and long, with much good worship.

Written at Framlingham, the 8th day of March.

Eleanor, *the Duchess of Norfolk*.[3]

[1444–60]

## 136. William[1] Paston to John[1] Paston[4]

*To my Master John Paston in Norfolk.*

Right well-beloved brother, I recommend me to you, certifying you that on Friday last was in the morning, Worcester and I were

[1] An officer who had charge of the table-linen, etc.
[2] Roger Hunt had sold his office to William subject to Lord Beaumont's approval.
[3] Wife of John Mowbray, third Duke of Norfolk.
[4] This letter gives an account of the steps taken by William Paston in behalf of his brother, who was Sir John Fastolf's principal executor, to secure the goods of the deceased knight immediately after his death which

F 752

come to London by eight of the clock; and we spake with my Lord Chancellor,[1] and I find him well disposed in all things, and ye shall find him right profitable to you, etc. And he desired me to write you a letter in his name, and put trust in you in gathering of the goods together, and pray you to do so and have all his [Fastolf's] goods out of every place of his, and his own place,[2] wheresoever they were, and lay it secretly where as ye thought best at your assignment, and till that he spake with you himself; and he said ye should have all lawful favour. I purpose to ride to him this day for writs of *diem clausit extremum*,[3] and I suppose ye shall have a letter sent from himself to you.

As for the goods at Paul's, it is safe enough; and this day we have a grant to have the goods out of Bermondsey[4] without advice of any man, saving Worcester, Plomer, and I myself, and nobody shall know of it but we three.

My Lord Treasurer[5] speaketh fair, but yet many advise me to put no trust in him. There is laboured many means to entitle the King in his [Fastolf's] goods. Southwell[6] is escheator, and he is right good and well disposed. My Lord of Exeter claimeth title in my master's place, with the appurtenances, in Southwark, and verily had purpose to have entered; and his counsel were with us, and spake with Worcester and me. And now afterward they have sent us word that they would my Lord to sue by means of the law, etc. I have spoken with my Lord of Canterbury and Master John Stokes, and I find them right well disposed both, etc.

---

occurred on 5th November 1459 at Caister Castle. Fastolf's last will, made immediately before his death, constituted a body of ten executors, of whom two were to have the sole and absolute administration. These two acting executors were John Paston and Thomas Howes. Furthermore, the effect of this will was to bequeath to John Paston the whole of Fastolf's lands in Norfolk and Suffolk, subject only to the obligation of founding a college of priests at Caister and of paying 4,000 marks to the other executors. These provisions gave rise to jealousy on the part of Yelverton and Worcester, two of the other executors, who claimed that the will put forward by Paston was in fact a forgery. The result was a protracted lawsuit and numerous troubles (particularly in respect of Hellesdon, Drayton, and Caister), to which many of the remaining letters in these volumes refer.

[1] William Waynflete, Bishop of Winchester.
[2] Caister.
[3] These were writs issued on the death of a tenant *in capite* of the Crown, and directed to the escheators in the different counties in which his lands lay, directing them to inquire by jury what lands he held, and of what value, and who was his nearest heir, and what was the heir's age.
[4] The Abbey of St Saviour, Bermondsey, where Fastolf had deposited certain goods for safe-keeping.
[5] James Butler, Earl of Winchester and Ormond.
[6] Richard Southwell: he was escheator of Norfolk and Suffolk.

Item, to-morrow or the next day ye shall have another letter, for by that time we shall know more than we do now.

My Lord Chancellor would that my master should be buried worshiply, and 100 marks alms done for him; but this day I shall wholly know his intent. Master John Stokes hath the same conceit and almsgiving. Harry Filongley is not in this town, nor the Lord Beauchamp.

Item, we have got men of the spiritual law withholding with us, what case soever hap. We have Master Robert Kenthe; but in any wise have all the goods there together, and tarry for no letting, though ye should do it by daylight openly, for it is my Lord Chancellor's full intent that ye should do so.

As for William Worcester, he trusteth verily ye would do for him and for his avail, in reason; and I doubt not, and he may verily and faithfully understand you so disposed to him-ward, ye shall find him faithful to you in like wise. I understand by him he will never have other master but his old master; and to my conceit it were pity but-if he shall stand in such case by my master that he should never need service, considering how my master trusted him, and the long years that he hath been with him in, and many shrew journey for his sake, etc.

I write you no more, because ye shall have another letter written to-morrow. Written at London, the 12th day of November, in haste, by

WILLIAM PASTON.

[1459]


137.      BISHOP WAYNFLETE'S ADVICE[1]

Be it remembered that, forasmuch as Sir John Fastolf, late deceased, of great affection, hath put me in trust to be one of his executors, and since it is desired me to know my disposition herein, mine advice is this, that first an inventory be made wholly of his goods and chattels in all places, and that they be laid in sure ward by your discretions till the executors, or the most part of those that he put his great trust upon, speak with me and make declaration to me of his last will, to the accomplishment whereof I will be special good lord.

Furthermore, as touching his burying and month's mind [2]

---

[1] William Waynflete, Bishop of Winchester, the first of Sir John Fastolf's executors, was at this time Lord Chancellor, to whom the others applied for his advice and directions concerning the execution of his will. He here gives them fully, but at the same time advises them to apply to someone learned in the spiritual law concerning the administration, etc.

[2] The month's mind was a Mass celebrated for the soul of a deceased person at the end of the first month following his death.

keeping, that it be done worshiply according to his degree and for the health of his soul, and that alms be given in Mass-saying, and to poor people to the sum of an hundred marks till that otherwise we speak together. And I can agree right well that his servants have their rewards betimes according to his will, to the intent that they may be better disposed and to pray for the welfare of his soul, taking advice of a learned man in spiritual law, for the charge of administration till the executors come together, or the most part that his trust was most upon, to take the administration.

W. Winton.

[November 1459]

138.  Friar Brackley to John[1] Paston[1]

*Carissimo suo magistro, Johanni Paston, armigero.  Jesus, Maria, etc.*

Right reverend master and most trusty friend in earth, as lowly as I can or may I recommend me, etc.

Sir, in faith I was sore afraid that ye had a great letting, that ye came not on Wednesday to meet, etc.  By my faith, an' ye had been here, ye should have had right good cheer, etc., and have fared right well after your pleasure, etc., with more, etc.

Sir John Tattershall is at one with Heydon, etc., and Lord Scales hath made a loveday [2] with the prior and Heydon in all matters, except the matter of Snoring, etc.  And the said prior spake masterly to the jurors, etc., and told them, an' they had dreaded God and hurt of their souls, they would have some

---

[1] This letter was written after the dispersion of the Duke of York's army near Ludlow, in October 1459, as the transactions here related refer to the direction of state affairs when in the hands of Henry's friends.  Commissions were granted to James Butler, Earl of Wiltshire, Thomas, Lord Scales, and others to apprehend all those who had been concerned in the late rebellion, and to punish them according to law.  It appears here that John Paston was supposed to favour the Yorkist party, and from the expressions contained in Dr Brackley's letters he certainly did so.

Brother John Brakle, or Brackley, the son of John Brakle, a dyer, was born at Norwich.  About 1418, when still very young, he joined Friars Minors at Norwich.  He afterwards took a doctor's degree of divinity, and became a famous preacher.  He was an intimate friend of and chaplain to Sir John Fastolf, who appointed him one of his executors; he was also much connected with the Paston family, being chaplain to the judge and tutor to Sir John Paston, his grandson.  He died in the year 1461 or 1462, and was buried in the church of his own convent.

[2] A day appointed for the settlement of disputes by arbitration.

instruction of the one party as well as of the other. But they were so bold they were not afraid, for they found no bones to say in their verdict as Thomas Tuddenham and John Heydon would, etc.

A lewd doctor of Ludgate preached on Sunday fortnight at Paul's, charging the people that no man should pray for these lords traitors; [1] and he had little thank, as he was worthy, etc. And for his lewd demeaning his brethren are had in the less favour at London, etc. Dr Pinchbeck and Dr Westhawe, great preachers and parsons at London, be now late made monks of Charterhouse at Sheen, one at the one place and another at the other place, etc.

The Chancellor is not good to these lords, etc., for he feareth the Earl of March will claim by inheritance the earldom of Ha . . . [2] etc., of which matter I heard great speech in Somerset-shire, etc.

Wyndham, Heydon, Tuddenham, Blake, W. Chamberlain, and Wentworth have late commissions to take for traitors and send to the next jail all persons fautorers and well-willers to the said lords, etc. Master Radcliff and ye have none of commissions directed to you, etc., for ye be holden favourable, etc.

Wyndham and Heydon be named here causers of these commissions, etc.

On Monday last at Cromer was the oar and the books of registry of the Admiralty taken away from my Lord Scales's men by a great multitude of my Lord Roos's men, etc. The Lord Scales is to my Lord Prince,[3] etc., to wait on him, etc. He saith, *per Deum sanctum*, as we say here, he shall be admiral or he shall lie thereby, etc. By my faith here is a coisy world. Walsham of Chancery, that never made lesing, told me that Bocking was with my Lord Chancellor this term; but I asked not how many times, etc.

As I have written to you often before this, '*Facite vobis amicos de mammona iniquitatis*' [4] *quia de facto.*

Thomas Tuddenham, Johannes Heydon, et J. Wyndham cum caeteris magistri Fastolf fallacibus famulis magnam gerunt ad vos invidiam, quod excelleritis eos in bonis, etc. Judas non dormit, etc. 'Noli zelare facientes iniquitatem quoniam tanquam fenum velociter arescent, et quemadmodum olera herbarum cito per Dei gratiam decident.' Ideo sic in Psalmo,

---

[1] The lords here meant were the earls of March, Warwick, and Salisbury, and others in the Duke of York's interest.

[2] The original letter is here defective.

[3] Edward, Prince of Wales.

[4] Luke xvi. 9.

'Spera in Domino et fac bonitatem et pascêris in divitiis ejus et delectare in Domino et dabit tibi petitiones cordis tui.' Et aliter, 'Jacta cogitatum tuum in domino, and ipse te enutriet.' 'Utinam,' inquit apostolus, 'abscindantur qui vos conturbant,' etc. Et alibi, 'Cavete vos a malis et importunis hominibus.'

Precor gratiosum Deum qui vos et me creavit et suo pretioso sanguine nos redemit, vos vestros et vestra gratiose conservet in prosperis, et gratiosius dirigat in agendis.

Scriptum, Walsham feria 4ta in nocte cum magnâ festinatione, etc. Utinam iste mundus malignus transiret et concupiscentia ejus. Vester ad vota promptissimus.

Frater JOHANNES BRACKLEY,

Minorum Minimus.

[1459]

139.    WILLIAM BOTONER TO JOHN BERNEY

To the right worshipful sir, John Berney, Esquire,[1] at Caister being.

Right worshipful Sir, I recommend me to you. [Here follow complaints against Friar Brackley, etc., concerning Sir John Fastolf's burial, affairs, etc.]

As for tidings here, I send some off hand, written to you and others, how the Lord Rivers,[2] Sir Anthony [3] his son, and others, have won Calais,[4] by a feeble assault made at Sandwich by Denham, Esquire,[5] with the number of 800 men, on Tuesday between four and five o'clock in the morning. But my Lady Duchess [6] is still again received in Kent. The Duke of York is at Dublin, strengthened with his earls and homagers, as ye shall see by a bill. God send the King victory of his enemies, and rest and peace among his lords!

[1] John Berney, Esq., appears to have been the son of John Berney, by Isabel, daughter and heiress of Sir John Heveningham, Kt, and died without issue in 1461. He had served under Sir John Fastolf in the wars in France, as appears by a part of this letter where William Worcester says, 'You had verrey and faythfull lofe to my maistr yn the yeers and dayes that ye dyd him s'vice yn the werrs and suffred prysonment and manye a sherp day for hys sake not rewarded.'

[2] Richard Woodville, Lord Rivers, afterwards created an earl by King Edward IV, who married his daughter Elizabeth.

[3] Sir Anthony Woodville, afterwards Lord Scales and Earl Rivers.

[4] This must be sarcastic. The truth, as recorded by Botoner himself in his annals, was that John Denham and others secretly sailed from Calais, and surprised Sandwich, where they took Lord Rivers and his son Anthony prisoners, and carried them back to Calais.

[5] James Denham or Dynham, afterwards Lord Dynham.

[6] Cecily, Duchess of York.

I am right greatly heavied for my poor wife, for the sorrow she taketh, and must leave her and her country. I shall nothing take from her more than a little spending-money till better may be. And the Blessed Trinity keep and send you health. Written at London hastily the Monday after I departed from you, 1459–60.

Your

W. BOTONER, *called* WORCESTER.

[January 1460]

## 140.   WILLIAM[1] PASTON TO JOHN[1] PASTON

*To his right worshipful brother, John Paston, be this letter delivered.*

After due recommendation had, please you to wete that we came to London upon the Tuesday by noon, next after our departure from Norwich, and sent our men to inquire after my Lord Chancellor and Mr John Stokes and Malmesbury. And as for my Lord Chancellor, he was departed from London, and was rode to the King two days ere we were come to London; and, as we understand, he hasted him to the King because of my Lord Rivers being taken at Sandwich,[1] etc.

[*Then follows a long account of private business, which is here omitted.*]

As for tidings, my Lord Rivers was brought to Calais and before the lords with eight score torches, and there my Lord of Salisbury rated him, calling him knave's son, that he should be so rude to call him and these other lords traitors, for they shall be found the King's true liege men when he should be found a traitor, etc.

And my Lord of Warwick rated him, and said that his father was but a squire, and brought up with King Henry V, and since made himself by marriage, and also made a lord, and that it was not his part to have such language of lords being of the King's blood.

And my Lord of March rated him in likewise.

And Sir Anthony was rated for his language of all the three lords in likewise.

Item, the King cometh to London-ward, and, as it is said, reareth the people as he come; but it is certain there be commissions made into divers shires that every man be ready in his best array to come when the King send for him.

---

[1] *See* footnote 4, page 142.

Item, my Lord Roos is come from Guisnes.

No more, but we pray to Jesu have you in His most merciful keeping. Amen.

Written at London the Monday next after St Paul's day.

Your brother,

WILLIAM PASTON.

[28th January 1460]

141. WILLIAM BOTONER TO ANONYMOUS [J. G.][1]

A very friend at need experience will show by deed, as well as by authority of Aristotle in the *Ethics* that he made of morality, also by the famous Roman Tullius in his little book *De Amicitia*. Thanking you for old continued friendship steadfastly grounded, as I feel by your letter of a good disposition made, as it appeareth. Whereas it showeth to the understanding of such as you write upon that I should, by crafty counsel of some men, suddenly have departed into these parts, etc., and that I estranged me from certain persons too much, etc.; as for the first, it shall be too openly known that I departed not hither by counsel of such persons as they imagine, for in truth no creature living, when I departed from Norwich, knew of it, save one that hath and evermore shall be next of my knowledge in voyages making, albeit I will not alway disclose the cause. I heard say since I came to London they which ye deemed to be of my counsel then were at Walsingham or Thepala [*sic in MS.*] when I departed. I have written the cause to him that of nature should be my best friend, that forasmuch as I had laboured as well as W. Paston do my master's friends, chevised, and laid money content out of his purse to the sum of £100 and more for cloth and other things for my said master's intention, promitting payment before Christmas, or right soon after, or to be at London, or acquitting me that I put me my devoir. And because my master's attorneys in those parts took not to heart to make the payments here so hastily as they did there, I had no comfortable answer of speeding the said payments here. And also I was not put in trust among the said attorneys there to give one penny for my master's soul, but I paid it of mine own purse before; neither in trust nor favour to give an alms-gown, but that I paid for it as a stranger should do, albeit mine authority is as great as theirs, and rather more as I told you. And also my Lord of Canterbury and Master John Stokes, his judge, had

[1] In this letter Fastolf's former secretary first reveals that growing jealousy of Paston and Howes which later developed into bitter enmity and suspicion.

given authority to minister to a certain sum till the testament
were proved. And these precedents considered would discourage any man to abide but a little amongst them that so
stranged themselves from me and mistrusted me, by that any
cause ye know well how that my master's manservants were put
in greater trust and familiarity to handle, give, and tell out of the
bags my master's money both at St Benet's and in Norwich in
divers places by great sums and little. And ye, as other my
master's servants and I, that helped get my master's goods and
bring them together, were stranged and, as it seemed by their
demeaning, mistrusted to our great villainy and rebuke; which
must be answered the causes why, and we declared,[1] and so shall
I make it for my poor person and for my master's soul's health.
It is not so ill known that I was one of the chief that kept both
my master Paston and mine uncle [2] in my master's favour and
trust; and if I would have laboured the contrary, by my soul—
that is the greatest oath I may swear of myself—they had never
been nigh my master in that case they stand now. And if they
will labour to damage or hinder me, all the world will misreport
of them and little trust them, neither they shall not have worship
nor profit by it. I would be to them as loving and as well-
willing as I gan, so I find cause; and other[wise] I will not be
to my father, an' he were alive. I require you answer for me
as I would and have done for you when some of them have said
full nakedly of you; and such as ye deem have misreported
causeless of me, I pray you that they see my letter as well as my
friends. My master also (God yeld his soul) granted me to
a livelode according to my degree, that I, my wife, and my
children should have cause to pray for him. My wife's uncle [3]
was present in his chapel at Caister as well as my wife, and
commanded her uncle to choose the land. This is truth by the
Blessed Sacrament that I received at Pasch. And because I
demanded my right and due of my master Paston, he is not
pleased. I have lost more than ten marks land in my master's
service, by God, and, not I be relieved, all the world shall know
it else that I have too great wrong. Would God I could please
both Master Paston and my uncle in reason; who preserve you.
Writ hastily the 7th day of February.

                    Your
              W. Botoner, *dit* Worcester.

[1460]

---

[1] i.e. declared free of suspicion, exculpated.
[2] Botoner's wife Margaret was a niece of Thomas Howes.
[3] Thomas Howes (*see* footnote 2).

142. WILLIAM LOMNER TO JOHN[1] PASTON [J. G.]

*To the right worshipful and reverend and my good Master Paston,*
*Esquire, be this taken.*

My right worshipful master, I recommend me to you, beseeching
you to hold me excused that I awaited none otherwise upon you
and my mistress at my coming from Norwich; for in good faith I
was so sick that I had much labour to come home, and since that
time I have had my part, etc. And, sir, as for Berney, he
beginneth to fall out of the people's conceit faster than ever he
fell in, for certain causes, etc. I shall tell you in haste. But,
sir, blessed be God, as for you, your love increaseth among
them, and so I pray God it may; for, an' I heard the contrary,
ye should soon have weting. The under-sheriff doth Mortoft
favour, and lets him go in Norwich as him list, and all the
country about me say right evil of him for a maintainer of the
King's enemies. For there be a hundred purposed to ride to
the King for him, an' he come near this country; for they say,
though he had never done with his hands, he hath said enough
to die. I have warned the under-sheriff thereof, etc. Sir,
further, I am in building of a poor house; I trust God that ye
shall take your lodging therein hereafter when ye come to your
lordships [1] in these parts. And I durst be so bold on your
mastership to ask of you twelve couple of oaken spars; I would
heartily pray you not to have them but there they may be
forebore best, and that is at a yard of yours in Saxthorpe, called
Barker's. I have ash, but none oak, but little now cometh the
felling thereof, etc. And meseemeth ye might take money for
wood there that stands and sereth, and doth no good but harm,
and within few years ye shall not wete where it is become, etc.
Also there be certain matters between some of your tenants and
me. I abide your coming and do naught at the reverence of
you; they be known well in the country. And God have you
in His keeping.
Written on Palm Sunday.

By your servant,

W. LOMNER.

[6th April 1460]

---

[1] i.e. the lands claimed to have been bequeathed to Paston by Sir John
Fastolf.

### 143. THE ABBOT OF LANGLEY TO JOHN STOKES

*To the right worshipful sir, Master John Stokes.*

Right worshipful sir, I recommend me to you. And forasmuch as it is informed me that it was appointed that all the executors of the worshipful knight Sir John Fastolf, whose soul God assoil, should be at London as on Monday next coming, of which executors I am named for one, as I understand; wherefore, inasmuch as ye be ordinary and one of the same executors, I pray you tender my labour without my coming, by your discretion, might be more profit to the dead. For I conceive it should be but charge to the dead and little available, considering that John Paston, Esquire, and Thomas Howes, parson of Blofield, shall come up at this time, which were the persons above all others that the said Sir John Fastolf put in his most singular love and trust, and would they should have the keeping and disposition of his goods, as well in his life as after his decease, to dispose for the weal of his soul; and that none other named his executors, but only they twain, should have any keeping or disposing of any part of his goods during their lives; and that all other named executors should support them, and give them to the said John Paston and Thomas Howes their good advice in performing of his desire in that behalf. Wherefore that it liketh you, in anything ye desire me to do in this cause or matter, to give your faith and credence to the said John Paston and Thomas Howes; and so desired me the said knight faithfully to do, that knoweth God, whom I beseech preserve you from all adversity. Written in the abbey of Langley, the 8th day of the month of May, the year of our Lord 1460.

Your priest,

ABBOT OF LANGLEY.

### 144. THE YORKIST LORDS TO THE AUTHORITIES IN NORFOLK[1]

*The earls of March, Warwick, and Salisbury.*

Right well-beloved, we greet you well. And where for the tender love that we have to the conservation of the King's peace, laws, and justice in this his realm of England, we have commanded the King's people in his name, by our letters and divers

[1] While the Yorkists were in power no acts of vengeance were committed or allowed. It was thought the Lancastrians had suffered sufficiently in the loss of so many of their leaders in the battle, and the avowed principle of the Earl of Warwick was to spare the lower and middle classes as much as possible, and to select as victims only the nobility and higher classes, both on the battlefield and in the courts.

writings, that no man should rob or despoil Sir Thomas Tuddenham, knight, John Heydon, John Wyndham, Harry and John Andrews, or any other of suspected fame be accorded with us, or any of us, for such wrongs as they, or any of them, have done to us, our servants, and tenants, or well-wishers, or that we should have them in tenderness or favour to discourage true people to sue against them by the law. We therefore notify to you, as we will that it be notified to all people, that we, nor none of us, intend not to favour or tender them, or any other of suspected fame, but rather to correct such by the law, for we made our said letters solely for keeping of the peace and justice, and not for favour of suspected conditions. And the Holy Trinity keep you. Written at London, the 23rd day of July.

To all Mayors, Sheriffs, Bailiffs, Constables, and all the King's Officers and Ministers in Norfolk, and each one of them.

[1460]

145. John[1] Paston to Margaret Paston

*To my worshipful cousin,[1] Margaret Paston, be this delivered in haste.*

I recommend me unto you, letting you wit that your uncle John Berney [2] is dead, on whose soul God have mercy; desiring you to send for Thomas Holler, and inquire of him where his [Berney's] goods are, and what he [Berney] is worth, and that he [Holler] take good heed to all such goods as he [Berney] had both moveable and unmoveable. For I understand that he [Berney] is worth in money 500 marks, and in plate to the value of other 500 marks, beside other goods. Wherefore I would ye should not let him [Holler] wete of his decease unto the time that ye had inquired of the said Thomas Holler of all such matters as be above written; and when he hath informed you thereof, then let him wete verily that he [Berney] is dead, desiring him [Holler] that no man come into his [Berney's] place at Reedham but himself [Holler], unto the time that I come.

Item, I let you wit that great part of his [Berney's] goods is at William Taverner's, as I understand. Thomas Holler will tell

[1] Between 1460 and September 1465, Paston addressed his wife as 'cousin' seven times. The reason is not clear.

[2] Second son of John Berney of Reedham. Owing to the troubled state of the times, his will, made on 2nd June 1460, was not proved until 1st December 1461. Administration was granted provisionally to Thomas Holler. Power was reserved of committing administration to John Paston; but the latter did not appear on the day, and left the undivided administration to Holler.

you justly the truth as I suppose, and desire him on my behalf
that he do so, and there is writing thereof; and tell Thomas
Holler that I and he be executors named, and therefore let him
take heed that the goods be kept safe, and that nobody know
where it shall lie but ye and Thomas Holler.  And Thomas
Holler, as your uncle told me, is privy where all his [Berney's]
goods lie, and all his writings; and so I will that ye be privy to
the same for casualty of death, and ye two shall be his executors
for me as long as ye do truly, as I trow verïly ye will.  Written
at London the 28th day of July.

I require you be of good comfort and be not heavy if ye will
do aught for me.

Your

JOHN PASTON.

[1461]


146.     FRIAR BRACKLEY TO JOHN[1] PASTON

*To my master, John Paston, Esquire, be this letter presented.
Jesus, Maria, etc.*

Right reverend sir, after due recommendation, we say in this
country that Heydon is for Berkshire in the Commons' House,
and the Lady of Suffolk[1] hath sent up her son and his wife[2] to
my Lord of York, to ask grace for a sheriff the next year—
Stapleton, Boleyn, or Tyrell, *qui absit.*   God send you Poynings,
W. Paston, W. Rokewood, or Arblaster.   Ye have much to do;
Jesu speed you.   Ye have many good prayers, what of the
convent, city, and country.   God save our good Lords, Warwick, all his brethren, Salisbury, etc., from all false covetise and
favour of extortion, as they will flee utter shame and confusion.
God save them, and preserve them from treason and poison.   Let
them beware hereof, for the pity of God; for if aught come to
my Lord Warwick but good, farewell ye, farewell I, and all our
friends; for by the way of my soul, this land were utterly
undone, as God forbid.   Their enemies boast with good to come
to their favour; but God defend them, and give them grace to
know their friends from their enemies, and to cherish and prefer
their friends and lessen the might of all their enemies throughout

---

[1] Alice, Duchess of Suffolk, widow of William, Duke of Suffolk, who was
beheaded at sea in 1450.
[2] John de la Pole, Duke of Suffolk, married Elizabeth, daughter of Richard
Plantagenet, Duke of York.

the shires of the land. And my good Lord Warwick (with my Lord his brother Chancellor [1] and my Lord their father [2]) would oppose, as did Daniel, Fortescue, Alexander, Hody, Dr Aleyn, Heydon, and Thorpe, of the writing made by them at Coventry Parliament, they should answer worse than *sub cino* or *sub privo*; and this generally would I say at Paul's Cross, etc., and I should come there, etc.

It is verified of them: *vere mendacium operatus est stilus mendax scribarum*,[3] etc. And think of two verses of your Psalter: *Scribantur haec in generatione alterâ* (hujus, scilicet, Parliamenti) *et populus qui creabitur laudabit Deum Dominum*;[4] *Deleantur etiam tales persversi scriptores de libro viventium et cum justis non scribantur*.[5] Et non plura, sed vos, vestros et vestra conservet Jesus graciose in prosperis et graciosius dirigat in agendis. Ex Norwico feria quarta,[6] nuntio festinante.

And I pray you for God's sake to be good master to John Lyster, etc. And I pray you think in this Parliament of the text of Holy Scripture: *quicunque fecerit contra legem Dei et contra legem regis judicium fiet de eo, vel in condemnationem substantiae ejus, vel in carcerem, vel in exilium, vel in mortem,* (1^mo Esdrae vii. v. 26, et p. 2° Esdrae, 8°.)

[October 1460]

147. CHRISTOPHER HANSSON TO JOHN[1] PASTON

*To the right worshipful sir and master, John Paston, Esquire, at Norwich, be this delivered in haste.*

Right worshipful sir and master, I recommend me unto you. Please you to wete, the Monday after Our Lady day [7] there came hither to my master's place,[8] my Master Bowser, Sir Harry Ratford, John Clay, and the harbinger of my Lord of March, desiring that my Lady of York [9] might lie here until the coming of my Lord of York and her two sons, my Lord George [10] and my

[1] George Neville, Bishop of Exeter.
[2] Richard Neville, Earl of Salisbury.
[3] Cf. Jeremiah viii. 8.
[4] Cf. Psalm cii. 18.
[5] Cf. Psalm lxix. 28.
[6] i.e. Wednesday.
[7] The Monday following 8th September; in 1460 this was on the 15th.
[8] Probably Sir John Fastolf's place in Southwark.
[9] Cecily, Duchess of York.
[10] Afterwards Duke of Clarence.

Lord Richard,[1] and my Lady Margaret [2] her daughter, which I granted them in your name to lie here until Michaelmas. And she had not lain here two days but she had tidings of the landing of my Lord at Chester.[3] The Tuesday next after, my Lord sent for her that she should come to him at Hereford, and thither she is gone. And since I left here both the sons and the daughter, and the Lord of March cometh every day to see them.

Item, my Lord of York hath divers strange commissions from the King for to sit in divers towns coming homeward; that is for to say, in Ludlow, Shrewsbury, Hereford, Leicester, Coventry, and in other divers towns, to punish them by the faults to the King's laws.

As for tidings here, the King is way at Eltham and at Greenwich to hunt and to sport him there, biding the Parliament, and the Queen and the Prince both in Wales alway. And is with her the Duke of Exeter and others, with a few meny, as men say here.

And the Duke of Somerset, he is in Dieppe; with him Master John Ormond, Wittingham, Andrew Trollope, and other divers of the garrison of Guisnes, under the King of France's safe conduct; and they say here, he purposes him to go to Wales to the Queen. And the Earl of Wiltshire [4] is still in peace at Utrecht at the Friars, which is sanctuary.

Item, Colbyne is come home to my master's place, and saith that, at your departing [5] out of London, ye sent him word that he should come hither to the place, and be here until your coming again; and so he is here it, and saith he will take no master but by your advice, nevertheless awaiteth upon Master Oldhall the most part at Redre [6] at his place.

Item, Master Poynings hath entered on two or three places upon the Earl of Northumberland, and he standeth in good grace of the King, my Lord of March, my Lord Warwick, and my Lord of Salisbury. Most part of the country about his livelode hold aythe with him. And my mistress your sister [7] is not delivered as yet; God give her good deliverance.

No more to you at this time; but, an' ye will command me any service I may do, it is ready. And Jesu have you in His

---

[1] Afterwards Richard III.
[2] Afterwards Duchess of Burgundy.
[3] The Duke of York had come over from Ireland following the victory of his party at the battle of Northampton.
[4] James Butler, Earl of Wiltshire and Ormond.
[5] Paston must have left London and gone to Norwich not long before the Parliament, which opened on 7th October.
[6] Redriff or Rotherhithe.
[7] Elizabeth, wife of Robert Poynings.

blessed keeping; and I beseech you this letter may commend me
to my mistress your wife, and all your household.
Written at London the 12th day of October.

Your own servant,

Christopher Hansson.

[1460]

148.    Margaret Paston to John[1] Paston

*To my right worshipful husband, John Paston, be this delivered in
haste.*

Right worshipful husband, I recommend me to you. Pleaseth it
you to wete that I received your letter that ye sent me by
Nicholas Colman on Sunday last past. And as for the matter
that ye desired me to break of to my cousin Rookwood, it
fortuned so that he came to me on Sunday to dinner soon, after
that I had your letter; and when we had dined, I moved to him
thereof in covert terms, as Playter shall inform you hereafter.
And as I thought by him, and so did Playter also by the language
that he had to us, that he would be as faithful as he could or
might be to that good lord that ye wrote of, and to you also, in
anything that he could or might do in case were that he were set
in office, so that he might aught do; and thereto he said he
would be bound in £1,000, an' he was so much worth.

As for the other that ye desired I should move to of the same
matter, meseemeth he is too too young to take any such things upon
him; and also I know verily that he shall never love faithfully
the other man that ye desired that he should do, for when he
remembereth the time that is past, and therefore I spake not to
him thereof.

This day was holden a great day at Acle before the under-
sheriff and the under-escheator for the matter of Sir John
Fastolf's lands; and there was my cousin Rookwood and my
cousin John Berney of Reedham, and divers other gentlemen and
thrifty men of the country; and the matter is well sped after your
intent, blessed be God! as ye shall have knowledge of in haste.

I suppose Playter shall be with you on Sunday or on Monday
next coming if he may. Ye have many good prayers of the poor
people that God should speed you at this Parliament; for they
live in hope that ye should help to set a way that they might
live in better peace in this country than they have done before,
and that wools should be purveyed for, that they should not go
out of this land, as it hath been suffered to do before, and then
shall the poor people more live better than they have done by

their occupation therein. Thomas Bone hath sold all your wool here for 20*d*. a stone, and good surety found to you therefore, to be paid at Michaelmas next coming; and it is sold right well, after that the wool was for the most part right feeble.

Item, there be bought for you three horses at St Faith's fair, and all be trotters, right fair horses, God save them, and they be well keeped.

Item, your mills at Hellesdon be let for twelve marks, and the miller to find the reparation. And Richard Calle hath let all your lands at Caister; but as for Mauteby lands, they be not let yet. William White hath paid me again this day his £10, and I have made him an acquittance thereof, because I had not his obligation.

There is great talking in this country of the desire of my Lord of York.[1] The people report full worshipfully of my Lord of Warwick. They have no fear here but that he and other should show too great favour to them that have been rulers of this country before time.

I have done all your errands to Sir Thomas Howes that ye wrote to me for. I am right glad that ye have sped well in your matters betwixt Sir Philip Wentworth and you,[2] and so I pray God ye may do in all other matters to His pleasance.

As for the writings that ye desired that Playter should send you, Richard Calle told me that they were at Harry Barber's, at the Temple Gate.

The mayor [3] and the mayoress sent hither their dinners this day, and John Damme came with them, and they dined here. I am beholden to them, for they have sent to me divers times since ye yed hence. The mayor saith that there is no gentleman in Norfolk that he would do more for than he would for you, if it lay in his power to do for you.

J. Perse [4] is still in prison, but he will not confess more than he did when ye were at home. Edmund Brome was with me, and told me that Perse sent for him to come speak with him; and he told me that he was with him and examined him, but he would not be aknow to him that he had no knowledge where no goods was of his master's more than he had knowledged to you. He told me that he sent for him to desire him to labour to you and to me for him if ye had been at home; and he told me that

---

[1] The claim made by Richard, Duke of York, to the Crown in Parliament on 17th October 1460.

[2] Concerning the wardship of Thomas Fastolf of Cowhaw.

[3] John Gilbert, mayor of Norwich.

[4] A servant first of John Berney and afterwards of the Paston family. The cause of his imprisonment is not stated; but it would appear that he had refused to disclose the whereabouts of some of Berney's property. (*See also* No. 199, page 207.)

he said to him again that he would never labour for him, but he might know that he were true to his master, though it lay in his power to do right much for him. I suppose it should do none harm though the said Perse were removed further. I pray to God give grace that the truth may be known, and that the dead may have part of his own goods. And the blessed Trinity have you in His keeping.

Written in haste, at Hellesdon, the Tuesday next after St Luke.

By yours,

M. P.

[21st October 1460]

149.    J. Perse to Margaret Paston [J. G.]

*To my right reverend and worshipful Mistress Paston, be this delivered.*

Right reverend and worshipful mistress, I recommend me unto you, beseeching you of your good mistress-ship to be my good mistress to help with your gracious word unto my right reverend and worshipful master and yours to take of me, his poor prisoner and yours, surety which I shall find to be bound for me to bring me unto all answer, into the time that my master and ye have dismissed me with my surety. And beseech your good mistress-ship to pray my master that he will give you licence with his worshipful counsel and yours, in case that my master may not tarry, that ye in his absence may take my said surety. And if it please his highness and yours, that I may have answer again by the bringer of this; and hereupon I shall send for my surcties, which I trust in God shall be to your pleasure. No more at this time. I pray God ever have you in keeping.

By your poor prisoner,

Perse, *sometime servant of*
*John of Berney.*

[1460]

150.    J. Perse to Sir Robert Rokesby

*To my right worshipful Sir Robert Rokesby.*

Right worshipful sir, I recommend me to you, beseeching you of your good mastership that ye will vouchsafe to speak to Richard Kowven, that he might bring me or send me the money that is between him and me in all the haste that he may. For in good faith, I had never more need for to have help of my goods as I have at this time; for, God wot, it stands right strange with me. For the false jailer that keepeth me entreateth me worse than it were a dog; for I am fettered worse than ever I was, and manacled in the hands both day and night, for he is afraid of me for breaking away. He maketh false tales of me, through the means of a false quean that was tending to a Frenchman that is prisoner to my Lord Roos,[1] and for because of that he bronde me every day by John of Berney, that is gone to the other lords;[2] but I trust to God once to quit his meed. And, sir, I thank you mickle of that ye have done for me or said. And, sir, I shall deserve it against you, by the grace of God; for, in faith, I am beholden to you more than to all men that ever I found since I came in prison.

No more to you at this time, but God have you in His keeping.

By your servant and beadsman,

PERSE.

[1460]

## 151. MARGARET PASTON TO JOHN[(1)] PASTON [J. G.]

*To my right well-beloved brother, Clement Paston, for to deliver to his brother John, in haste.*

Right worshipful husband, I recommend me to you. Pleaseth you to wete that I received a letter on St Simon's eve and Jude, that came from John Paston;[3] in the which letter he wrote that ye desired that I should do John Paston or Thomas Playter look in the great standing chest, in one of the great canvas bags which standeth against the lock, for the copies of the false inquest of office that was found in Norfolk, and for the copy of the commission that came to John Andrews and Philpot and Heydon, and other things touching the same matter I have done. John Paston sought all three great bags in the said coffer at right good leisure, and he can none such find. Pleaseth you to remember ye sent me word in the first letter that ye sent me, that ye would that Playter should have sent them up to you to London, and I showed him your writing how that ye wrote to me therein. I suppose because he purposed to come up to London himself hastily, he sent you none answer thereof. Richard Calle told me that all such things were left with Harry Barber at the Temple Gate when the last term was done; and so I sent you word in a letter[4] which was written on the Tuesday next after

---

[1] Thomas, Lord Roos.  [2] i.e. the lords of the Yorkist party.
[3] The addressee's elder son of that name.  [4] No. 148, page 153.

St Luke, and therein was an answer of all the first letter that ye sent me. I sent it you by young Thomas Ellis. I sent you another letter by Playter, the which was written on Saturday last past.

Item, I received another letter from you on Sunday, of the which I sent you an answer of my letter on St Simon's even and Jude by Edmund Clere of Stokesby; and as soon as I had the said letter on Sunday, I sent to Sir Thomas Howes for the matter that ye desired that he should inquire of to Bocking, and I sent again since to the said Sir Thomas for to have knowledge of the same matter yesterday, and I have none answer of him yet. He sent me word he should do his part therein, but other answer have I none yet of him. I send you in a canvas bag, ensealed by Nicholas Colman, as many of Christopher Hansson's accounts as John Paston can find thereas ye sent word that they were. Richard Harbard recommendeth him to you, and prayeth you that ye will vouchsafe to remember the letter that should be sent from my Lord of Warwick to a man of his being at Lowestoft; and if it be not sent to him, that it please you to do purvey that it may be sent to him in haste, if it may be, as to-morrow there shall be kept a day at Bungay for Master Fastolf's lands before the escheator,[1] and there shall be William Barker and Richard Calle. Ye shall knowledge in haste what shall be done there. And the Blessed Trinity have you in His keeping.

Written in haste at Norwich on the Wednesday next after SS Simon and Jude.

By your

M. P.

[29th October 1460]


152.            Sir Geoffrey Boleyn to
                John[1] Paston [J. G.]

*To my right worshipful sir, John Paston, Esquire.*

Right worshipful sir, after right heartily recommendation, liketh you to wete that my master Fastolf, whose soul God assoil, when I bought of him the manor of Blickling, considering the great payment that I payed therefor, and the yearly annuity during his life after his intent, was to me great charge; and the same time, in his place at Southwark, by his oath made on his primer there, granted and promitted me to have the manor of Guton with all the appurtenances for a reasonable price afore any other man.

[1] The inquisition on Fastolf's lands in Suffolk was held at Bungay on 30th October 1460.

And, sir, as I understand ye be that person that my said master, considering your great wisdom, most trusted to have rule and direction of his livelode and goods—and, sir, truly, if I had been near unto you, I would have spoken hereof to you before this time; nevertheless, I would desire and pray you to show me your good will and favour in this behalf, wherein ye shall discharge my said master's soul of his oath and promise, and I shall do you service in that I can or may to my power.  And of your good will and favour herein I pray you to let me have weting, and I shall be ready to wait on you at any time and place where ye will assign.  And our Blessed Lord have you in His keeping. Writ the 5th day of December.

By your own,

GEOFFREY BOLEYN.[1]

[1460]


153.    CLEMENT PASTON TO JOHN[(1)] PASTON

*To his right worshipful brother, John Paston.*

Right reverend and worshipful brother, I recommend me to you, certifying you that your letter was delivered to me the 23d day of January about noon season; and Richard Calle rode in the morning, and therefore I brake your letter,[2] if there were any after matter.  And I did Christopher Hansson go to my Lord of Canterbury [3] to tell him, as your letter rehearsed; and my Lord said he had spoken with your man thereof the day before, and if the Bishop of Norwich would not do so much for him, he is the less beholden to him.  Notwithstanding, he said he would save you harmless against John Young; but, an' ye do well, remember this lord have many matters to think on, and if it be forgotten, the harm is yours, and also if the world turn, John Young will not do at his prayer.

And my Lord Fitzwalter [4] is ridden northwards, and it is said in my Lord of Canterbury's house that he hath taken 200 of Andrew Trollope's [5] men.  And as for Colt,[6] and Sir James Strangwyse, and Sir Thomas Pykering, they be taken or else dead: the common voice is that they be dead.

---

[1] This man was an ancestor of Queen Anne Boleyn.
[2] i.e. he broke the seal and read the letter.
[3] Archbishop Bourchier.
[4] *See* footnote 1, page 113.
[5] Andrew Trollope, whose desertion of the Duke of York at Ludlow in 1459 caused the dispersal of the Yorkist leaders.  He was killed at Towton.
[6] Thomas Colt.

Hopton [1] and Hastings [2] be with the Earl of March, and were not at the field.[3]

What word that ever ye have from my Lords that be here, it is well done, and best for you to see that the country be always ready to come, both footmen and horsemen, when they be sent for; for I have heard said the farther lords will be here sooner than men ween, I have heard said ere three weeks to an end; and also that ye should come with more men and cleanlier arrayed than another man of your country should, for it lieth more upon your worship and toucheth you more near than other men of that country, and also ye be more had in favour with my Lords here. In this country every man is well willing to go with my Lords here, and I hope God shall help them, for the people in the north rob and steal, and be appointed to pill all this country, and give away men's goods and livelodes in all the south country, and that will ask a mischief. My Lords that be here have as much as they may do to keep down all this country, more than four or five shires; for they would be up on the men in the north, for it is for the weal of all the south.

I pray you recommend me to my mother, and that I prayed her of her blessing. I pray you excuse me to her that I write her no letter, for this was enough to do. I dare not pray you to recommend me to my sister your wife, and the messenger I trow be so wise he cannot do it. Ye must pay him for his labour, for he tarried all night in this town for this letter.

Written the 23rd day of January in haste, when I was not well at ease. God have you in His keeping.

By CLEMENT PASTON,
*Your Brother.*

[1461]


## 154. JOHN, PRIOR OF BROMHOLM TO JOHN[1] PASTON

*Amicabili magistro nostro, Johanni Paston, Armigero.*

Full reverend and worshipful, after all due reverence and recommendation, your poor priest beseecheth humbly it please your good mastership to understand by this simple bill that on the Friday next after the Feast of the Conversion of Saint Paul last past I was at your place at Caister to have told you what answer I had of Sir Thomas Howes, parson of Blofield. And inasmuch as ye were not at home, I told it to my mistress your

---
[1] Walter Hopton.    [2] William, afterwards Lord Hastings.
[3] The battle of Wakefield.

wife; and God thank her of her gentleness, she made me great cheer, and moreover advised me to send you a bill thereof to London. This was his answer, when I had talked to him as I could in like wise as ye adverted me to do. He answered again in these words: 'Near is my kirtle, but nearer is my smock.' And this was his meaning: that ye should be more near us and tender to us than him he; and that ye should rather owe us good will than he; and that we should labour rather to your mastership than to him; and also, that good that he had to dispose he had beset it, and of passel he told me he had delivered the Abbot of Langley fourscore pounds, whereof, as he said to me, ye grudged and were in manner displeased, notwithstanding ye said again to him ye should give as much. And he said to me ye named the places where; and therefore he advised me to labour effectually to your good mastership, for ye might help us well. For he said ye had [1] much good of the dead to dispose, what of your father (God bless that soul), what of Berney, and what now of his good master Fastolf. And as for Sir John Fastolf, on whose soul Jesus have mercy, he said to me ye had of his good 'four, four, and four more' than he —— in these same terms, without any sum.

And after all other talkings he told me he should be with you at London hastily, and that he would say good word to you to relieve our poor place. Sir, I beseech, be thee not displeased; for truly, an' I wist to have your heavy mastership therefore, I had lever it had been unthought. And is this, that when Sir Thomas Howes and ye be soon at London, we might be so in your good grace, that our place might be brother to Langley, for that should glad us more than the commission that the Bishop of Norwich sent us on Thursday last past to gather the dimes, for that is a shrewd labour for us, a great cost and a shrew jeopardy.

Evermore that high and mighty celestial Prince preserve you body and soul, and send you comfort of the Holy Ghost well to perform all your heart's desire in all your matters to His pleasance and your worship, and solace to all your well-willers. Written at Bromholm on the Saturday next after the feast of the Conversion of Saint Paul last past.

From your priest and beadsman,

JOHN, *prior of Bromholm.*

[31st January 1461]

----

[1] i.e. as executor of three deceased persons whom he proceeds to name.

155. MARGARET PASTON TO JOHN⁽¹⁾ PASTON[1]

Please it you to wit that it is let me wit, by one that oweth you good will, that there is laid a wait upon you in this country if ye come here at large, to bring you to the presence of such a lord in the north as shall not be for your ease, but to jeopardy of your life, or great and importable loss of your goods. And he that hath taken upon him this enterprise now was under-sheriff to Giles St Loe; [2] he hath great favour hereto by the means of the son of William Baxter that lieth buried in the Grey Friars. And, as it is reported, the said son hath given great silver to the lords in the north to bring the matter about; and now he and all his old fellowship put out their fins, and are right flygge and merry, hoping all thing is and shall be as they will have it. Also, it is told me that the father of the bastard in this country said that now should this shire be made sure for him and his heirs henceforward, and for the Baxters' heirs also; whereby I conceive they think that they have none enemy but you, etc.

Wherefore like it you to be the more wary of your guiding for your person's safeguard, and also that ye be not too hasty to come into this country till ye hear the world more sure. I trow the bearer of this shall tell more by mouth, as he shall be informed of the rule in this country. God have you in His keeping. Written in haste, the second Sunday of Lent, by candlelight at even.

By yours, etc.

MARGARET PASTON.

[1st March 1461]

156. MARGARET PASTON TO JOHN⁽¹⁾ PASTON [J. G.]

*To my right worshipful husband, John Paston.*

Right reverend and worshipful husband, I recommend me to you, desiring heartily to hear of your welfare, thanking you for your letter and for the things that ye sent me therewith. And touching John Estgate, he come, neither none sent hither, nought yet; wherefore I suppose I must borrow money in short time but-if ye come soon home, for I suppose I shall none have of him, so God help me. I have but four shillings, and I owe near as much money as comes to the foresaid sum. I have done

¹ This letter has no direction, and lest it should be opened, the paper which fastens the seal is, along the edge, marked with lines by a pen which communicate with the letter, by which means the receiver might easily have discovered any attempts to have opened it, as the lines would not then have exactly coincided again.
² Giles St Loe was sheriff of Norfolk and Suffolk in 1458.

your errands to your mother and my uncle; and as for the feoffees of Stokesby, my uncle saith that there be no more than he wrote to you of that he knoweth. And also I have delivered the other thing that ye sent me, ensealed in the box as ye commanded me. And the man saith, that I delivered it to, that he will nought of the bargain that ye sent him, but such things be done ere he come there that ye sent him word of; he said that he would not be noised with no such things of that is, that it were done in his time for twenty marks. I suppose he shall send you word in short time how he will do. I pray you that ye will vouchsafe to buy for me such laces as I send you example of in this letter, and one piece of black lace. As for caps that ye sent me for the children, they be too little for them; I pray you buy them finer caps and larger than those were. Also I pray you that ye will vouchsafe to recommend me to my father and my mother, and tell her that all her children be in good health, blessed be God. Heydon's wife had child on St Peter's day; I heard say that her husband will nought of her, nor of her child that she had last neither. I heard say that he said, if she come in his presence to make her excuse, that he should cut off her nose to make her be known what she is; and if her child come in his presence, he said he would kill it. He will not be entreated to have her again in no wise, as I heard say. The Holy Trinity have you in His keeping and send you health. Written at Gelderstone on the Wednesday next after St Thomas. By yours,

M. PASTON.

[Year uncertain]

## 157. A WHITSUNDAY SERMON OF FRIAR BRACKLEY

*An ancient Whitsunday sermon, preached by Friar Brackley (whose hand it is) at the Friars Minors Church in Norwich.*[1]

Friends, this holy time, as our mother Holy Church maketh mention, the Holy Ghost came from heaven, and lighted on the disciples of Christ, inflaming them with cunning, and strengthening them with grace. And because the doctrine and preaching of them should go throughout all the world, first they were to be informed and taught cunning, and to be strengthened with audacity and grace, and then to be endued and given all manner of languages that they might preach to all manner of nations, so that those nations that they preached to might understand them, and every nation his own tongue. And so these Apostles, after

[1] This is written on the back of the paper containing the original sermon.

that they were inspired with the Holy Ghost, wheresoever they preached, were there never so many nations present, each nation thought that they spoke in their own language—*etenim illud loquebantur variis linguis Apostoli.*

Friends, three things be necessary in preaching, to him that shall preach through the world as the Apostles did, that is to say, cunning, boldness, and languages. If they had had cunning and none audacity, but have feared to have preached, it should little have profited, as we have examples daily at Cambridge, *exempli gratia, de clerico quis studuit sermonem,* etc. And if they have both cunning and audacity, and have none eloquency nor copiousness of language, so that he preach that his audience is most exercised in, that they may understand him, else it profiteth not.

Therefore these holy Apostles, before they should preach, first they were to be confirmed and strengthened. Our Lord strengthened them by under-nemyng, informing, and helping, *culpando ut in evangelium recumbentibus,* etc.

He strengthened them with His help and grace when He breathed on them, saying: '*Accipite Spiritum Sanctum, et quorum remiseritis peccata, remittuntur eis, et quorum retinueritis retenta sunt,* etc.' [1] He strengthened them also by His doctrine when He said: '*Petite et accipietis; si quid petieritis Patrem in nomine meo, dabit vobis.*' [2] How that ye should pray to God and ask, I taught you on Easter day. Therefore ye shall pray God by good working, right full labouring, and in good deeds persevering.

Friends, ye ought for to ask of God that your joy may be a full joy and perfect; we may never have a full joy in this world, whereas ever among followeth heaviness. A man joyeth some-times in gold and silver, and in great substance of earthly goods, in beauty of women, but this joy is not perfect—but this joy is not stable, but it is mutable as a shadow; for he that thus joyeth in the beauty of his wife, it may fortune to-morrow he shall follow her to church upon a bier. But if ye will know what is a full and a very joy, truly forgiveness of sin and everlasting bliss, whereas is never sickness, hunger, nor thirst, nor no manner of disease, but all wealth, joy, and prosperity, etc. There be three manner of joys, the one void, another half full, the third is a full joy. The first is plenty of worldly goods, the second is ghostly grace, the third is everlasting bliss. The first joy, that is affluence of temporal goods, is called a vain joy; for if a man were set at a board with delicate meats and drinks, and he saw a cauldron boiling afore him with pitch and brimstone, in the which

---

[1] John xx. 22, 23. [2] John xvi. 23, 24.

he should be thrown naked as soon as he had dined—for he should joy much in his delicious meats, it should be but a vain joy. Right so doth the joy of a covetous man, if he see what pain his soul shall suffer in hell for the miskeeping and getting of his goods, he should not joy in his treasure, *ut in libro Decalogorum,* '*Quidam homo dives,* etc.'

*Semiplenum gaudium est quando quis in praesenti gaudet et tunc cogitans de futuris dolet, ut in quodam libro Graeco,* '*Quidam Rex Graeciae,*' etc. Here ye may see but half a joy; who should joy in this world if he remembered him of the pains of the other world? '*Non glorietur fortis in fortitudine suâ, nec sapiens in sapientiâ suâ, nec dives in divitiis suis.*'[1] *De quibus dicitur,* '*qui confidunt in multitudine divitiarum suarum, quasi oves in inferno positi sunt*';[2] '*Qui gloriatur, in Domino glorietur*'[3] Therefore let us joy in hope of everlasting joy and bliss.

'*Gaudete quia nomina vestra scripta sunt in caelo*'[4] *ut gaudium vestrum sit plenum.*

A full joy is in heaven.

*Et in hoc apparet, quod magnum gaudium est in caelo, quoniam ibi est gaudium quod,* '*oculus non vidit, nec auris audivit, et in cor hominis non ascendit, quae Deus preparavit diligentibus.*'[5] *Et ideo, fratres, variis linguis loquens precor ut gaudium vestrum sit plenum, vel habeatis gaudium sempiternum.*

[Year uncertain]

## 158. THE EARL OF OXFORD TO JOHN[(1)] PASTON

*To my right trusty and right well-beloved John Paston.*

Right trusty and right well-beloved, I greet you well. And I am informed that William Mathew of Norwich, butcher, hath brought an action of debt against Nicholas Hart, a tenant of mine, bearer hereof, and hath supposed by his action that my said tenant should owe him seventy shillings for his hire of time that he should have been servant to my said tenant; where it is said to me for truth that he was apprentice to my said tenant, and never otherwise withheld but as apprentice, and oweth no money to have of him. I send to you my said tenant to give you clear information of the matter, and I pray you that ye will call the jury before you that are empanelled between them, and open them the matter at large at mine instance, and desire them

---

[1] Jeremiah ix. 23.  [2] Psalm xlix. 6, 14.
[3] 1 Corinthians i. 31.  [4] Luke x. 20.
[5] 1 Corinthians ii. 9.

to do as conscience will, and to eschew perjury. And the Trinity keep you. If ye take the matter in rule, I pray thereof, and will be content. Written at Wivenhoe the 28th day of December.

THE EARL OF OXFORD.

[Year uncertain]

159. SIR JOHN WINGFIELD TO JOHN[1] PASTON

*To my well-beloved brother, John Paston, Esquire.*

Brother Paston, I recommend me unto you, praying you that ye take the labour to speak with Thomas Ratcliff of Framsden, for the deliverance of part of an house which lieth in his wood at Framsden; which house the owner hath carried part thereof to Orford, which so departed, the remnant that remaineth there in his wood shall do him little good, and it shall hurt greatly the workmen and the owner thereof also, which is my tenant, and the house should be set upon ground.

I write unto you in this behalf, because I understand he will be much advised by you, and if he do anything at my request, I shall do as much that shall please him; and also the poor man shall give him two nobles or twenty shillings rather than fail. I pray you be as good a mean for him as ye may in this behalf, as my very trust is in you, and I shall be ready at all times to do that may be to your pleasure. I trust to Jesu, who have you in His keeping, and send you joy of all your ladies.

Written at Letheringham, this Tuesday in Whitsun week.

Your brother and friend,

WINGFIELD, J.

[Year uncertain]

160. JOHN[1] PASTON TO RICHARD SOUTHWELL [J. G.]

Brother Southwell, I commend me to you, certifying you that, on Thursday by the morrow, I spake with my cousin Wichingham at London, where he let me wete of the letter sent to Lee, whereby I conceive the steadfast good lordship and ladyship of my Lord and my Lady [1] in this matter,[2] etc., which giveth cause to all their servants to trust verily in them and to do them true service.

[1] Probably the Duke and Duchess of Norfolk.
[2] The matter here referred to is probably the impending marriage of Southwell with Amy, daughter of Sir Edward Wichingham.

I let you wete that the said Wichingham, when I departed from him, had knowledge that Jane Boys should that night be come to London, and he put in a bill to the lords for to have deliverance of her and to have his adversaries arrested. And this night at Norwich was told me new tidings, that she should on Thursday after my departing have been before the lords and there have said untruly of herself, as the bearer hereof shall inform you if ye know it not before; of which tidings, if they be true, I am sorry for her sake, and also I fear that her friends should sue the more faintly, which God defend. For her saying untruly of herself may hurt the matter in no man but herself; and though she will mischief herself, it were great pity but-if the matter were laboured forth, not for her sake, but for the worship of the estates and others that have laboured therein, and in punishing of the great horrible deed. Wherefore I send you divers articles in a bill closed herein, which prove that she was ravished against her will, whatsoever she say.

These be proofs that Jane Boys was ravished against her will, and not by her own assent.

One is that she, the time of her taking, when she was set upon her horse, she reviled Longstrather and called him knave and wept, and cried out upon him piteously to her, and said as shrewdly to him as could come to her mind, and fell down off her horse until that she was bound, and called him false traitor that brought her the rabbits.

Item, when she was bound, she called upon her mother, which followed her as far as she might on her feet; and when she said Jane saw she might go no farther, she cried to her mother and said that whatsoever fell of her, she should never be wedded to that knave, to die for it.

Item, by the way, at Shragger's house at Cockley Cley, and at Beachamwell, and in all other places where she might see people, she cried out upon him, and let people wete whose daughter she was, and how she was ravished against her will, desiring the people to follow her and rescue her.

Item, Longstrather's priest of the Eagle in Lincolnshire, which shrove her, said that she told him in confession that she would never be wedded to him, to die for it; and the same priest said he would not wed them together for £1,000.

Item, she sent divers tokens of message to Southwell by Robert Inglose, which proveth well at that time she loved not Longstrather.

Item, a man of the master of Carbrooke's came divers times in the week before she was ravished to Wichingham's house, and inquired of her maid whether her mistress was ensured to Southwell or nay, the which proveth well that Longstrather was not sure of her good will nor knew not of her counsel, for if he had, he needed not to have sent no spies.

Which seen, I advise you to move my Lord and my Lady to do in this matter as effectually as they have done before; for this matter toucheth them, considering that they have begun. And doubt not, whatsoever fall of the woman, well or evil, my Lord and my Lady shall have worship of the matter if it be well laboured, and also ye shall have avail thereof and the adverse part shall great trouble.

Also it were necessary that Wichingham were sent to and comforted in his suit; and that he advised him of such articles and proofs of the matter as I have sent to you and put them in writing, but not to disclose none of those proofs to none creature unto that time that it fortune the matter to be tried by inquest, or otherwise take end. But advise him for to say to the lords, and all in general terms, that whatsoever Longstrather or his daughter say now, it shall be well proved that she was ravished against her will. And let him desire of the lords that his daughter might be in his keeping, and at large from Long-strather until the matter were duly examined. I would this matter sped the better because my Lady spoke so faithfully to me therein, and that moveth me to write to you this long simple letter of mine intent. God keep you.

Writ at Norwich the Sunday next before the feast of St Margaret.

Item, if she had been of his assent after the time she was in his possession in Lincolnshire, it had been better . . . [*Sentence left unfinished*].

[Year uncertain]

# EDWARD IV (1461–1470)

## 161.    JOHN[3] PASTON TO ANONYMOUS

I recommend me to you, and let you wete that notwithstanding tidings come down, as ye know, that people should not come up till they were sent for, but to be ready at all times; this notwithstanding, most people out of this country have taken wages, saying they will go up to London.    But they have no captain nor ruler assigned by the commissioners to await upon; and so they straggle about by themselves, and, by likeliness, are not like to come at London half of them.    And men that come from London say, there have not passed Thetford, not passing 400. And yet the towns and the country that have waged them shall think they be discharged; and therefore, if these lords above wait after more people in this country, by likeliness it will not be easy to get without a new commission and warning.    And yet it will be thought right strange of them that have waged people to wage any more, for every town hath waged and sent forth, and are ready to send forth, as many as they did when the King sent for them before the field at Ludlow; [1] and they that are not gone be going in the same form.

Item, there was shrewd rule toward in this country; for there was a certain person forthwith after the journey at Wakefield gathered fellowship to have murdered John Damme, as is said.

And also there is at the castle of Rising, and in other two places, made great gathering of people and hiring of harness; and it is well understood they be not to the King-ward, but rather the contrary, and for to rob.

Wherefore my father is in a doubt whether he shall send my brother up or not, for he would have his own men about him if need were here; but notwithstanding, he will send up Dawbeney, his spear and bows with him, as Stapleton and Calthorp or other men of worship of this country agree to do.    Wherefore demean you in doing of your errands thereafter, and if ye shall bring any message from the lords, take writing, for Darcort's message is not verily believed because he brought no writing.

Item, this country would fain take these false shrews that are

[1] Battle of Mortimer's Cross near Ludlow, won by Edward IV before he was king, 3rd February 1461.

of an opinion contrary to the King and his council, if they had any authority from the King to do so.

Item, my brother is rode to Yarmouth for to let bribers that would have robbed a ship under colour of my Lord of Warwick, and belong nothing to them-ward.

[1461]


162. WILLIAM[1] PASTON AND THOMAS PLAYTER TO JOHN [1] PASTON

*To my master, John Paston, in haste.*

Please you to know and wete of such tidings as my Lady of York hath by a letter of credence under the sign-manual of our sovereign lord King Edward, which letter came unto our said Lady this same day Easter even [1] at 11 o'clock, and was seen and read by me, William Paston.

First, our sovereign lord hath won the field; [2] and upon the Monday next after Palm Sunday he was received into York with great solemnity and processions. And the mayor and commons of the said city made their means to have grace by Lord Montagu [3] and Lord Berners,[4] which, before the King's coming into the said city, desired him of grace for the said city, which granted them grace.

On the King's part is slain Lord Fitzwalter,[5] and Lord Scrope sore hurt; John Stafford and Horne of Kent be dead; and Humphrey Stafford and William Hastings made knights with others; Blount is knighted, etc.

On the contrary part is dead Lord Clifford, Lord Neville, Lord Welles, Lord Willoughby, Anthony, Lord Scales,[6] Lord Harry [Stafford], and by supposition the Earl of Northumberland,[7] Andrew Trollope, with many others, gentle and commons, to the number of twenty thousand.

[1] 4th April.
[2] Towton, Palm Sunday, 29th March 1461.
[3] John Neville, Lord Montague, was, in 1464, created Earl of Northumberland, and, on his resignation of that title in 1470, Marquis of Montague; he fell in the battle of Barnet in 1471, fighting against King Edward.
[4] Sir John Bourchier, Lord Berners, in the battle of St Albans, in 1450, fought on the part of Henry VI; but after that time he and his family espoused the cause of the Yorkists; he died in 1474.
[5] He was actually killed in the preliminary skirmish at Ferrybridge.
[6] Scales was not killed at Towton; he succeeded his father as Earl Rivers, and died in 1491.
[7] Henry Percy, Earl of Northumberland, who commanded jointly with the Duke of Somerset.

Item, King Harry, the Queen, the Prince, Duke of Somerset,[1] Duke of Exeter, Lord Roos be fled into Scotland, and they be chased and followed, etc.   We sent no earlier unto you, because we had none certain till now; for unto this day London was as sorry city as might.   And because Spordauns had no certain tidings, we thought ye should take them a worth [2] till more certain.

Item, Thorp Waterfield is yielded, as Spordauns can tell you.

And Jesu speed you.   We pray you that this tidings my mother may know.

By your brother,

W. PASTON.
TH. PLAYTER.

[4th April 1461]

163.     THOMAS PLAYTER TO JOHN[(1)] PASTON

*To my right reverend and worshipful John Paston, Esquire, or to
my mistress his wife.*

After my most special recommendation, like your mastership wete that the matter for you and my mistress your mother against Poutrell and Tanfield hath been called upon as diligently and as hastily this term as it might be, and alway days given them by the court to answer; and then they took small exceptions and trifled forth the court, and alway excused them because the bill is long and his counsel had no leisure to see it.   And they prayed hearing of the testament of my master your father,[3] and thereof made another matter, and argued it to put them from it, because they had emparled [4] to us before.   And then Hillingworth, to drive it over this term, alleged variance betwixt the bill and the testament, that John Damme was named in the testament Joh Dawme,[5] in which case now the court must have sight of the said testament.   Wherefore ye must send it up the beginning

---

[1] Henry Beaufort, Duke of Somerset.   He was taken prisoner at the battle of Hexham (1464) and beheaded.

[2] i.e. at their worth.

[3] William Paston, the Judge, who died in 1444.

[4] *Emparled* refers to the licence or privilege of a defendant, granted on motion, to have delay of trial, to see if he could settle the matter amicably by talking to the plaintiff, and thus to determine what answer he should make to the plaintiff's action.

[5] This is a most curious objection to have made at a time when the orthography of the language was wholly unsettled, and when proper names were diversely written, even by their owners.   In the originals of these letters variations are constantly occurring.

of the next term, or else we shall have no speed in the matter.
And therefore, mistress, if my master be not come home, and ye
have not the said testament in your keeping, that then it please
you to speak unto my mistress your mother-in-law [1] for the said
testament, that I might readily have it here, and that it be sealed
in a box and sent to me, and I shall keep it safe with God's
grace.

And as for tidings, in good faith we have none, save the Earl
of Wiltshire's [2] head is set on London Bridge.

Master William is ridden home to my mistress Poynings; and
as for Master Poynings himself, she letteth as though she wist
not where he were.

A gentleman that came from York told me my master was hale
and merry, and rode to meet the King coming [3] from Middleham
castle.

Berwick [4] is full of Scots, and we look by likelihood after
another battle now betwixt Scots and us.

And I pray Jesu have you in His blessed keeping.

Your

Thomas Playter.

[May 1461]

164.  John Smith to John[(1)] Paston [J. G.]

*To his worshipful master, John Paston the eldest, Esquire.*

Right worshipful and my singular master, I recommend me to
you.   If it please your mastership to wete, the cause of my
writing is this.   I have understood by communing with other
credible men that many and the more part of the feoffees of the
lands late Sir John Fastolf's, and also they that pretend to be
executors of the said Sir John, purpose them to sell to my Lord
of Suffolk, though he recover not by tail, or to other mighty
lords, a great part of the lands of the said Sir John, to the intent
that ye shall not have them; upon which sale they will make
estate and enter and put you to your action, and though ye
recover in the law, as I am informed, ye shall recover of hard and

[1] Agnes Paston, widow of the Judge.
[2] James Butler, Earl of Wiltshire and Ormond, was taken at the battle of
Towton, and soon afterwards beheaded.   He had been twice Lord High
Treasurer.
[3] This shows that the King had not yet returned from Yorkshire to London
since the battle of Towton.
[4] Henry VI and his queen escaped after Towton to Berwick, and from
thence retired to Edinburgh.

but a part, the which should be dear of the suit. Where[fore] it seemeth to me, it were necessary to you to see remedy for this matter, and either put it in award or else that my Lord of Warwick, the which is your good lord, may move that the King, or himself, or my Lord Chamberlain, or some other witty men, may take a rule betwixt you and your adversaries. For if ye may not hold the foresaid lands, there shall grow great loss both to the dead and to you, and men shall put you in default thereof; your friends shall be sorry. It is better to bear a little loss than a great rebuke. Your matter hangeth long in the audience. If ye had there your intent your adversaries should cease the rather. I believe verily if ye do your part to have peace, God of His great grace shall grant it to you, the which give you the spirit of wisdom to guide you unto His pleasure. Amen.

We desire to see your mastership in Norfolk; your presence there be necessary.

From Norwich the 10th day of May.

Your clerk,<br>JOHN SMITH.

[1461]

---

165. THOMAS DENYS TO JOHN[1] PASTON

*To my master, Paston.*

Right worshipful and mine especial good master, I recommend me to you with all my service, beseeching you heartily, at the reverence of God, to help me now in the greatest extremity that I came at since my great trouble with Ingham.[1]

It is not out of your remembrance how Twyer in Norfolk vexeth me both by noise and searching mine house for me,[2] so that there I cannot be in quiet; and all that, I am verily ascertained, is by Heydon's craft. And here in the King's house anenst Howard,[3] where I had hoped to have relieved myself, I am supplanted and cast out from him by a clamour of all his servants at once; and ne were only that his disposition accordeth not to my poor conceit, which maketh me to give less force, because I desire not to deal where bribery is like to be used, else by my troth this unhappy unkindness would, I trow, have killed me. I pray you, at the reverence of Jesu Christ, to inform my Lord of Warwick of me. Pardee, I have done him service; I was with him at Northampton, that all men know, and

---

[1] *See* Nos. 74, 75, pages 80–1.
[2] Denys had mentioned this search in an earlier letter to Paston.
[3] Sir John Howard, who was sheriff of Norfolk this year.

now again at St Albans,[1] that knoweth James Ratcliff; and there lost I £20 worth horse, harness, and money, and was hurt in divers places. I pray you to get me his good lordship, and that I may be toward him in Norfolk in his courts holding, or else, if anything he have to do; and that ye will get me a letter to Twyer to let me sit in rest. For now if I made any fellowship against Twyer, I can have no colour now the sheriff and I be out; so I must keep me apart, which I am loth to do, by God, if I might better do.

I beseech you to send me your intent by the next man that come from you. I should have come to you, but, so help me God, my purse may no farther.

The Trinity preserve you. Written hastily at York, etc.

Yours, to his power,

Denys.

[May 1461]

166.    Thomas Playter to John[1] Paston

*To my right good master, John Paston, in all haste.*

After my most special recommendation, please your mastership wete, the King, because of the siege of Carlisle, changed his day of coronation to be upon the Sunday [2] next after Saint John Baptist, to the intent to speed him northward in all haste; and howbeit, blessed be God, that he hath now good tidings that Lord Montagu hath broken the siege, and slain of Scots six thousand, and two knights, whereof Lord Clifford's brother is one, yet notwithstanding he will be crowned the said Sunday.

And John Jenney informed me, and as I have verily learned since, ye are inbilled to be made a knight at this coronation.[3] Whether ye have understanding beforehand, I wot not; but, an' it like you to take the worship upon you, considering the comfortable tidings aforesaid, and for the gladness and pleasure of all your well-willers, and to the pine and discomfort of all your ill-willers, it were time your gear necessary on that behalf were purveyed for. And also ye had need hie you to London, for as I conceive the knights should be made upon the Saturday before the coronation. And as much as may be purveyed for you in secret wise without cost I shall bespeak for you, if need be, against your coming, in trust of the best; nevertheless, if ye

---

[1] The second battle of St Albans, 17th February 1461.
[2] 28th June.
[3] John Paston was not knighted at the coronation of Edward IV, but his eldest son John was made a knight, probably as a substitute for himself, within two years after.

be disposed, ye had need send a man before in all haste, that nothing be to seek. William Calthorp is inbilled. And Yelverton is inbilled, which caused Markham; because Yelverton looked to have been chief judge, and Markham thinketh to please him thus. And as for the matter against Poutrell, we can no farther proceed till we have my master your father's testament. I sent my mistress a letter for it.[1] No more, but I pray Almighty Jesu have you in His keeping.

Your

THOMAS PLAYTER.

[1461]

### 167.    RICHARD CALLE TO JOHN[(1)] PASTON

*To my right reverend and worshipful master, my master John Paston.*

Right reverend and worshipful master, I lowly recommend me unto your good mastership. Pleaseth you to wit that I have been at Framlingham, and spake Richard Southwell to have his advice in this matter; wherein he would give me but little counsel, and said ye were strangely disposed, for ye trusted no man, and had much language, which the bearer hereof shall inform your mastership.

And as for the letters, they were delivered my Lord [2] at the lodge, but I could not speak with his Lordship. And such time as they were delivered Fitzwilliam was there, which is now keeper of Caister; and what time as my Lord had seen the letters, he commanded him to avoid, and so he did. And then my Lord sent for Southwell. And in the meantime my Lord sent a man to me and asked me where ye were, and I told him ye were with the King; and so he sent me word that an answer should be made by Southwell to the King, saying that two or three heirs had been with my Lord and showed their evidence, and delivered it to my Lord, saying they have great wrong, beseeching my Lord that it might be reformed. Wherefore he commanded me that I should go home, for other answer could I none have. So I abode upon Southwell to have known my Lord's answer to the King; which answer Southwell told me was, that he writeth to the King that certain points in your letters be untrue, and that he shall prove such time as he cometh before the King, beseeching the King to take it to no displeasure; for he is advised to

---

[1] No. 163, page 169.
[2] The Duke of Norfolk, who had recently taken possession of Caister, and appointed a keeper.

keep it still unto the time that he hath spoken with his Highness, for he trusteth to God to show such evidence to the King and to the lords, that he should have best right and title thereto; and so he sent a man forth to the King this day. It were right well done ye awaited upon his man coming, that ye might know the ready intent of my Lord's writing.

Bartholomew Ellis hath been with my Lord, and made a release to my Lord; and Sir Will. Chamberlain was there two days before I came hither, I can think for the same matter. And Thomas Fastolf was there the same time that I was there; and, as I am informed, they have delivered my Lord certain evidence. Wherefore meseemeth it were right well done, saving your better advice, to come home and seal up your evidence, and have them with you to London, to prove his title nought. There be but two or three men within the place; and if ye think it best to do it, send word, and I suppose a remedy shall be had.

Also, I hear no word of Master William, nor of the writs for the Parliament. Also, it is told here that Tuddenham and Heydon have a pardon of the King, and that they shall come up to London with the Lady of Suffolk to the coronation. Also, as for the letter that ye sent to Thomas Wingfield, I have it still, for he is at London. Some men say he moved my Lord for to enter, and some say Fitzwilliam is in default; so I can see there is but few good. Also my master Sir Thomas Howes shall send a letter to the person ye wot of, for to deliver you the gear at London the next week. My right worshipful and reverend master, Almighty God preserve you. Written at Norwich, on the morrow after Corpus Christi day.

Your poor servant and beadsman,

R. C.

[5th June 1461]


168.     JAMES GRESHAM TO JOHN[1] PASTON

*To my right worshipful master, John Paston, at Hellesdon, in Norfolk, in haste.*

After due recommendation had, please it your mastership to wit that as for Playter, he shall excuse the writ of the Parliament, etc. As touching my Master Howard,[1] I cannot yet speak with him nor with Montgomery[2] neither. But as for the day of coronation of the King, it shall be certainly the Monday next

[1] Sir John Howard.          [2] Sir Thomas Montgomery.

after Midsummer, and it is told me that ye among others are named to be made knight at the coronation, etc.

Item, it is said, that the coronation done, the King will into the north part forthwith; and therefore shall not the Parliament hold, but writs shall go into every shire to give them that are chosen knights of the shire day after Michaelmas; this is told me by such as are right credible.

Master Brackley shall preach at Paul's on Sunday next coming, as he told me, and he told me, that for cause Childermas day fall on the Sunday, the coronation shall on the Monday.[1]

Written in haste at London, the Sunday next before Midsummer.

Your right poor servant,

JAMES GRESHAM.

[21st June 1461]

### 169. CLEMENT PASTON TO JOHN[(1)] PASTON [J. G.]

*To my right worshipful brother, John Paston, be this delivered in haste.*

Brother, I recommend me to you, desiring to hear of your welfare, the which I pray God maintain. Please you to wete that I have sent my mother a letter for money for my sister;[2] and if ye will agree that I may have £20, I shall give you accounts thereof, and ye shall be paid again of the obligation that my mother hath, or else I shall take a surety of my sister. I wis obligation must needs be sued, and a dozen actions more in her name, and she do well this term; and it will be done within fortnight. The Countess of Northumberland and Robert Fenys occupy all her land, and that is a great mischief. I pray you speak to my mother hereof, and let me have an answer within this se'nnight. Also, brother, Wyndham is come to town, and he said to me he will go get him a master; and methought by him he would be in the King's service, and he saith that he will have Felbrigg again ere Michaelmas, or there shall be 500 heads broke

---

[1] Childermas, or Holy Innocents' day (28th December), fell on Sunday in 1461. The day of the week on which it fell used to be considered unlucky during the whole ensuing year. Edward's coronation, however, was not postponed till Monday. It took place on the Sunday as arranged, but the processions and pageantry were deferred till next day. (*See* Cotton MS. Vitellius A. XVI.)

[2] Elizabeth, widow of Robert Poynings. Her husband had been killed at the second battle of St Albans (17th February 1461), and her lands were immediately seized by Eleanor, widow of Henry Percy, third Earl of Northumberland, who had been slain at Towton.

therefore. Brother, I pray you deliver the money that I should have unto some prior of some abbey or some master of some college to be delivered when I can espy any land to be purchased. I pray you send me word whether ye will do thus or no. No more, but our Lord have you in His keeping. Written on Friday next after St John's day.

By your brother

CLEMENT PASTON.

[26th June 1461]

170. MARGARET PASTON TO JOHN[1] PASTON [J. G.]

*To my right worshipful husband, John Paston, be this delivered in haste.*

Right worshipful husband, I recommend me to you. Please you to wete that this day in the morning the parson of Snoring came to Thomas Denys and fetched him out of his house, and beareth him a hand that he should have made bills against Twyer and him, and hath led him forth with them. His wife hath no knowledge of it. Furthermore, the said parson saith that the said Thomas Denys should have taken soldiers out of his fellow-ship when he went to St Albans; that is another of his com-plaints. Item, another of his complaints is, he beareth the said Thomas a hand that he had away a horse of John Copping of Brisley, and another of King of Downham, the which horses were stolen by the said two persons. Wherefore the said Thomas took them as a commissioner and delivered them to the escheator, Francis Costard, and one of them he bought of the said Francis. And the said parson hath away the said horses, and saith that he will the said thieves should be recompensed by Thomas Denys. Thus I am informed of all these matters by his wife; and she prayeth you in the reverence of God ye will be her good master, and help that her husband may have some remedy by your labour in this matter, for she saith since that her husband is the King's officer,[1] that they ought to spare him the rather . . .[2]

I pray you heartily that ye will send me word in haste how that ye do with my Lord of Norfolk, and with your adversaries. Item, I have done purveyed in this warren eleven score rabbits and sent up by the bearer hereof. The Blessed Trinity have

---

[1] After his release from prison, Denys had entered the King's service, and was at this time coroner of Norfolk.

[2] The next eight lines of the manuscript are badly mutilated and are there-fore omitted here.

you in His keeping, and send you the better of all your adversaries, and good speed in all your matters. Written in haste, the same day that ye departed hence.

Item, I pray you that ye will remember my uncle Berney's matter touching the executing of his will, and how ye will that we be demeaned for keeping of his year-day, and that it liketh you to send me word by Mr John Smith.

[June 1461]

## 171. THOMAS DENYS TO MARGARET PASTON[1]

*To my right noble and worshipful mistress, my mistress Paston, or to William Paston, if she be absent.*

Right noble and worshipful mistress, I recommend me to you with my poor service. And forsomuch as I hear nothing of my master your husband's coming hastily home—and though he come or come not, it were expedient that the King were informed of the demeaning of the shire—therefore I send to you a testimonial which is made by a great assent of great multitude of commons to send to the King. I pray you for the good speed thereof that in all haste possible ye like to send it to my said master, if he be with the King; else find the mean to send it to the King though my master be thence; beside further that ye vouchsafe to let diligent labour be made to a sufficient number to asseal for my master Paston alone, for if both hold not I would one hold.

I pray you that it like you to send for my master William Paston, and show him all this, and that it were hasted; for on the adversary's part Judas sleepeth not.

Berney promised to have sent; but for Our Lord's love trust not that. For I see his sloth and silly labour, which is no labour. And I would full fain speak with you, etc.

My master, your husband, will peradventure blame us all if this matter be not applied; for he may not of reason do so largely herein by his might, because he is elected, as the commons might wisely do with help of his favour, if it were wisely wrought. If my master William Paston ride hastily from a ten days [2] to London, I will with him if he send me word. The Holy Trinity preserve you.

[1] This letter must have been written in the last days of June or on 1st July. We know from the records of the King's Bench that on Thursday, 2nd July, a labourer named Robert Grey, of Warham, with a number of other people, attacked Denys and dragged him from his house at Gately to Egmere near Walsingham, where they murdered him on the Saturday following (4th July).

[2] i.e. within ten days.

*G 752

Written rudely in haste the Sunday, etc.

Men say, send a wise man on thy errand and say little to him; wherefore I write briefly and little.

THOMAS DENYS.

[1461]

## 172. MARGARET PASTON TO JOHN[1] PASTON [J. G.]

*To my right worshipful husband, John Paston, be this delivered in haste.*

Right worshipful husband, I recommend me to you. Please you to wete that I have spoken with Thomas Denys's wife; [1] and she recommends her to your good mastership, and she prayeth you to be her good master, and prayeth you of your good mastership that ye will give her your advice how to be demeaned for her person and her goods. For as touching her own person, she dare not go home to her own place; for she is threatened, if that she might be taken, she should be slain or be put in fearful place in shorting of her live days, and so she standeth in great heaviness, God her help. Furthermore, she is now put by her brother in Norwich with Awbry, and she thinketh the place is right conversant of people for her to abide in, for she keepeth her as close as she may for spying. Item, as I went to St Leonard's-ward, I spake with Master John Salet and communed with him of her, and methought by him that he oweth her right good will. And then I asked him how she might be demeaned with his [Denys's] goods and hers. He counselled me that she should get her a trusty friend, that were a good, true, poor man that had not much to lose, and would be ruled after her, and to have a letter of ministration; and so I told her. Then she said she would have her brother's advice therein. Item, she saith there be no more feoffees in his lands but ye and Rookwood; and she prayeth you that it please you to speak to Rookwood that he make no release but by your advice, as she trusteth to your good mastership. Item, the last time that I spake with her she made such a piteous moan and said that she wost not how to do for money, and so I lent 6s. 8d. Item, I sent my cousin Berney the bill that John Pampyng wrote by your commandment to me, and he hath sent a letter of his intent to you and to Rookwood thereof. And also but-if it please you to take better heed to his matter than he can do himself, I can think he shall else fare the worse; for in faith he standeth daily in great fear for the false

[1] This letter relates to the affairs of Thomas Denys's wife five days after the murder of her husband. John Paston and William Rookwood were trustees of his lands.

contrary party against him. Item, at the reverence of God, beware how ye ride or go for naughty and evil-disposed fellowships. I am put in fear daily for mine abiding here, and counselled by my mother and by other good friends that I should not abide here but-if the world were in more quiet than it is. God for His mercy send us a good world, and send you health in body and soul, and good speed in all your matters. Written in haste the Thursday next after St Thomas.

By your

M. P.

[9th July 1461]

### 173. John Berney to John[1] Paston and William Rookwood

*To the worshipful John Paston, and William Rookwood, Esquire, and to every of them.*

Right worshipful cousins, I recommend me to you. And forasmuch as I am credibly informed how that Sir Miles Stapleton, knight, with other ill-disposed persons, defame and falsely noise me in murdering of Thomas Denys the coroner, and how that I intend to make insurrections contrary unto the law; and that the said Stapleton furthermore noiseth me with great robberies; in which defamations and false noisings the said Stapleton, and in that his saying, he is false, that knoweth God, etc. And for my plain acquittal, if he or any substantial gentleman will say it and avow it, I say to it contrary, and by licence of the King to make it good as a gentleman. And in this my plain excuse I pray you to open it unto the lords, that the said Stapleton, etc., make great gatherings of the King's rebellions lying in wait to murder me. And in that I may make open proof. Written in haste the 10th day of July, in the 1st year of the reign of Edward IV.

John Berney.

Remember to take a writ to choose coroners in Norfolk.

[1461]

### 174. John[1] Paston to Margaret Paston

*To my cousin,[1] Margaret Paston.*

I recommend me to you, letting you wete that the under-sheriff doubteth him of John Berney; wherefore I pray you bring them

[1] *See* footnote 1, page 148.

together, and set them accord, if ye can, so that the said under-
sheriff be sure that he shall not be hurt by him nor of his
countrymen. And if he will not, let him verily understand that
he shall be compelled to find him surety of the peace to agree
on this head, and that shall neither be profitable nor worshipful.
And let him wete that there have been many complaints of him
by that knavish knight, Sir Miles Stapleton, as I sent you word
before; but he shall come to his excuse well enough, so he have
a man's heart, and the said Stapleton shall be understood as he
is, a false shrew. And he and his wife [1] and other have blavered
here of my kindred in hedermoder; but, by that time we have
reckoned of old days and late days, mine shall be found more
worshipful than his and his wife's, or else I will not for his gilt
gypcer.

Also tell the said Berney that the sheriff is in a doubt whether
he shall make a new election of knights of the shire, because of
him and Grey, wherein it were better for him to have the sheriff's
good will.

Item, methinketh for quiet of the country it were most
worshipful that as well Berney as Grey should get a record of all
such that might spend forty shillings a-year, that were at the
day of election, which of them that had fewest to give it up as
reason would.[2] Written at London, on Relic Sunday.

Item, that ye send about for silver according to the old bill
that I sent you from Lynn.

John Paston.

[12th July 1461]

[1] Probably his second wife, Catherine, daughter of Thomas de la Pole,
second son to the Duke of Suffolk.
[2] Paston had again been elected to Parliament; but Berney and Grey were
suspected of having overawed the electors, and the sheriff was contemplating
a fresh poll. Berney gave assurances (No. 177) that he meant no harm to the
under-sheriff; rather than agree to the measures suggested by Paston here,
he proposed a different course: he asked that the under-sheriff should either
tell the people that the election should stand, or procure a new writ and
publicly announce the date of a new election. Paston, in a letter to his wife
written on 1st August, expressed himself satisfied with this proposal, provided he were not put to further expense; if there were to be a new election,
he only desired it might be held on a holiday so as not to interfere with the
people's work. The matter was discussed before the King, Paston and the
under-sheriff being present, and a writ was granted for a new election to be
held on St Laurence's day. But from what he had seen of the under-
sheriff's conduct, Paston feared that the day might be changed to his dis-
advantage. In an interview with the under-sheriff, he got him to place the
writ in his hands and sent it to his wife for safe keeping until the election
date, asking her to see that the under-sheriff had it again on that day. The
election was duly held; but it was the occasion of a violent scene between
Paston and the sheriff, which is referred to in No. 180.

## 175. MARGARET PASTON TO JOHN[1] PASTON[1]

I recommend me to you; please you to wete that I have sent to my cousin Berney, according to your desire in the letter that ye did write on Relic Sunday to me, whereupon he hath written a letter to you and another bill to me, the which I send you. He told the messenger that I sent to him that the under-sheriff needeth not to fear him, nor none of his; for he said, after the election was done, he spake with him at the Grey Friars, and prayed him of his good mastership, and said to him that he feared no man of bodily harm but only Twyer and his fellowship.

Item, Sir John Tattershall and the bailiff of Walsingham and the constable hath taken the parson of Snoring and four of his men, and set them fast in the stocks on Monday at night; and, as it is said, they should be carried up to the King in haste. God defend it but they be chastised as the law will. Twyer and his fellowship beareth a great weight of Thomas Denys's death in the country about Walsingham; and it is said there, if John Osbern had ought him as good will as he did before that he was acquainted with Twyer, he should not have died, for he might have ruled all Walsingham as he had list, as it is said.

Item, William Lynes, that was with Master Fastolf, and such other as he is with him, go fast about in the country, and bear men a hand, priests and other, they be Scots, and take bribes of them [2] and let them go again. He took the last week the parson of Fritton, and but for my cousin Jerningham the younger, there would have led him forth with them; and he told them plainly if they made any such doings there, but they had the letter to show for them, they should aley on their bodies. It were well done that they were met with betimes. It is told me that the said Will reporteth of you as shamefully as he can in divers places. Jesu have you in His keeping. Written in haste, the Wednesday after Relic Sunday.

If the under-sheriff come home I will assay to do for him as ye desired me in your letter. As for money, I have sent about, and I can get none but 13s. 4d. since ye went out. I will do my part to get more as hastily as I may.

By your

M. P.

[15th July 1461]

---

[1] This letter is in answer to the previous one (No. 174).
[2] This means either that they pillaged them or held them to ransom.

176. JOHN BERNEY TO JOHN⁽¹⁾ PASTON AND WILLIAM ROOKWOOD

*To the worshipful John Paston, and to my cousin, William Rookwood, Esquire, with my Lord of Canterbury.*

Right worshipful sir, I recommend me to you, praying you heartily to labour for that the King may write unto me, giving me thanking of the goodwill and service that I have done unto him, and in being with him against his adversaries and rebellions, as well in the north as in this country of Norfolk. And in that the King should please the commons in this country; for they grudge and say how that the King receiveth such of this country, etc., as have been his great enemies, and oppressors of the commons; and such as have assisted his Highness be not rewarded; and it is to be considered, or else it will hurt, as meseemeth by reason. And in aid of this changeable rule it were necessary to move the Lords Spiritual and Temporal, by the which that might be reformed, etc. And in case that any of mine old enemies, Tuddenham, Stapleton, and Heydon, with their affinity, labour the King and lords unto my hurt, I am and will be ready to come to my sovereign lord for my excuse, so that I may come safe for unlawful hurt purveyed by my said enemies. No more at this time, but God preserve you in grace. Written at Witchingham, the 16th day in the month of July, in the first year of the reign of Edward IV.

JOHN BERNEY.

Please it you move this unto my Lords Canterbury, Ely, Norwich, etc.

[1461]

177. JOHN BERNEY TO JOHN⁽¹⁾ PASTON

*To the right worshipful John Paston, Esquire, in haste.*

Sir, I recommend me to you, etc. And as for my plain disposition towards the under-sheriff, I will him no bodily hurt, nor shall not be hurt by me, nor by no man that I may rule. But the commons through all the shire be moved against him for cause of his light demeaning towards them for this election of knights of the shire for the Parliament. And I suppose if that he will, he may be hastily eased as thus: let him make notice unto the said commons that this their election shall stand, or else let him purchase a new writ, and let him make writing unto them what day they shall come, and they to make a new election according unto the law. And, sir, I pray you say to him that it is not his

honesty to lie upon too many men, noising them rebellions of
Norfolk, and Berney their captain. No more to you at this
time, but I have sent you two letters within this eight days.
Written the 17th day of July, in the 1st year of the reign of
Edward IV.

JOHN BERNEY.

[1461]


178. MARGARET PASTON TO JOHN[1] PASTON

*To my worshipful husband, John Paston, this letter be delivered in
haste.*

Right worshipful husband, I recommend me to you. Please it
you to wete that I am desired by Sir John Tattershall to write
to you for a commission, or an oyer and terminer, for to be sent
down into this country to sit upon the parson of Snoring, and
on such as was cause of Thomas Denys's death, and for many and
great horrible robberies. And as for the costs thereof, the
country will pay therefor, for they be sore afraid but the said
death be chastised, and the said robberies; they are afraid that
more folks shall be served in like wise. As for the priest and
six of his men that be taken, they be delivered to Twyer, and
four be with them of the country's cost for to be sent with to
the King; and if they be brought up, at the reverence of God
do your part that they escape not, but that they may have the
judgment of the law, and as they have deserved, and be committed to prison, not to depart till they be inquired of their foresaid robbery by such a commission that ye can get, that the King
and the lords may understand what rule they have been of, not
only for the murders and the robberies, but as well for the great
insurrection that they were like to have made within the shire.
The priests of Caister, they be straitly take heed at by Robert
Harmerer and other; so that the said priests may have nothing
out of their own, nor of other men's, but they be ransacked, and
the place is watched both by day and night. The priests think
right long till they have tidings from you. At the reverence of
God, beware how ye go and ride, for it is told me that ye be
threatened of them that be naughty fellows that hath been
inclining to them that hath been your old adversaries.

The Blessed Trinity have you in His keeping. Written in
haste, the Saturday next before Saint Margaret.

By yours,

MARGARET PASTON.

[18th July 1461]

179.  THOMAS PLAYTER TO JOHN[1] PASTON [J. G.]

*To Master John Paston, Esquire, in haste.*

Please your mastership wete that Daniel of Gray's Inn informed me that King of Downham, which slew Thomas Denys, is arrested and in hold at Wisbeach, and had been delivered nor had Francis Costard a-taken surety of peace of him; and so he is kept in by none other mean but alonely by surety of peace. And as I felt by the said Daniel, if he be craftily handled he will accuse many others; but Daniel is loth to name them, but I suppose he meant by Twyer and yet others more, right sufficient, and called of substance. Item, Heydon harh paid 400 marks and is delivered. Item, it is talked the Parliament shall be pro-rogued till the 4th day of November and the King will into Scotland in all haste. Written in haste upon the day of the Advention.[1]

Yours,

THOMAS PLAYTER.

[1st August 1461]

180.    JOHN[2] PASTON TO JOHN[1] PASTON

*To my right reverend and worshipful father, John Paston, Esquire, dwelling in Hellesdon, be this letter delivered in haste.*

Most reverend and worshipful father, I recommend me heartily, and submit me lowlily to your good fatherhood, beseeching you for charity of your daily blessing. I beseech you to hold me excused that I sent to you none erst no writing, for I could not speed to mine intent the matters that ye sent to me for. I have laboured daily my Lord of Essex,[2] Treasurer of England, to have moved the King both of the manor of Dedham and of the bill copy of the court roll every morning afore he went to the King, and often times inquired of him and he had moved the King in these matters. He answered me nay, saying it was no time, and said he would it were as fain sped as I myself, oft times delaying me, that in truth I thought to have sent you word that I feeled by him that he was not willing to move the King therein. Nevertheless, I laboured to him continually, and prayed Berners, his man, to remember him of it. I told often times to my said Lord that I had a man tarrying in town that I should have sent to you for other sundry matters, and he tarried for nothing but

¹ The feast of St Peter ad Vincula.
² Henry, Viscount Bourchier, Lord Treasurer of England, was created Earl of Essex in 1461.

that I might send you by him an answer of the said matters; other times beseeching him to speed me in these matters for this cause, that ye should think no default in me for remembering in the said matters.

And now of late, I remembering him of the same matter, inquired if he had moved the King's Highness therein; and he answered me that he had felt and moved the King therein, rehearsing the King's answer therein; how that when he had moved the King in the said manor of Dedham, beseeching him to be your good lord therein, considering the service and true part that ye have done and owe to him, and in especial the right that ye have thereto, he said he would be your good lord therein, as he would be to the poorest man in England. He would hold with you in your right; and as for favour, he will not be understood that he shall show favour more to one man than to another, not to one in England.

And as for the bill copied of the court roll, when he moved to him of it, he smiled and said that such a bill there was, saying that ye would have oppressed sundry of your countrymen of worshipful men, and therefore he kept it still. Nevertheless, he said he should look it up in haste, and ye should have it.

Berners undertook to me twice or thrice that he should so have remembered his lord and master that I should have had it within two or three days. He is often times absent, and therefore I have it not yet; when I can get it, I shall send it you, and of the King's mouth, his name that take it him.

I send you home Peacock again. He is not for me. God send grace that he may do you good service; that, by estimation, is not likely. Ye shall have knowledge afterward how he hath demeaned him here with me. I would, saving your displeasure, that ye were delivered of him, for he shall never do you profit nor worship.

I suppose ye understand that the money that I had of you at London may not endure with me till that the King go into Wales and come again, for I understand it shall be long ere he come again. Wherefore I have sent to London to mine uncle Clement to get an hundred shillings of Christopher Hansson your servant, and send it me by my said servant, and mine harness with it, which I left at London to make clean.

I beseech you not to be displeased with it, for I could make none other chevisance but I should have borrowed it of a strange man, some of my fellows, which I suppose should not like you an' ye heard of it another time. I am in surety where as I shall have another man in the stead of Peacock.

My Lord of Essex saith he will do as much for you as for any esquire in England, and Berners his man telleth me, saying,

'Your father is much beholden to my Lord, for he loveth him well.' Berners m@ved me once, and said that ye must needs do somewhat for my lord and his, and I said I wost well that ye would do for him that lay in your power. And he said that there was a little money betwixt you and a gentleman of Essex called Dyrward, saying that there is as much between my said Lord and the said gentleman, of the which money he desireth your part.

It is talked here how that ye and Howard should have striven together on the Shire day,¹ and one of Howard's men should have stricken you twice with a dagger, and so ye should have been hurt but for a good doublet that ye had on at that time. Blessed be God that ye had it on! No more I write to your good fatherhood at this time, but Almighty God have you in His keeping, and send you victory of your enemies, and worship increasing to your life's ending.

Written at Lewes, on St Bartholomew's eve.

By your servant and elder son,

JOHN PASTON.

[23rd August 1461]

181. CLEMENT PASTON TO JOHN⁽¹⁾ PASTON

*To his right reverend and worshipful brother, John Paston.*

Right reverend and worshipful brother, I recommend me to your good brotherhood, desiring to hear of your welfare and good prosperity, the which I pray God increase to His pleasure and your heart's ease; certifying you that I have spoken with John Russe, and Playter spoke with him both, on Friday before St Bartholomew. He told us of Howard's guiding, which made us right sorry till we heard the conclusion that ye had none harm.

Also I understand by William Peacock that my nephew ² had knowledge thereof also upon Saturday next before St Bartholomew in the King's house. Notwithstanding, upon the same day Playter and I wrote letters unto him, rehearsing all the matter, for cause, if there were any questions moved to him thereof, that he should tell the truth, in case that the questions were moved by any worshipful man, and named my Lord Bourchier,³ for my Lord Bourchier was with the King at that time.

I feel by W. Peacock that my nephew is not yet verily

¹ *See* footnote 2, page 180.
² John Paston, the elder son of that name, who had been for a while in the King's household.
³ Henry, Viscount Bourchier, who had been created Earl of Essex about two months earlier. Clement had apparently forgotten his new dignity.

acquainted in the King's house, nor with the officers of the King's house; he is not taken as none of that house. For the cooks be not charged to serve him, nor the sewer [1] to give him no dish, for the sewer will not take no men no dishes till they be commanded by the comptroller. Also, he is not acquainted with nobody but with Wykes; [2] and Wykes had told him that he would bring him to the King, but he hath not yet done so. Wherefore it were best for him to take his leave and come home till ye had spoken with somebody to help him forth, for he is not bold enough to put forth himself. But then I considered that if he should now come home, the King would think that when he should do him any service somewhere, that then ye would have him home; the which should cause him not to be had in favour, and also men would think that he were put out of service. Also, W. Peacock telleth me that his money is spent, and not riotously, but wisely and discreetly, for the costs is greater in the King's house when he rideth than ye weened it had been, as William Peacock can tell you. And therefore we must get him one hundred shillings at the least, as by William Peacock's saying; and yet that will be too little, and I wot well we cannot get forty pence of Christopher Hansson. So I shall be fain to lend it him of mine own silver. If I knew verily your intent were that he should come home, I would send him none. There I will do as methinketh ye should be best pleased, and that methinketh is to send him the silver. Therefore I pray you, hastily as ye may, send me again five marks, and the remnant, I trow, I shall get upon Christopher Hansson and Lukett. I pray you send me it as hastily as ye may, for I shall leave myself right bare; and I pray you send me a letter how ye will that he shall be demeaned. Written on Tuesday after St Bartholomew, etc. *Christus vos conservet!*

CLEMENT PASTON.

[25th August 1461]

## 182. LORD BEAUCHAMP[3] TO THOMAS HOWES

*To mine well-beloved friend, Sir Thomas Howes, parson of Blofield.*

Well-beloved friend, I greet you well. And forasmuch as I understand that William Worcester, late the servant unto Sir

---

[1] An officer responsible for the service of dishes, etc.

[2] John Wykes, an usher of the King's chamber, was a cousin of John Paston.

[3] John Beauchamp, Lord Beauchamp of Powick, in Worcestershire, was so created in 1447. In 1450 he was appointed Lord Treasurer, and became a Knight of the Garter. He died in 1475, and was buried in the Church of the Dominican Friars at Worcester.

John Fastolf, knight, whose soul God assoil, is not had in favour
nor trust with my right well-beloved friend John Paston, neither
with you, as he saith, namely in such matters and causes as
concerneth the will and testament of the said Sir John Fastolf;
and as I am informed the said William purposeth him to go into
his country, for the which cause he hath desired me to write
unto you that ye would be a special good friend unto him, for his
said master's sake, to have all such things as reason and conscience requireth, and that ye would be mean unto Paston for
him in this matter, to show him the more favour at this time for
this my writing in doing of any trouble to him, trusting that he
will demean him in such wise that he shall have no cause unto
him but to be his good master, as he saith.   And if there be
anything that I can do for you, I will be right glad to do it, and
that knoweth Almighty God, which have you in His keeping.
Written at Greenwich, the 28th day of August.

J. Beauchamp.
[1461]

183.   Lord Hungerford and Robert Whittingham
to Margaret of Anjou

*A la Reine d'Angleterre en Escote.*[1]

Madam, please it your good God, we have since our coming
hither written to your Highness thrice.   The first we sent by
Bruges, to be sent to you by the first vessel that went into
Scotland; the other two letters were sent from Dieppe, the one
by the carvel in the which we came, and the other in another
vessel.   But, madam, all was one thing in substance, of putting
you in knowledge of the king [2] your uncle's death, whom God
assoil, and how we stand arrested, and do yet; but on Tuesday
next we trust and understand we shall up to the king,[3] your
cousin german.   His commissaries, at the first of our tarrying,
took all our letters and writings, and bear them up to the king,
leaving my Lord of Somerset in keeping at castle of Arques, and
my fellow Whittingham and me (for we had safe conduct) in the
town of Dieppe, where we are yet.   But on Tuesday next, we
understand that it pleaseth the said king's highness that we shall
come to his presence; and are charged to bring us up to Monsieur
de Cressell, now Bailiff of Caen, and Monsieur de la Mot.

[1] To the Queen of England in Scotland.
[2] Charles VII of France, who died on 22nd July 1461.
[3] Louis XI, son of Charles VII.

Madam, fear you not, but be of good comfort; and beware that ye adventure not your person, nor my Lord the Prince,[1] by the sea, till ye have other word from us, in less than your person cannot be sure there as ye are, and that extreme necessity drive you thence.   And for God's sake, the King's Highness be advised the same; for, as we be informed, the Earl of March [2] is into Wales by land, and hath sent his navy thither by sea. And, madam, think verily we shall not sooner be delivered but that we will come straight to you, without death take us by the way, the which we trust he will not till we see the King and you peaceable again in your realm; the which we beseech God soon to see, and to send you that your Highness desireth.   Written at Dieppe the 30th day of August.[3]

Your true subjects and liege men,

HUNGERFORD.

WHITTINGHAM.

[1461]

*At the bottom of the copy of the letter is added:*

These are the names of those men that are in Scotland with the queen.

The King Harry is at Kirkcudbright with four men and a child.

Queen Margaret is at Edinburgh, and her son.

| | |
|---|---|
| The Lord Roos and his son. | Sir Edmund Hampden. |
| John Ormond. | Sir Henry Roos. |
| William Taylboys. | John Courtenay. |
| Sir John Fortescue. | Dauson. |
| Sir Thomas Fyndern. | Thomas Burnby. |
| Waynesford of London. | Borret of Sussex. |
| Thomas Thompson of Guines. | Sir John Welpdale. |
| Thomas Brampton of Guines. | Mr Roger Clerk of London. |
| John Audeley of Guines. | John Retford late Coubitt. |
| Langheyn of Ireland. | Giles St Loe. |
| Thomas Philip of Ipswich. | John Hawt. |

---

[1] Edward, son of Henry VI.

[2] Edward IV, whom the Lancastrians did not yet recognize as king.

[3] A copy of this letter was enclosed by Henry Windsor in his letter of 4th October to John Paston (No. 185, page 191).

184.         JAMES GLOYS TO JOHN[1] PASTON

*To the right reverend and worshipful sir, and my good master,*
*John Paston, Esquire.*

Right reverend and worshipful sir, I recommend me to your
good mastership, praying you to wete that I was at Blake's and
spake with his wife; and she saith he was not at home this three
weeks—he rideth up the country to take accounts of bailiffs—
and that this day se'nnight he should have sat in Caister by you
upon accounts, and from thence he should have ridden to Lynn,
and that he shall be at home on Monday at night next coming.
Wherefore I have left my errand with her. But she saith that
he shall not mown coming to you, for my Lady [1] have sent for
him in great haste, both by a letter and by a token, to come to
her as hastily as he may; notwithstanding she shall do the errand
to him.

As for Yelverton, I did a good feel to inquire of James Skinner
when the said Yelverton should go to London. He said not this
se'nnight. He could not tell what day till he had spoken with
his son. His son should come to him ere his master should ride.
I shall inquire more at Walsingham. And for God's love be not
too long from London, for men say there, as I have been told,
that my Lord of Gloucester [2] should have Caister, and there is
great noise of this revel [3] that was done in Suffolk by Yelverton
and Jenney; and your well-willers think that if they might prevail
in this they would attempt you in others. But cease their power
and malice, and preserve you from all evil. And at the reverence
of God let some interposition go a-twixt you and my mistress
your mother ere ye go to London, and all that ye do shall speed
the better; for she is set on great malice, and every man that she
speaketh with knoweth her heart, and it is like to be a foul noise
over all the country without it be soon ceased.

Also, sir, it is told me that my Lord of Norfolk is coming to
Framlingham, and that ye be greatly commended in his household. Therefore it were well done, meseemeth, that ye spake
with him.

The Holy Trinity keep you. Written at Norwich, the
Thursday after St Matthew.

                              Your poor priest,

                                   JAMES GLOYS.

[24th September 1461]

---

[1] Alice, Duchess of Suffolk.
[2] Richard, the King's brother, afterwards Richard III.
[3] *See* No. 187, page 193.

185.     HENRY WINDSOR TO JOHN[1] PASTON

*To my full worshipful, special good master, John Paston, Esquire,*
*abiding at Norwich.*

Right worshipful sir, and some time my most special good
master, I recommend me unto your good mastership with all my
poor service, if it may in any wise suffice.   And farthermore, sir,
I beseech you, now being in your country where ye may daily
call unto you my master Sir Thomas Howes, once to remember
my poor matter, and by your discretions to take such a direction
therein, and so to conclude, as may be to your discharge and to
my furtherance, according to the will of him [Fastolf] that is
passed unto God, whose soul I pray Jesu pardon!   For truly,
sir, there was in him no fault, but in me only, if it be not as I
have remembered your mastership afore this time.   For truly,
sir, I dare say I should have had as special and as good a master
of you as any poor man, as I am, within England should have had
of a worshipful man, as ye are, if ye had never meddled the goods
of my master F.; and as much ye would have done, and laboured
for me, in my right, if it had been in the hands of any other man
than of yourself only.   But, I trust in God, at your next coming,
to have an answer such as I shall be content with.   And if it may
be so, I am and shall be your servant in that I can or may; that
knoweth our Lord Jesu, whom I beseech save and send you a
good end in all your matters, to your pleasure and worship everlasting.   Amen.   Written at London, the 4th day of October.

As for tidings, the King will be at London within three days
next coming; and all the castles and holds both in South Wales
and in North Wales are given and yielded up into the King's
hand.   And the Duke of Exeter and the Earl of Pembroke are
flown and taken the mountains, and divers lords with great
puissance are after them; and the most part of gentlemen and
men of worship are come in to the King, and have grace, of all
Wales.   The Duke of Somerset, the Lord Hungerford, Robert
Whittingham, and other four or five squires are come into
Normandy out of Scotland, and as yet they stand straight under
arrest; and, as merchants that are come late thence say, they
are like to be deemed and judged prisoners.   My Lord Wenlock,
Sir John Cley, and the Dean of St Severin's have abode at
Calais these three weeks, and yet are there, abiding a safe
conduct, going upon an embassy to the French king.   And Sir
Walter Blount, treasurer of Calais, with a great fellowship of
soldiers of Calais, and many other men of the marches, have lain,
and yet do, at a siege afore the castle of Hammes, beside Calais,
and daily make great war, either party to other.

Item, I send unto you a copy of a letter [1] that was taken upon the sea, made by the Lord Hungerford and Whittingham.

Item, we shall have a great embassy, out of Scotland in all haste, of lords.

At your commandment, and servant,

HENRY WINDSOR.

[4th October 1461]

186.   CLEMENT PASTON TO JOHN[(1)] PASTON [J. G.]

*To his right reverend and worshipful brother, John Paston, Esquire, be this delivered in great haste.*

Brother, I recommend me to you.   After all due recommendations, etc., sir, it was told me by right a worshipful man that loveth you right well, and ye him (and ye shall know his name hereafter, but put all things out of doubt he is such a man as will not lie), on the 11th day of October the King said: 'We have sent two privy seals to Paston by two yeomen of our chamber, and he disobeyeth them; but we will send him another to-morrow, and by God's mercy, and if he come not, then he shall die for it. We will make all other men beware by him how they shall disobey our writing.[2]   A servant of ours hath made a complaint of him.   I cannot think he has informed us all truly, yet not for that, we will not suffer him to disobey our writing; but since he disobeyeth our writing, we may believe the better his guiding is as we be informed.'   And therewith he made a great avow that if ye come not at the third commandment ye should die therefor. This man that told me this is as well learned a man as any is in England; and the same 11th day of October, he advised me to send a man to you in all the haste that might be to let you have knowledge, and that ye should not let for none excuse, but that ye should make the man good cheer and come as hastily as ye might to the King, for he understandeth so much that the King will keep his promise.   Notwithstanding, by mine advice, if ye have this letter ere the messenger come to you, come to the Kingward ere ye meet with him, and when ye come ye must be sure of a great excuse.   Also, if ye do well, come right strong; for

---

[1] No. 183, page 188.

[2] Complaints had been made to the King about Paston's election to Parliament.   Edward summoned both Paston and the sheriff of Norfolk, Sir John Howard (a close relation of the Duke of Norfolk), to appear before him.   Paston delayed to obey the royal summons owing to a dispute with his co-executors Yelverton and Jenney.   Clement's letter spurred him to action; but his enemies had already prevailed, and immediately on his arrival in London he was committed to the Fleet.

Howard's wife made her boast that if any of her husband's men might come to you, there should go no penny for your life; and Howard hath with the King a great fellowship.

This letter was written the same day that the King said these words, and the same day that it was told me, and that day was the 11th of October as abovesaid. And on the next morning sent I forth a man to you with this letter, and on the same day sent the King the third privy seal to you. Also, he that told me this said that it were better for you to come up than to be fotte out of your house with strength and to abide the King's judgment therein, for he will take your contumacy to great displeasure. Also, as I understand, the Duke of Norfolk hath made a great complaint of you to the King, and my Lord of Suffolk [1] and Howard and Wingfield help well to every day and call upon the King against you. The King is at this day at Greenwich, and there will be still till the Parliament begin. Some say he will go to Walsingham, but Mr Sotehill said in the Hall in the Temple that he heard no word of any such pilgrimage. No more, etc. Written the 11th day of October at midnight.

My nephew John told me also that he supposed there were out proclamations against you, etc., the same day.

By CLEMENT PASTON,<br>your Brother.

[1461]

## 187. RICHARD CALLE TO JOHN[(1)] PASTON [J. G.]

*To my right reverend and worshipful master, my master John Paston.*

Pleaseth your mastership to wit that Mr John and I, with other more, have been at Cotton on Friday last passed; and there Jenney had done warn the court there to be the same Friday, and he was at Eye at the Sessions the Thursday before. And on the Friday, in the morning, he was coming to Cotton to hold the court there. And it fortuned we had entered the place ere he came; and he heard thereof and turned back again to Hoxne to

---

[1] John de la Pole, son and heir of William, Duke of Suffolk, who was attainted in 1450, was not restored to the dukedom until 23rd March 1463; but being in favour at court, and having married the King's sister, he was called 'my Lord of Suffolk.'

my Lord of Norwich, and there dined with him. And my Lord sent Mr Jack Coleman to Cotton Hall to speak with you. And at his coming he understood ye were not there; and if ye had, my Lord desired you to come and spoken with him, and that my Lord desired to put your matter in a treaty; insomuch that Mr John Coleman told to my master, John Paston, that divers of your enemies had laboured to my Lord to have a treaty if he could bring it about, etc. As for the tenants, they would not come at the place on to the time that I sent for them, for they say plainly they will not have ado with them; and so the court was holden in your name, and the tenants right well pleased thereof (except Thurnberne and Agas). And as for any succour, they have there right none at all. And so Mr John was there Friday all day and Saturday till noon; and then he took his horse, with thirty men with him, and rode to Jenney's place, and took there thirty-six head of neat, and brought them into Norfolk; and so was I left still at Cotton with twelve men with me, because they report, an' we abode there two days, we should be put out by the heads. And so we abode there five days and kept the place, and I walked about all the lordships and spake with all the farmers and tenants that belong to the manor to understand their disposition and to receive money of them; and I find them right well disposed to you. And because the court was warned in their name and not in yours, therefore they purvey no money; but they have promised me to pay no money to no man but to you, so that ye will save them harmless. They have appointed with me to make ready their money within a fortnight after Hallowmas, etc. I have received of the tenants that I understood owed worst will eight marks, etc. And as for Edward Dale's money, it is ready, so that your mastership will see that he be not hurt by his obligation. Furthermore, please it your mastership to send word, if they enter into the manor again, how we shall be ruled and guided. For the tenants fear them they will enter when we be gone, and then will they dis- train the tenants; for they say there that my Lord of Canterbury and other lords will release to them, notwithstanding that I have informed them otherwise. Wherefore, saving your better advice, meseemeth it were right well done that ye had a letter of my Lord of Canterbury and other, to the tenants of Cotton, that it is their will and intent that ye should have the rule and governance, and receive the money of that manor and others that were Sir John Fastolf's (on whom God have mercy); for I doubt not, an' such a letter came down to the tenants there, should no man say nay to it. Beseeching your mastership to have an answer of how we shall be guided and ruled, etc. Item, to send word how we shall do with the gear that we took out at the

White Friars, whether it shall be sent to you or not. And Jesu preserve you. Written at Norwich upon St Edward's day.

By your servant and beadsman,

RIC. CALLE.[1]

[13th October 1461]


## 188. WILLIAM NAUNTON TO JOHN[(1)] PASTON

*To my master Paston, the elder, be this letter delivered in haste.*

Right worshipful sir, I recommend me to your good mastership. The cause why I write: I let you have knowledge of the men that be in Cotton Hall, how they be strangely disposed against you; for, as I hear say, they make revel there. They melt lead and break down your bridge, and make that no man go into the place but on a ladder, and make them as strong as they can against you by the supportation of Jenney and Debenham, and his son.[2] For they say there that Jenney hath sold the livelode unto Debenham, and that his son the knight shall dwell there; and therefore they have warned a court against Monday, and now they are advised to keep it on Saturday before Monday. What they mean thereby I wot never, but as for the fellowship in the place that is there now, and have been there all this week, there is no man of substance, as we hear, and there have been but seven or eight all this week; but there will be a great fellowship this night or to-morrow upon Saturday, for then they will keep the court. And as for Edward Dale, he dare not abide well at home, they threaten him so, because he will send them no victuals. And as for myself, Edward Dale dare not let me well be there for taking in suspicion. And as for the tenants, they be well disposed, except one or two, so that ye will support them in haste, for they may not keep their cattle off the ground longer; and specially they desire to have your own presence, and they would be of great comfort.

No more I write to you, but the Holy Ghost have you in keeping. Written on the Friday after my departing.

By your servant,

WILLIAM NAUNTON.

[October 1461]

[1] It was at this juncture that Paston received the third summons to London. Yelverton and Jenney (as appears from the next two letters) did not re-enter the manor; but Jenney sold his interest therein to Gilbert Debenham, with disastrous consequences.

[2] Sir Gilbert Debenham, for whom his father intended Cotton Hall as a residence.

## 189.    MARGARET PASTON TO JOHN[1] PASTON

Right worshipful husband, I recommend me to you. Please it you to wete that I received your letter that ye sent me by John Holme on Wednesday last past, and also I received another letter on Friday at night, that ye sent me by Nicholas Newman's man; of the which letters I thank you, for I should else have thought that it had been worse with you than it hath been or shall be, by the grace of Almighty God. And yet I could not be merry since I had the last letter till this day that the mayor [1] sent to me, and sent me word that he had knowledge for very truth that ye were delivered out of the Fleet, and that Howard was committed to ward for divers great complaints that were made to the King of him. It was talked in Norwich and in divers other places in the country, on Saturday last past, that ye were committed to the Fleet; and in good faith, as I heard say, the people was right sorry thereof, both of Norwich and in the country. Ye are right much bound to thank God, and all those that love you, that ye have so great love of the people as ye have. Ye are much beholden to the mayor and to Gilbert,[2] and to divers others of the aldermen, for faithfully they owe you good will to their powers.

I have spoke with Sir Thomas Howes for such things as ye wrote to me for, and he promised me that he should labour it after your intent as fast as he could; and in good faith, as my brother and Playter can tell you, as by his saying to us, he is and will be faithful to you. And as for William Worcester, he hath been set so upon the hone,[3] what by the parson and by others, as my brother and Playter shall tell you, that they hope he will do well enough. The parson said right well and plainly to him. The parson told me that he had spoke with Sir William Chamberlain,[4] and with his wife, and he thinketh that they will do well enough after your intent, so that they be pleasantly entreated. The parson told me that he wist well that Sir William Chamberlain could do more ease in such matters as ye wrote of touching my Lord of Bedford than any man could do that liveth at this day; also he told me that he felt by them that they would owe you right good will, so that ye would owe them good will. The parson hopeth verily to make you accorded when he cometh to London.

---

[1] William Norwich, mayor of Norwich in 1461.
[2] John Gilbert was mayor in 1459 and in 1464. He died in 1472.
[3] This expression is taken from setting a razor, and means that he had been talked to not only in a smooth, but likewise in a sharp and severe manner.
[4] Sir William Chamberlain, K.G., of Gedding in Suffolk. He had served under the Regent Bedford in the French wars.

Item, my brother and Playter were with Calthorpe to inquire of the matter that ye wrote to me of; what answer he gave them they shall tell you. I sent the parson of Hellesdon [1] to Gurney [2] to speak to him of the same matter; and he saith faithfully there was no such thing desired of him, and though it had been desired, he would neither have said nor done against you. He said he had ever found you loving and faithful to him, and so he said he would be to you to his power, and desiring me that I would not think him the contrary.

As for John Gros, he is at Sloley; therefore he might not be spoke with.

I pray you that ye will send me word whether ye will that I shall remove from hence, for it beginneth to wax cold abiding here. Sir Thomas Howes and John Russe shall make an end of all things after your intent, as much as they can do therein this week, and he purposeth to come forward to you on the Monday next after St Leonard's day.

My brother and Playter should have been with you ere this time, but that they would abide till this day were past, because of the shire. I spoke to my brother William as ye bade me, and he told me, so God him help, that he hired two horses two days before that ye rode that he might have ridden forth with you; and because that ye spoke not to him to ride with you, he said that he weened ye would not have had him with you.

Thomas Fastolf's mother was here on the next day after ye were ridden, to have spoken with you for her son. She prayeth you, at the reverence of God, that ye will be his good master, and to help him in his right, that he may have home his livelode out of their hands that have it in his nonage. She saith that they would make him a year younger than he is, but she saith that he is more than twenty-one, and upon that she dare take an oath.

And the blessed Trinity have you in His keeping, and send you good speed in all your matters, and send the victory of all your enemies. Written in haste, on Soulmas day.

By yours,<br>M . P .

[2nd November 1461]

---

[1] Thomas Hert.
[2] Thomas Gurney of Norwich, died in 1471.

190. Roger Taverham to John[1] Paston

*To my reverend and most-betrusted master, John Paston, Esquire, dwelling in the Inner Temple, be this delivered.*

Right reverend and most betrusted master, I recommend me in the most lowly wise unto your good and proved mastership, and desiring many days to hear of your welfare, which I beseech God increase unto His pleasance and unto the prosperity and welfare of your person and of all yours. And I beseech you of the good continuance of your mastership at divers times before this writing showed unto me; and, sir, there is none man alive that I trust more to than I do unto you, and I am your beadsman, and so shall remain by the grace of God all the days of mine life. And, sir, I suppose I shall never see you no more, nor none of mine friends, which is to me the greatest lamentation that might come unto mine heart; for, sir, by the grace of God, I shall go to Rome and into other holy places, to spend mine days of this present life in the service of God. For I had lever live in great tribulation in the service of God in this present life, than for to follow the wretchedness of this world.

And, sir, of one thing I beseech specially your good mastership, that ye will show your good mastership unto my father in time of his need, and that ye will recommend me in the most lowly wise with all reverence unto his good fatherhood, beseeching him that he will give me every day, during the days of his life, his paternal blessing. And I have marvel, since that I have written so many letters unto him before this time, that I had never none letter again, which is to me the greatest lamentation that ever came to my heart. And now knowing that I shall never see him more, nor you, nor none other of mine friends, marvel ye not that sorrow is imprended in mine heart.

But, reverend master, mine singular trust remaineth now in your person; for, sir, an' it please you, I must needs write unto your good mastership, in the which my most trust remaineth. For, sir, an' it please you, as for mine inheritance and other things which should come to me after the death of my father, whose life God preserve to His long pleasance, knowing that I shall never come there, I had lever that by your good advice that ye would take it unto you; for I had lever that ye had it rather than any person in the world during my life, with all the profits thereof; and if that ye will make as good evidences for you in that part as ye can, and I shall seal them. And as you seemeth best, and in the most secret wise, rule you in this matter.

And, sir, I beseech you to recommend me in the most lowly

wise to mine reverend master William Lomner, saying him that
I am and shall be his perpetual beadsman; and, as ye think best,
ye may tell him of all these matters.    And, sir, I beseech you
to recommend me with all reverence unto my mistress your wife,
and to all other masters and friends there.    And, sir, that ye
will thank the bringer of this letter, which hath been in my great
tribulation my good friend.    And, sir, when ye speak with my
father, recommend me unto him with all reverence, and say
unto him I shall send him a letter in all haste possible.

And, sir, as for this matter, demean you as ye will, and I shall
do your pleasance as much as in me is.    And, reverend master,
remit me some letter by the bringer hereof of all these matters,
for he dwelleth with my lord, and he is right much betrusted, for
I know well he will give attendance unto you for to have some
letter from you; for, sir, it shall not be long ere that I go to
Rome, by the grace of God.    And as soon as I have a letter from
you at this time I shall send you another again.

No more at this time, but the Holy Trinity have you in His
blessed keeping.    Written at Sarum, the Monday after Midsummer day.    And let these matters be kept secret by your best
advice.

By your poor servant,

ROGER TAVERHAM.

[Year uncertain]

## 191.    ROGER TAVERHAM TO JOHN[1] PASTON

*To my right worshipful master, John Paston, Esquire, be this letter
delivered.*

Right worshipful master, I recommend me unto your mastership, and I thank your mastership that it pleased your mastership
to send me word again of my letter that I sent you by the bringer
hereof.    Sir, as I am informed, ye sent me word how that my
father was dead long time passed, and also ye desired to know
my title of right.    Sir, I am very heir, by the decease of my
father, to a place called Keswick, in Taverham, with all the
appurtenances; and that cometh by inheritance and descent to
me, for I am the elder and heir.    And though my Lord Cromwell [1] hath taken Thomas Taverham, my younger brother, as
ward for the same inheritance, that maketh no matter to me,
insomuch I am elder brother.    Wherefore I beseech you to send
me a letter of attorney made to you in my name in the strongest
wise that ye can, for to enter into the same livelode, and I shall

---

[1] Humphrey Bourchier, Lord Cromwell, so created in 1461.

asseal that, and then I shall do my service and fealty to the said
Lord Cromwell in all things as by the tenure of the same livelode
of old time ought to be done. And herein I know well the King
shall cause my Lord Cromwell to do me both law and right; and
also my Lord Chancellor, with other lord divers, shall do the
same. And, sir, I beseech your mastership to do and to take
possession in the said place with the appurtenances in short time,
for losing [1] of the rent this year passed.

And, sir, as for the place of Attlebridge that my mother-in-
law now dwelleth in, sir, your mastership shall right nought
attempt there now in; for my Lord of Warwick hath seen how
the same place was given me by testament, by Sir Roger Dalling
after the decease of my father, which is ready to be showed.
And thereupon my Lord of Warwick hath commanded certain
gentlemen to enter in the same place, and your mastership had
been moved therein ere this, but for cause that ye love well
Lomner, and that my mother-in-law is his sister; but I know
well it will cost £300, but that she shall be dispossessed of that
place in short time. And, master, how ye will be ruled in the
said place of Keswick, I beseech you to send me word, as my
singular trust is in you. For, an' ye would not take possession
in the said place, my Lord Wenlock would have that full fain;
for all the country knoweth that while I live I am heir and none
other. And therefore I beseech you in all haste send me word
by the bringer hereof in haste, quia mora trahit periculum.
And, sir, I would come speak with you. I am sick and may not
go; but tell the bringer hereof all your intent. For my life
during I had lever that ye had that place for one penny than
another man, though he would give me much money, for your
mastership there showed to me in my young age. And God
keep you, etc.

Your chaplain,

ROGER TAVERHAM.

[1461-6]

192.          SIR JOHN[2] HEVENINGHAM TO
                    JOHN[1] PASTON [J. G.]

*To mine worshipful cousin, John Paston the elder, Esquire, be this
letter delivered in haste.*

Right worshipful cousin, I recommend me unto you in as
heartily wise I can, desiring ever to hear of your welfare, which
I beseech our Lord Jesu to preserve to your heart's pleasure, etc.

[1] i.e. for fear of losing.

Sir, ye sent me a letter of attorney to receive and to occupy in your name the manor called Burneviles in Nacton. Sir, as for that occupation, I can little skill in, nor I will not take upon me none such occupations; wherefore I beseech you hold me excused, for it is no world for me to take such occupations. I have as much as I may to gather my own livelode, and truly, cousin, I cannot gather that well. And therefore, cousin, I pray you take it none displeasure. Sir, that I may worshipfully do for you, ye shall find me ready by the grace of Jesu, whom I heartily beseech to have you in His merciful keeping. Written at Heveningham on St Lucy's Eve.

By your cousin,
JOHN HEVENINGHAM, *Knight.*

[12th December 1461]

193.    MARGARET PASTON TO JOHN<sup>(1)</sup> PASTON

*To my right worshipful husband, John Paston.*

Right worshipful husband, I recommend me to you. Please it you to wete that mine aunt is deceased, whose soul God assoil! And if it please you to send word how ye will that we do for the livelode that she had at Walcot, whether ye will that anybody take possession there in your name or not. And if it like you to have with you my cousin William her son, I trow ye should find him a necessary man to take heed to your household, and to buy all manner of stuff needful thereto, and to see to the rule and good guiding thereof. It hath been told me before that he can good skill of such things; and if ye will that I send for him, and speak with him thereof, I shall do as ye send me word; for in faith it is time to crone your old officers for divers things, whereof I have known part by Dawbeney, and more I shall tell you when ye come home.

Also, it is thought by my cousin Elizabeth Clere and the vicar and others that be your friends, that it is right necessary for you to have Hugh Fenn to be your friend in your matters. For he is called right faithful and trusty to his friends that trust him; and it is reported here he may do much with the King and the lords, and it is said that he may do much with them that be your adversaries. And therefore, God's sake, if ye may have his good will, forsake it not. Also it is thought the more learned men ye have of your own country of your counsel, the more worshipful it is to you.

Also, if ye be at home this Christmas, it were well done ye should do purvey a garnish or twain of pewter vessel (two basins

H 752

and two ewers, and twelve candlesticks), for ye have too few of
any of these to serve this place. I am afraid to purvey much
stuff in this place till we be surer thereof. The blessed Trinity
have you in His blessed keeping. Written the Thursday next
after St Andrew.

By your

M. P.

[? 3rd December 1461]

194.          RICHARD CALLE TO JOHN[1] PASTON

*To my right reverend and most worshipful master, my master John
Paston.*

Right worshipful and my most reverend master, I recommend
me unto your good mastership. Like you to weet that on
Childermas day [1] there were much people at Norwich at the
shire, because it was noised in the shire that the under-sheriff [2]
had a writ to make a new election; wherefore the people was
grieved because they had laboured so often, saying to the sheriff [3]
that he had the writ, and plainly he should not away unto the
time the writ were read. The sheriff answered and said that he
had no writ, nor wist who had it. Hereupon the people peaced
and stilled unto the time the shire was done; and after that done,
the people called upon him, 'Kill him! head him!' And so
John Damme, with help of others, gat him out of the shire-house,
and with much labour brought him into Spurrier Row; [4] and
there the people met against him, and so they avoided him into an
house, and kept fast the door unto the time the mayor was sent
for, and the sheriff, to strengthen him and to convey him away,
or else he had been slain. Wherefore divers of the thrifty men
came to me, desiring that I should write unto your mastership
to let you have understanding of the guiding of the people, for
they be full sorry of this trouble; and that it please you to send
them your advice how they shall be guided and ruled, for they
were purposed to have gathered an hundred or two hundred of
the thriftiest men, and to have come up to the King to let the
King have understanding of their mocking. And also the people
fear them sore of you, and of Master Berney, because ye come
not home.

¹ 28th December.
² Sir Thomas Montgomery.
³ The word 'sheriff' here and in line 8 must be understood as referring
to the under-sheriff.
⁴ Now London Street.

Please you that ye remember the bill I sent you at Hallowmas for the place and lands at Beighton which Cheeseman had in his farm for five marks. There will no man have it above forty-six shillings and eight pence, for Arblaster and I have done as much thereto as we can, but we cannot go above that. And yet we cannot let it so for this year without they have it for five or six years.[1] I wrote to your mastership hereof, but I had none answer; wherefore I beseech that I may have answer of this by Twelfth,[2] for an' we have an answer of this by that time, we shall enfeoff them with all, etc.

My right worshipful and my most reverend master, Almighty Jesu preserve you, and send you the victory of your enemies, as I trust to Almighty Jesu ye shall.

Written at Norwich on St Thomas's Day after Christmas Day.

Your poor servant and beadsman,

RICHARD CALLE.

[29th December 1461]

195.   ANONYMOUS TO MARGARET PASTON

*To my right worshipful Mistress Paston.*

I recommend me to your good mistress-ship, beseeching you in the way of charity, and as I may be your beadsman and servant, that ye will let me have weting how I may be ruled against the next shire. It is said there shall be much more people than were the last; and also if I be in my Lady's place, or in any other in the town, I shall be taken out. Also, mistress, that my master Radcliff shall take all my cattle and all other poor goods that I have, and so-but I may have help of my master and of you, I am but lost. Also my servant Mariot will go from my wife, to my right great hurt. Wherefore, mistress, I beseech your help in all these, and I shall content the costs as ye shall be pleased, by the grace of God, who ever preserve you, etc.

Also, mistress, I cannot be without your continual help, but I must sell or let to farm all that I have.

Mistress, my lady sent to Cambridge for a doctor of physic; if ye will anything with him, he shall abide this day and to-morrow. He is right a cunning man and a gentle.

[? 1461]

---

[1] Farmers were then evidently aware of the value of a fixed term, and, though rents were declining, would not take a farm at a reduced rent, except under a lease for five or six years.
[2] 6th January 1462.

## 196. Elizabeth Mundeford to John[1] Paston

*To my right worshipful sir and my right good nephew, John Paston, Esquire, be this letter delivered, etc.*

Right worshipful sir and my right good nephew, I recommend me unto you with all mine heart. Please it you to understand the great necessity of my writing to you is this, that there was made an exchange by the grandsire of my husband Mundeford, on whose soul God have mercy, of the manor of Gressenhall with the ancestors of Rous for the manor of East Lexham, the which is part of my jointure; and my grandfather Mundeford recovered the said manor of East Lexham by assize [1] against the ancestors of Rous, and so made it clear. And now have Edmund Rous [2] claimed the said manor of East Lexham by the virtue of an entail, and hath taken possession and made a feoffment to my Lord of Warwick,[3] and Walter Gorge,[4] and to Curde.[5] And on Friday before St Valentine's day Walter Gorge and Curde entered and took possession for my said Lord of Warwick, and so both the foresaid manors were untailed; and at the time of the exchange made, the entails and evidence of both foresaid manors were delivered unto the parties indifferently by the advice of men learned. Wherefore I beseech you that it please you to take the great labour upon you to inform my Lord's good lordship of the truth in the form above written, and that it please you to understand whether that my Lord will abide by the feoffment made to him or not; and that it shall please my Lord that I may have right, as law require it, for I trust to God by such time as my Lord shall be informed of the truth by you, that his Lordship will not support the foresaid Rous against my right. And if I had very understanding that my Lord would take no part in the matter abovesaid, I would trust to God's mercy, and to you and other of my good friends, to have possession again in right hasty time. Beseeching you to pardon me of my simple writing, for I had no leisure. Right worshipful and my right good nephew, I beseech the Blessed Trinity have you in His gracious

[1] Assize was a writ directed to the sheriff of the county for recovery of the possession of things immovable, whereof oneself or one's ancestors had been dispossessed.

[2] Edmund Rous was second son of Henry Rous, Esq., of Dennington, in Suffolk, and ancestor of the earls of Stradbroke.

[3] Richard Neville, Earl of Warwick.

[4] Walter Gorges, Esq., married Mary, the daughter and heiress of Sir William Oldhall, and was at this time lord of the manor of Oldhall in Great Fransham; he died in 1466.

[5] John Curde was lord of the manor of Curde's Hall in Fransham.

keeping. Written at Norwich in great haste the Tuesday next after St Valentine's day.

Your own

ELIZABETH MUNDEFORD.[1]

[1461-6]


## 197. ROBERT WILLIAMSON[2] TO AGNES PASTON

*To my right reverend mistress, Agnes Paston, be this letter delivered in haste.*

Right worshipful mistress, I recommend me unto you, thanking you of the great cheer that ye made me the last time that I was with you. Mistress, in all your goods and occupations that lieth in my simple power to do in word, will, and deed, I have done my diligence and my power thereto, so I be saved before God, and have owed to your person right hearty love; for the which I am right ill acquit, an' it be as I understand it. For it is done me to wete that I am sued with more of my parishioners for a rescue-making upon the officers of the sheriff, and I take God to record that it is wrongfully done unto us. And the great fray that they made in the time of Mass, it ravished my wits and made me full heavily disposed. I pray Jesu give them grace to repent them thereof, that they that caused it may stand out of peril of soul.

Mistress, at the reverence of God, and as ever I may do service that may be pleasing unto you, send me justly word by the bringer of this bill how ye will that I be guided; for it is told me that if I be taken I may no other remedy have but straight to prison. For the which I have sold away 20s. worth of stuff; and the residue of my stuff I have put it in sure hand, for truly I will not abide the jeopardy of the suit—I have lever to go as far as my feet may bear me. Nevertheless as ye command me to do, so it be not to my great hurt, I will fulfil it. No more to you at this time, but God send you that grace that ye may come to His bliss. Written at Bromholm, in great haste.

By your

SIR[3] ROBERT WILLIAMSON.

[1460-4]

---

[1] *See* footnote 1, page 112.
[2] Vicar of Paston from 1460 until 1464.
[3] *See* footnote 1, page 44.

## 198. Margaret Paston to John[1] Paston [J. G.]

*To my right worshipful husband, John Paston, be this delivered in haste.*

Right worshipful husband, I recommend me to you. Please you to wete that I sent you a letter by my cousin Berney's man of Witchingham which was written on St Thomas's day in Christmas; and I had no tidings or letter of you since the week before Christmas, whereof I marvel sore. I fear me it is not well with you, because ye came not home or sent ere this time. I hoped verily ye should have been home by Twelfth at the furthest. I pray you heartily that ye will vouchsafe to send me word how ye do as hastily as ye may, for my heart shall never be in ease till I have tidings from you. People of this country beginneth to wax wild, and it said here that my Lord of Clarence and the Duke of Suffolk, and certain judges with them, should come down and sit on such people as be noised riotous in this country. And also it is said here, that there is returned a new rescue upon that that was done at the shire. I suppose such talking cometh of false shrews that would make a rumour in this country. The people saith here that they had lever go up whole to the King and complain of such false shrews as they have been wronged by afore, than they should be complained of without cause and be hanged at their own doors. In good faith, men fear sore here of a common rising but-if a better remedy may be had to appease the people in haste, and that there be sent such down to take a rule as the people hath a fantasy in, that will be indifferent. They love not in no wise the Duke of Suffolk nor his mother. They say that all the traitors and extortioners of this country be maintained by them and by such as they get to them with their goods, to that intent to maintain such extortion still as hath been done by such as hath had the rule under them beforetime. Men ween, an' the Duke of Suffolk come, there shall be a shrewed revel but-if there come other that be better beloved than he is here. The people feareth them much the more to be hurt, because that ye and my cousin Berney come not home; they say they wot well it is not well with you, and if it be not well with you, they say they wot well, they that will do you wrong will soon do them wrong, and that maketh them almost mad. God for His holy mercy give grace that there may be set a good rule and a sad in this country in haste, for I heard never say of so much robbery and man-slaughter in this country as is now within a little time. And as for gathering of money, I saw never a worse season; for Richard Calle saith he can get but little in substance of that is owing,

neither of your livelode nor of Fastolf's either.  And John
Paston [1] saith, they that may pay best they pay worst; they fare
as though they hoped to have a new world.  And the Blessed
Trinity have you in His keeping and send us good tidings of
you.  Yelverton is a good threadbare friend for you and for
other in this country, as it is told me.

Written in haste on the Thursday next after Twelfth.

By your

MARGARET PASTON.

[7th January 1462]

## 199.  MARGARET PASTON TO JOHN[(1)] PASTON [J. G.]

Right worshipful husband, I recommend me to you.  Please it
you to wete that Perse was delivered out of prison [2] by the
general pardon that the King hath granted, which was openly
proclaimed in the Guildhall.  Anon as he was delivered, he
came hither to me, God wot in an evil plight, and he desired me
weeping that I would be his good mistress and to be mean to you
to be his good master, and swore sore that he was never defaulty
in that ye have thought him defaulty in.  He said that if there
were any coin in the coffer that was at William Taverner's, it was
there without his knowledge; for his master would never let him
see what was in that coffer, and he told me that the keys were
sent to Thomas Holler [3] by Master John Smith.  What Holler
laid in or took out he wot not, as he sweareth.  He offered me
to be ruled as ye and I would have him, and, if I would command him, to go again to prison, whether I would to the Castle
or to the Guildhall, he would obey my commandment; and saith
that he came of his own free will without any commandment of
anyone or desire.  I said I would not send him again to prison,
so that he would abide your rule when ye came home.  And so
he is here with me, and shall be till ye send me word how ye will
that I do with him.  Wherefore I pray you that ye will let me
have knowledge in haste how ye will that I do with him.

Item, I have spoke with John Damme and Playter for the
letter testimonial, and John Damme hath promised to get it, and
Playter shall bring it to you to London.  Item, I have purveyed
you of a man that shall be here in Barsham's stead an' ye will,
the which can better cherish your wood, both in felling and
fencing thereof, than Barsham can.  And he shall make you as
many hurdles as ye need for your fold, of your own wood at

[1] The writer's eldest son.
[2] *See* Nos. 148–50, pages 152–4.
[3] He was John Berney's executor.  (*See* No. 145, page 148.)

Drayton, and shall take as little to his wages as Barsham doth;
and he is holden a true man. Item, Playter shall tell you of a
woman that complained to the Duke of Suffolk of you, and the
said Playter shall tell you of the demeaning of the sheriff for you,
and also of the demeaning of the said duke, and of other matters
the which were too long matter to put in writing. The people
of this country be right glad that the day yed with you on
Monday as it did. Ye were never so welcome into Norfolk as
ye shall be when ye come home, I trow. And the Blessed
Trinity have you in His keeping. Written in haste on Wednesday next after St Agnes the first.[1]

By your

M. P.

Item, Ric. Calle told me that he hath sent you an answer
of all errands that ye would should be done to Sir Thomas
Howes. Sir Thomas Howes came neither to me nor sent since
that he came home from London.

Will. Worcester was at me in Christmas at Hellesdon, and he
told me that he spake with you divers times at London the last
term; and he told me that he hoped that ye will be his good
master, and said he hoped ye should have none other cause but
for to be his good master. I hope, and so do my mother and my
cousin Clere, that he will do well enough, and that he be fair
with Dawbeney and Playter. Advise me let Perse go at large
and to take a promise of him to come to me among unto your
coming home, and in the meanwhile his demeaning may be
known and espied in more things.

[27th January 1462]

200.     RICHARD DOWBIGGING TO
         JOHN[1] PASTON[2] [J. G.]

*To the right reverend and worshipful sir, John Paston, sometime
Lord of Gresham, and now farmer thereof, as it is said.*

Perse of Legh came to Lynn upon Christmas Eve in the freshest
wise, and there he dined so as was. But when my Lord of
Oxford heard hereof, he with his fellowship and such as I and
other your prisoners came riding into Lynn, and even unto the
bishop's jail where the said Perse dined with other of his fellowship. My Lord pulled him out of the said jail and made to cast

---

[1] The first feast of St Agnes is on 21st January; there is a second on 28th.
(*See* vol. ii, footnote 2, page 127.)

[2] This letter is placed here for convenience, since it refers, as does the
previous number to J. Perse. Its date is uncertain.

him upon an horse, and tied an halter by his arm, and so led him forth like himself. And even forthwith the said bishop, the mayor, and other their fellowship met with my said Lord and your prisoners, and also the said Perse tied by an halter, the bishop having these words unto my Lord with his pillion in his hands: 'My Lords, this is a prisoner, ye may know by his tippet and staff. What will ye do with him?' Thereto my Lord said: 'He is my prisoner now.' Whereto the bishop said: 'I have warrant sufficient to me.' And thus they departed, the mayor and all the commonalty of Lynn keeping their silence. But when we were gone, and Perse of Legh fast in Rising Castle, then the gates of Lynn, by the bishop's commandment, were fast sperred and kept with men of arms. And then the bishop and his squires rebuked the mayor of Lynn, and said that he had shamed both him and his town for ever, with much other language, etc.

The bishop should have kept his Christmas at Gaywood, but yet he came not out of Lynn. In faith, my Lord did quit him as courageously as ever I wist man do. The bishop came to the town with sixty persons the same time, and made to sper the gates after him; but when we met, there bode not with him over twelve persons at the most, with his serjeant at arms—which serjeant was fain to lay down his mace. And so at the same gates we came in we went out, and no blood drawn, God be thanked.[1]

If ye will anything that I may do, send me word; it shall be done to my power, etc. Commend me to your mistress your wife, etc. And if ye dare jeopardize your surety of 100 marks I shall come and see you. And else have me excused, for, etc.

From your own,

JOHN DOWBIGGING.

201.     THOMAS HOWES TO JOHN[(1)] PASTON

*To my right worshipful sir and master, mine master John Paston, Esquire.*

Right worshipful sir and master, I recommend me to you. And please you that the church of Drayton is or shall be resigned in haste into the bishop's hands by Sir [2] John Bullock, desiring you heartily that ye like I may have the presentation of the next avoidance for a nephew of mine, called Sir [2] Reynold Spende-love, which I trust your mastership will agree to make in your

---

[1] Nothing more is known of the events here described.
[2] *See* footnote 1, page 44.

name and mine as was last, etc.[1]  And, sir, please you also that I have had divers communications with Worcester since Christmas.  And I feel by him utterly that he will not appoint in other form than to have the lands of Fairchilds and other lands in Drayton to the sum of ten marks of you properly, beside that that he desireth of mine master, whom God assoil; which matter I remit to your noble discretion.

And as for answer of the bills that I have, I have been so sickly since Christmas that I might not yet done them, but I shall in all haste; wherein ye may excuse you by me if ye please till the next term, at which time all shall be answered, by God's grace, who preserve you and send you the accomplishment of your desires, etc.

Item, sir, please your mastership, it was letten me wete in right secret wise that a puissance is ready to arrive in three parts of this land (by the mean of King Harry and the queen that was, and by the Duke of Somerset and others), of six-score thousand men; and their day, if wind and weather had served them, should have been here soon upon Candlemas.  At Trent, to Londonward, they should have been by Candlemas, or soon after, one part of them, and another part coming from Wales, and the third from Jersey and Guernsey.  Wherefore it is well done ye inform mine Lord Warwick, that he may speak to the King that good provision be had for withstanding their malicious purpose and evil will, which God grant we may overcome them; and so we should, I doubt not, if we were all one.  There be many meddlers, and they be best cherished which would hurt much if these come too, as God defend, etc.

                                        THOMAS HOWES.

[February 1462]


202.    MARGARET PASTON TO JOHN[(1)] PASTON

*To my right worshipful husband, John Paston, be this delivered in haste.*

Pleaseth you to wete that John Welles and his brother told me this night that the King lay at Cambridge as yesternight to Sandwich-ward, for there is great division betwixt the lords and the shipmen there, that causeth him to go thither to see a remedy therefor.

---

[1] It appears from the Institution books in the registry of the Bishops of Norwich that the living of Drayton was resigned by John Bullock, and that on 15th March 1462 John Flowerdew was presented thereto instead of Reynold Spendelove.

I thank God that John Paston yed none erst forth, for I trust to God all shall be done ere he cometh. And it is told me that Sir John Howard is like to lose his head.

If it please you to send to the said Welles, he shall send you more tidings than I may write at this time.

God have you in His keeping.

Written in haste at Thetford, at 11 of the clock in the night, the same day I departed from you.

I thank Pampyng of his good will, and them that were cause of changing of my horse; for they did me a better turn than I weened they had done, and I shall acquit them another day, an' I may.

By your
M. P.

[March 1462]

## 203.      JOHN[2] PASTON TO JOHN[1] PASTON

*To mine right reverend and worshipful father, John Paston, being in the Inner Temple.*

Right reverend and worshipful father, I recommend me unto you, beseeching you of your blessing and good fatherhood. Please it you to understand the great expense that I have daily travelling with the King, as the bearer hereof can inform you; and how long that I am like to tarry here in this country ere I may speak with you again, and how I am charged to have mine horse and harness ready, and in hasty wise. Beseeching you to consider these causes, and so to remember me that I may have such things as I may do my master service with, and pleasure; trusting in God it shall be to your worship and to mine avail. In especial, I beseech you that I may be sure where to have money somewhat before Easter, either of you or by mine uncle Clement, when need is. Of other causes the bearer hereof can inform you. No more to you at this time, but God have you in His keeping.

Written at Stamford, the 13th day of March.

By your son and servant,
JOHN PASTON, *the Older.*

[1462]

## 204.    Anonymous: Report of French Prisoners

*Memorandum.    This is the confession of sixteen Frenchmen with the master, taken at Sheringham the third week of Lent.*

Right worshipful sir, I recommend me to you, and let you wit that I have been at Sheringham and examined the Frenchmen, to the number of sixteen with the master.    And they tell that the Duke of Somerset is into Scotland; and they say the Lord Hungerford was on Monday last past afore Sheringham into Scotland-ward in a carvel of Dieppe, no great power with him, nor with the said duke neither.    And they say that the Duke of Burgundy [1] is poisoned and not like to recover.

And as for powers to be gathered against our welfare, they say there should come into the Seine 200 great forstages [2] out of Spain from the king there; [3] and 300 ships from the Duke of Brittany[4] with the navy of France, but they be not yet assembled, nor victual there purveyed, as they say, nor men.    And the King of France [5] is into Spain on pilgrimage with few horse, as they say; what the purpose is they cannot tell certain, etc.

In haste, at Norwich.

The King of France hath committed the rule of Bordeaux unto the merchants of the town, and the browd [6] that be therein to be at their wages; and like as Calais is a staple of wool here in England, so is that made staple of wine.

John Farmer, prisoner, saith, one John Giles, a clerk that was with the Earl of Oxford, which was some time in King Harry's house, was a privy secretary with the Earl of Oxford; and if any writing were made by the said earl, the said Giles knew thereof in this great matter.

[March 1462]

## 205.    James Gresham to John[(1)] Paston

*To my right singular master, J. Paston, Esquire, in haste, etc.*

After due recommendation, please it your mastership to wit Master Yelverton, justice, said in the sessions that the King should keep his Easter at Bury, and from thence come into this

---

[1] Philip the Good.    This rumour was incorrect.
[2] Large ships with forestages or forecastles (*see* footnote 1, page 131).
[3] Henry IV, King of Castile.
[4] Francis II, last Duke of Brittany, died in 1488.
[5] Lewis XI, King of France, died in 1483.
[6] This word is imperfect in the original.    It may be meant for 'troops' or 'garrison.'

country, and see such riots as have been in this country punished
in such form as happily some should hang by the neck.   And he
told what thank he had of the King at Cambridge for cause he
declared so well the charge of extortion done by sheriffs and
other officers, etc.; for the which declaration the King took him
by the hand, and said he owed him great thanks, and prayed him
so to do in this country.

In haste, at Norwich, the Wednesday next before the Annun-
ciation.

Your poor

JAMES GRESHAM.

[24th March 1462]

205.        JOHN WYKES TO JOHN⁽¹⁾ PASTON

*To my right trusty and well-beloved friend, John Paston, Esquire.*

Right worshipful and mine entirely well-beloved friend, I
recommend me unto you, heartily thanking you of your great
present of fish, and of the fellowship that my cousin your son
showed unto me at Norwich, purposing by the grace of God to
deserve it unto you in time to come, in such place as I may do
for you.   Desiring you specially, whereas a tenant of mine of
Lavenham, called John Farmer, is seized and arrested within the
town of Yarmouth, because he dwelled with the Earl of Oxford's
son, and purposed to have passed the sea without licence, and
standeth out of the conceit of much people, I would desire you
that ye would write to the bailiffs of Yarmouth to deliver the
said John Farmer to my servant John Brenerigg, bringer of this,
with an officer of the said town, to be carried unto the King's
castle of Rising at my cost, there to be examined of certain
articles which I may not disclose till I have spoken with the
King's highness; praying you to write to the said bailiffs, that
I shall be their sufficient discharge against the King.   Desiring
you to give credence to the bringer hereof, as my very trust is in
you.

Written at Lavenham, the 25th day of March.

Your true and faithful friend, having no blame for my good
will,

JOHN WYKES,
*Usher of the King's Chamber.*

[1462]

207.          JOHN RUSSE TO JOHN⁽¹⁾ PASTON

*To the right reverend and worshipful sir, my right honourable*
*master, John Paston.*

Right worshipful sir, and my right honourable master, I recommend me to you in my most humble wise. And please it your
good mastership to wete that it is said here that my Lord
Worcester is like to be Treasurer,¹ with whom I trust ye stand
right well in conceit, with which God continue. Wherefore I
beseech your mastership that if my said Lord have the said
office, that it like you to desire the nomination of one of the
offices, either of the Controller or Searchership of Yarmouth,
for a servant of yours, and I should so guide me in the office as
I trust should be most profit to my said Lord. And if your
mastership liked to get grant thereof, that then it please you to
licence one of your servants to take out the patent of the said
office; and if it cost five, or six, or eight marks, I shall truly
content it again; and yearly as long as I might have the offices,
or any of them, I shall give my master your son five marks
toward an hackney.

It should be to me right a good mean to stand as well in the
trust as in the conceit amongst merchants, with whom, and with
all men, I call myself a servant of yours, and so will do, if it
please you, which boldeth me the more to call upon your right
worshipful mastership in this matter, wherein I beseech you to
forgive me my boldness in this behalf. And if I knew that my
Lord should have the office in certain, then I would wait upon
your good mastership there to obtain the patent, if it pleased
your good mastership to get me the grant, etc.

No more unto you, my right honourable master, at this time,
but Jesu I beseech send you a good conclusion in all your
matters, and grant you ever your heart's desire.

Your continual servant and beadsman,

JOHN RUSSE.

[? April 1462]

¹ John Tiptoft, Earl of Worcester, was appointed Lord Treasurer on 14th
April 1462, which office he had before held in the late king's reign. On
the reaccession of Henry VI he was taken prisoner, unjustly accused of
cruelty, convicted, and beheaded in October 1470.

208.      JOHN[2] PASTON TO JOHN[1] PASTON

*To my right worshipful father, John Paston.*

Please you to wete that I am at Lynn, and understand by divers persons, as I am informed, that the master of Carbrooke [1] would take a rule in the *Mary Talbot* as for captain, and to give jackets of his livery to divers persons which be waged by other men, and not by him, being in the said ship.  Wherefore, inasmuch as I have but few soldiers in mine livery here to strengthen me in that which is the King's commandment, I keep me your two men Dawbeney and Calle, which I purpose shall sail with me to Yarmouth; for I have purveyed harness for them.  And ye shall well understand, by the grace of God, that the said master of Carbrooke shall have none rule in the ships, as I had purposed he should have had, because of his business, and for this is one of the special causes I keep your said men with me, beseeching you ye take it to none displeasure of their tarrying with me.  Notwithstanding, their herden at Wiggenhall shall be done this day, by the grace of God, who have you in His keeping.  Written at Lynn, the morrow after my departing from you.

Item, as for such tidings as be here Th. shall inform you.

JOHN PASTON.

[May 1462]


209.      JOHN DAWBENEY TO JOHN[1] PASTON

*To my most reverend and worshipful master, John Paston, dwelling at Hellesdon, be this delivered.*

IHS

Most reverend and worshipful master, I recommend me unto your good mastership.  Please you to have knowledge, on the Friday at afternoon next after Saint Peter, there was at the tavern in London old Debenham and young Debenham, Thomas Edmonds and I; and there the said Thomas Edmonds fell in communication with old Debenham, and said that my Lord Treasurer [2] had put him to a great charge for the victualling of

---

[1] Possibly Sir Thomas Walgrave, who, with Sir John Howard, was commissioned on 29th May 1462 to arrest the *Mary Talbot* and the *Mary Thomson*, both of Lynn, and other vessels in Norfolk, Suffolk, and Essex, for a fleet which the King was fitting out.  At Carbrooke, in Norfolk, was a commandry formerly belonging to the Knights Templars, which, like most of the possessions of that Order, when it was suppressed in Edward II's time, was given to the Knights of St John.

[2] John Tiptoft, Earl of Worcester.

*Mary Talbot* [1] saying to old Debenham that he heard say that he had a hundred bullocks to sell, the which the said Edmonds will buy, so that they may accord of the price. Then the said old Debenham answered again, and said he would, so that he might have good payment, or else the said Edmonds to be bound in an obligation to pay him at such days as they might accord. Anon upon this same language, young Debenham spake to his father: 'Sir, I pray you that ye will take avisement of this matter till to-morrow, for I trust to your good fatherhood that ye will let me have a certain of your bullocks for the victualling of the *Barge of Yarmouth*, and I shall find you sufficient surety for the payment thereof for Edmonds. I will that ye know I have been there, and spoke with the owner and with the master of the said barge, and they know my appointment.'

Then the said Edmonds answered to young Debenham, and told him that the city of Norwich and Yarmouth hath granted, and sent writing to the King and to the lords, that they will man and victual the said barge of their own costs from the time of her going out till her coming home; and thus the said Edmonds told him that my Lord Treasurer and all the lords that be at London think they do right well their devoir, and be worthy much thank of the King. 'Well,' quoth young Debenham, 'I had in commandment for to have the rule of the said barge, and I will be at Yarmouth as this day four days, and man her and bring her down to the *Giles of Hull*, for that is my ship.'

Also, he said more, without that he might have the said barge, he will not go to sea but himself and his twenty-four men. And thus, if please your mastership, he departed from the tavern; and at his departing he told the said Thomas Edmonds: 'This is Paston's labour.' Then the said Edmonds answered him again, and said plainly he was to blame for to report so of your mastership, for he knoweth verily he said untruly of you and of my master your son both, and thereon he would take an oath. And so, if it please your good mastership, let the city of Norwich and Yarmouth have knowledge of his great cracking and boasts, and let him of his purpose by the authority that they have.

Item, my master your son will have to his jackets murrey [2] and tawney, and that it please you some of my fellowship may speak to one of the drapers for to ordain it against his coming home, for I trow it shall be this day se'nnight ere he cometh home.

Item, sir, if please you, Scrope hath sent to you to London by Bingham for the money that ye know of, yet I spake not with him; but I shall tell him that I suppose ye will be here in the

---

[1] *See* No. 208, page 215.
[2] Dark red or purple and yellowish colour.

last end of the term, and I shall send your mastership word what answer I have of him.

Item, sir, if please such tidings as I hear of, I send you word. My Lord of Warwick hath been in Scotland and taken a castle of the Scots, and upon this there came the Queen of Scots [1] with other lords of her country, as ye shall hear the names, in basetry to my said Lord of Warwick, and a truce is taken betwixt this and Saint Bartholomew's day in August. This is the last tidings that I know. No more to your good mastership at this time, but Jesu have you in keeping. Written on the Saturday next after Saint Peter.

By your poor servant,

J. DAWBENEY.

[3rd July 1462]

210. RICHARD CALLE TO JOHN[(2)] PASTON

*To my master John Paston, the younger, be this delivered.*

Sir, I have received your letter, wherein I understand that my master desired that my master your brother might have the guiding and governance of the *Barge of Yarmouth*. As to that, an' men of Yarmouth had known my master's intent a fortnight ago, he had been sure of it, but now it is so that Debenham hath a commission of the King expressed only for that ship named in his commission; and he hath been here at Yarmouth, and spoken with the bailiffs and with the owners of the said ship, and taken such a direction that they may grant it no man but him. And moreover he hath indented with the owners of the ship what day it shall be ready as well victualled as manned. And also he hath brought down letters from my Lord Treasurer to all priors and gentlemen in this country to help him and assist him to victual and man the said ship; and his men is here daily, and goeth about and gathereth wheat, malt, money, and whatsoever any man will give, etc.

The Blessed Trinity preserve you. Written at Caister, the Friday next after I received your letter.

Item, it is talked here that my master your brother and Debenham were at words at London, and that Debenham should have stricken him, had not Howard been, etc., whereof I am right sorry, etc. Nevertheless I trust to God all shall be well.

Your servant,

RIC. CALLE.

[1462]

[1] Mary, daughter of Arnold, Duke of Gelders, and mother to James III, King of Scotland.

## 211.   RICHARD CALLE TO JOHN[1] PASTON

*To my master, John Paston.*

Pleaseth your mastership to wit that I was at Scole, and spake with Arblaster and John Sadler, and with other good yeomen of the country, to understand how they were guided for the victualling of the *Barge of Yarmouth*. And I understand by them that their hundred have paid; nevertheless it is but little. There was gathered in that hundred eighteen shillings and certain corn, and some other hundreds six marks and corn, and so they have paid in all the hundreds and towns here about, that is to say, East Flegg and West Flegg and up to Blofield, Tunstead, and up to Stalham, I understand by the commission that Debenham hath. It is more large than Master John's, as ye shall understand, whereof I send you a copy, which causeth me that I labour no farther therein. Notwithstanding your mastership shall have knowledge what every hundred gives, and Yarmouth both.

Written at Winterton, the morrow after I departed from your mastership.

Your poor beadsman,

RICHARD CALLE.

[1462]

## 212.   JOHN RUSSE TO JOHN[1] PASTON

*To the right worshipful my right honourable master, John Paston.*

Right worshipful sir, and my right honourable master, I recommend me to you in my most humble wise, and please your mastership to wete that here is one Thomas Chapman, an evil-disposed man alway against you, as I have informed your mastership many times, and now he hath laboured to my Lord Treasurer to supplant me,[1] and brought down writing from the King and my Lord Treasurer. But ere his writing came, Wydwell[2] found the means, by the supportation of Master Fenn, that we had a discharge for him out of the Chancery; wherefore the said Chapman proposeth to be at London in all haste, and to advertise the King and my Lord Treasurer against me, to the greatest hurt he can imagine. Wherefore I beseech your mastership, considering his evil disposition to you, and also the rather at my poor instance, that ye like that my Lord Treasurer might understand that the said Chapman is of no

---

[1] i.e. in the office which he had asked Paston to obtain for him in No. 207 (page 214), and which had evidently been granted.
[2] Bailiff of Yarmouth.

reputation, but evil disposed to bribery of strangers, and by colour of his office of supervisor of the search shall greatly hurt the port. The said Chapman's supporters is Blakeney, clerk of the signet, and Avery Cornburgh, yeoman of the King's chamber. He hath here of Avery's twenty-four tuns wine, whereof at the long way he shall make the said Avery a lewd reckoning. The said Chapman loveth not you, nor no man to you-wards, etc.

Sir, I pray God bring you once to reign among your country-men in love, and to be dreaded. The longer ye continue there the more hurt groweth to you. Men say ye will neither follow the advice of your own kindred, nor of your counsel, but con-tinue your own wilfulness, which, but grace be, shall be your destruction.

It is my part to inform your mastership as the common voice is, God better it, and grant you once heart's ease; for it is half a death to me to hear the general voice of the people, which daily increaseth, etc.

Sir, I beseech your mastership to remember my mistress for the little silver, which for certain things delivered to your use is due to me. I have need of it now. I have bought salt and other things, which hath brought me out of much silver. I would trust, and I needed to borrow £20, your mastership would ease me for a time, but this that I desire is mine own due. And Jesu grant you ever your heart's desire to your worship and profit, and preserve you, my right honourable master, from all adversity.

Written at Yarmouth, the 15th day of July. Here is a carvel of Caen, in Normandy, and he taketh Dutchmen and ransometh them grievously.

Your servant and beadsman,

JOHN RUSSE.

[? 1462]

213. THOMAS PLAYTER TO JOHN[1] PASTON

*To my right good master, John Paston the oldest, being at Hellesdon, beside Norwich, in haste.*

Please your mastership wete that Christopher Hansson is dead and buried; and as for executor or testament, he made none.

As for tidings, the Earls of Warwick, of Essex, Lord Wenlock, Bishop of Durham, and other, go into Scotland of inbassat.

And as for the siege of Calais, we hear no more thereof, blessed be God, who have you in His keeping.

Item, as for Christopher's papers that longeth to your

tenants, I have gotten them of William Worcester; and as for all the remnant of Christopher's goods, William Worcester hath the rule as him seemeth most convenient.

Your

THOMAS PLAYTER.

[July 1462]

214.    THOMAS PLAYTER TO JOHN[1] PASTON[1]

*To my master, John Paston, at Hellesdon.*

Item, please you wete of other tidings. These lords in your other letter, with Lord Hastings and others, been to Carlisle to receive in the Queen of Scots. And upon this appointment Earl Douglas[2] is commanded to come thence, and as a sorrowful and a sore rebuked man lieth in the Abbey of Saint Albans; and by the said appointment shall not be reputed, nor taken, but as an Englishman, and if he come in the danger of Scots they to slay him. Item, King Harry and his adherents in Scotland shall be delivered; and Lord Dacre of the North is won and yielded, and the said lord, Sir Richard Tunstall, and one Billingham in the said castle be taken and headed. Item, the queen and prince have been in France and have made much ways and great people to come to Scotland and there trust to have succour, and thence to come into England: what shall fall I cannot say, but I heard that these appointments were taken by the young lords of Scotland, but not by the old.

Your

PLAYTER.

Christopher died on the Saturday next before Saint Margaret[3] in the second year of Edward IV.

[July 1462]

215.    JOHN RUSSE TO JOHN[1] PASTON

*To my right honourable and worshipful master, my master Paston.*

Please it your worshipful mastership to wete, that it is informed me this day secretly, that there is directed out a commission to Master Yelverton and Master Jenney which shall to-morrow sit

---

[1] This letter was evidently written immediately after the last was dispatched.

[2] James, Earl of Douglas, who had been banished from Scotland, but was made by Edward IV a Knight of the Garter.

[3] 17th July.

by virtue of the same at Saint Olave's;[1] and the substance of gentlemen and yeomen of Lothingland be assigned to be afore the said commissioners. And it is supposed it is for my master's lands, for as the said person informed me, the said commissioners have been at Cotton, and there entered and holden a court. I cannot inform your mastership that it is thus in certain, but thus it was told me, and desired me to keep it secret; but because I conceive it is against your mastership, it is my part to give you relation thereof.

I send you a letter which cometh from Worcester[2] to my master your brother. I would ye understood the intent of it, for as for Worcester I know well he is not good.

Some men are busy to make war; for by the absenting of my master, the parson cometh not of his own motion, but I would your mastership knew by whom it is moved. I heard you never call him false priest, by my troth, nor other language that is rehearsed him; but God send a good accord, for of variance cometh great hurt often time, and I beseech Jesu send your mastership your heart's desire, and amend them that would the contrary.

Sir, yestereven a man came from London, and he saith the King came to London on Saturday, and there did make a proclamation that all men that were between sixty and sixteen should be ready to wait upon him whensoever they were called. And it is said that my Lord Warwick had sent to the King, and informed his Highness that the Lord Somerset had written to him to come to grace; but of the fleet of ships there is no tidings in certain at London on Monday last past.

Your beadsman and servant,

JOHN RUSSE.

[September 1462]

216.     JOHN RUSSE TO JOHN[(1)] PASTON

*To my right honourable and worshipful master, my master John Paston.*

Please your worshipful mastership to wete, here is a ship of Hythe, which saith that John Cole came from the west coast on Wednesday last past; and he saith that the fleet of ships of this land met with sixty sail of Spaniards, Bretons, and Frenchmen, and there took of them fifty, whereof twelve ships were as great

---

[1] St Olave's, a village in the hundred of Lothing, in Suffolk.
[2] William Worcester.

as the *Grace de Dieu*; and there is slain on this part the Lords Clinton and Dacre,[1] and many gentlemen, juve [2] and others, the number of four thousand; and the said Spaniards were purposed with merchandise into Flanders. My Lord of Warwick's ship, the *Mary Grace*, and the *Trinity*, had the greatest hurt, for they were foremost. God send grace this be true. On Thursday last past at London was no tidings in certain where the fleet was, nor what they had done, and therefore I fear the tidings the more.

Item, sir, as for tidings at London, there were arrested by the Treasurer forty sail lying in Thames, whereof many small ships; and it is said it is to carry men to Calais in all haste, for fear of the King of France for a siege. And it was told me secretly there were two hundred in Calais sworn contrary to the King's weal, and for default of their wages; and that Queen Margaret was ready at Boulogne with much silver to pay the soldiers in case they would give her entrance. Many men be greatly afraid of this matter, and so the Treasurer hath much to do for this cause.

Item, sir, as for tidings out of Ireland, there were many men at London at the fair of the countries next them of Ireland, and they say this three weeks came there neither ship nor boat out of Ireland to bring no tidings; and so it seemeth there is much to do there by the Earl of Pembroke.[3] And it is said that the King should be at London as on Saturday or Sunday last past, and men deem that he would to Calais himself; for the soldiers are so wild there, that they will not let in any man but the King or my Lord Warwick. Other tidings there were come to London, but they were not published; but John Welles shall abide a day the longer to know what they are. No more unto you, my right honourable master, at this time, but Jesu send you your heart's desire, and amend them that would the contrary.

Your beadsman and continual servant,

JOHN RUSSE.

[1462]

---

[1] John, Lord Clinton, and Richard Fynes, Lord Dacre of the South. The rumour was false: Clinton was summoned to Parliament in 1463, while Dacre died in 1481.
[2] This word is doubtful in the original.
[3] Jasper Tudor, Earl of Pembroke.

217.        JOHN[3] PASTON TO JOHN[1] PASTON

*To my right reverend and worshipful father, John Paston, be this delivered in haste.*

Right reverend and worshipful father, I recommend me unto you, beseeching you lowly of your blessing.   Please it you to have knowledge that my Lord [1] is purposed to send for my Lady, and is like to keep his Christmas here in Wales, for the King hath desired him to do the same.   Wherefore I beseech you that ye would vouchsafe to send me some money by the bearer hereof; for, in good faith, as it is not unknown to you that I had but two nobles in my purse, which that Richard Calle took me by your commandment when I departed from you out of Norwich.

The bearer hereof should buy me a gown with part of the money, if it please you to deliver him as much money as he may buy it with.   For I have but one gown at Framlingham, and another here, and that is my livery gown; and we must wear them every day for the more part, and one gown without change will soon be done.

As for tidings, my Lord of Warwick yed forwards into Scotland as on Saturday last past with twenty thousand men; and Sir William Tunstall is taken with the garrison of Bamborough and is like to be headed, and by the means of Sir Richard Tunstall [2] his own brother.

As soon as I hear any more tidings, I shall send them you by the grace of God, who have you in His keeping.   Written in haste at the castle of the Holt,[3] upon Hallowmas day.

Your son and lowly servant,

J. PASTON, *jun.*

[1st November 1462]

218.        JOHN[3] PASTON TO JOHN[2] PASTON

*To my right worshipful brother, John Paston, the elder son of John Paston, Esquire, be this delivered in haste.*

Right worshipful brother, I recommend me to you.   Please it you to wete, that as this day we had tidings here that the Scots will come into England within seven days after the writing of this letter, for to rescue these three castles, Alnwick, Dunstanborough, and Bamborough, which castles were besieged as on

¹ John Mowbray, who had succeeded his father as fourth Duke of Norfolk in 1461 at the age of seventeen.   The writer was at this time in his household.
² Sir Richard Tunstall was a partisan of Queen Margaret, while his brother William sided with Edward IV.
³ In Denbighshire.

yesterday. And at the siege of Alnwick lieth my Lord of Kent [1] and the Lord Scales; and at Dunstanborough castle lieth the Earl of Worcester and Sir Ralph Grey; and at the castle of Bamborough lieth the Lord Montague and the Lord Ogle, and other divers lords and gentlemen that I know not. And there is to them out of Newcastle ordnance enough, both for the sieges and for the field, in case that there be any field taken, as I trow there shall none be not yet, for the Scots keep no promise. My Lord of Warwick lieth at the castle of Warkworth, but three miles out of Alnwick, and he rideth daily to all these castles for to oversee the sieges; and if they want victuals, or any other thing, he is ready for to purvey it for them to his power. The King commanded my Lord of Norfolk for to conduct victuals and the ordnance out of Newcastle into Warkworth castle, to my Lord of Warwick; and so my Lord of Norfolk commanded Sir John Howard, Sir William Peche, Sir Robert Chamberlain, Ralph Asheton and me, Calthorpe, and Gorge, and others, for to go forth with the victuals and ordnance unto my Lord of Warwick; and so we were with my Lord of Warwick with the victuals and ordnance as yesterday.

The King lieth at Durham, and my Lord of Norfolk at Newcastle. We have people enough here. In case we abide here, I pray you purvey that I may have here more money by Christmas eve at the farthest, for I may get leave for to send none of my waged men home again; no man can get no leave for to go home but-if they steal away, and if they might be known they shall be sharply punished. Make as merry as ye can, for there is no jeopardy toward, not yet. An' there be any jeopardy, I shall soon send you word, by the grace of God. I wot well ye have more tidings than we have here, but these be true tidings.

Yelverton and Jenney are like for to be greatly punished, for because they came not hither to the King. They are morken well enough, and so is John Billingforth and Thomas Playter; wherefore I am right sorry. I pray you let them have weting thereof, that they may purvey their excuse in haste, so that the King may have knowledge why that they came not to him in their own persons. Let them come or send their excuse to me in writing, and I shall purvey that the King shall have knowledge of their excuse. For I am well acquainted with my Lord Hastings and my Lord Dacres, which be now greatest about the King's person; and also I am well acquainted with the younger Mortimer, Ferrers, Hawte, Harpur, Crowmer, and Bosewell, of the King's house.

I pray you let my grandam [2] and my cousin Clere [3] have

---

[1] William Neville, Lord Fauconberg, now Earl of Kent.  [2] Agnes Paston.
[3] Elizabeth, widow of Robert Clere of Ormesby.

knowledge how that I desired you to let them have knowledge of the tidings in this letter, for I promise for to send them tidings. I pray you let my mother have knowledge how that I, and my fellowship, and your servants are, at the writing of this letter, in good health, blessed be God.

I pray you let my father have knowledge of this letter, and of the other letter that I sent to my mother by Felbrigg's man; and how that I pray both him and my mother lowly of their blessings.

I pray you that you will send me some letter how ye do, and of your tidings with you, for I think that I hear no word from my mother and you.

I pray you that this bill may recommend me to my sister Margery, and to my Mistress Joan Gayne, and to all good masters and fellows within Caister.

I sent no letter to my father never since I departed from you, for I could get no man to London, and never since.

I pray you, in case ye speak with my cousin Margaret Clere, recommend me to her; and Almighty God have you in His keeping.  Written at Newcastle on Saturday next after the Conception of Our Lady.

Your

JOHN PASTON, the Youngest.

[11th December 1462]

## 219.  JOHN[1] PASTON TO MARGARET PASTON [J. G.]

I recommend me to you and have received your letter, which causeth me to write in the letter that I send to you, Dawbeney and Richard Calle, certain articles touching the rule of mine house and mine livelode, as ye shall understand when ye see them.  Also, I send you in the same letter a bill of all the malt that remained at Michaelmas.  I suppose ye have none such of it.  Nevertheless, it had been convenient it had been had amongst your servants and you.  Also, I will that ye warn both Dawbeney and Richard Calle that they disclose not what malt I have, nor what I shall sell, nor that one merchant know not what another hath, for there is great spies laid here at London for engrossers of malt to heighten the price; howbeit mine is not but of mine own growing and my tenants'.

Also I let you wete I fail money here and must needs have up money at this time for speed of my matters, so that it may come up safely when James Gresham and other attorneys come up at the beginning of this term, with whom Richard Calle may come the same time.  And peradventure some trusty carrier . . . [1]

---

[1] Gap in the manuscript.

at this time; and with him might some money come trussed in some fardel, not known to the carrier that it is no money but some other cloth or vestment of silk or thing of charge. Wherefore take advice of such as ye trust, and purvey that I may have up at this time £100 of gold after the old coinage, and £20 in groats.

Item, if I might have sure carriage, I would have hither all the gilt plate that Richard Calle laid up, he can tell where and I trow ye know also; and two pottle pots and a roasting iron of silver lieth at the same place, for it should stand me in great store if it might be done closely and surely. Item, take true men of your counsel.

Writ the morrow next after St Hilary.

Item leave a bill endorsed what ye take away if ye take any. Your own, etc.

[*Unsigned; perhaps only a draft never sent.*]

[14th January ? 1463]

220.   Margaret Paston to John[1] Paston

*To my right worshipful husband, John Paston, be this letter delivered in haste.*

Right worshipful husband, I recommend me to you. Please you to wete that I received a letter from you on the Sunday [1] next after Twelfth day, which was sent by a priest of St Gregory's parish of Norwich. And whereas ye marvelled I sent you no writings of such letters as ye sent me before, I sent you an answer of the substance of such matters as ye have written of to me before, the which he [2] told me he sent them to you to London. And as touching the errands that ye sent to me for to do to Richard Calle, I have done as ye commanded me to do, and called upon him therefore, both before your writing and since; he therefore have none excuse for default of leisure, for he hath been but right little here since ye departed hence. He is out at this time, and when he cometh home I shall make him make you a clear bill of the receipt of your livelode and Fastolf's both; and I shall send you a clear bill of my receipts, and also of my payments out thereof again. And as for such errands that should be done to Sir Thomas Howes, I have showed Richard Calle your writing, and told him your intent, as for such things as ye would he should say to him on his own head. Also I

---

[1] 9th January.
[2] Thomas Playter, who had carried her letter.

have done your errands to my mother and to my cousin Clere after your writing. Item, I have spoke to John Adam and to Playter of your intent of the last bill that ye sent me, and they say they will do after your intent as much as they may, and ye shall have an answer thereof in haste.

Item, Sir Robert Conyers dined with me this day, and showed me a letter that came from the King to him, desiring him that he should await upon his well-beloved brother the Duke of Suffolk, at Norwich, on Monday next coming, for to be at the election of knights of the shire; and he told me that every gentlemen of Norfolk and Suffolk that are of any reputation hath writing from the King in likewise as he had. I feel him by his saying that he is right well disposed to you-ward; he saith there shall no man make him to be against you in no matter. Skipworth shall tell you such tidings as beeth in this country, and of Thomas Gurney [1] and of his man. Himself [Gurney] is clerk convict, and his man is hanged; ye shall hear hereafter what they and others were purposed to have done to their master.

I thank you heartily of your writing to me before that John Paston came home,[2] for God knoweth I thought right long till I heard from you; I shall send word in writing of such tidings as we have here on Monday in haste. Dawbeney desireth to wete what time that it please you that he should come again to you.

My mother and many other folks maketh much of your son John the elder, and right glad of his coming home, and liketh right well his demeaning. Heydon's son [3] hath borne out the side stoutly here this Christmas, and when that he rideth he hath four or five men with him in a clothing; but he hath but little favour in this country but-if it be of the bishop [4] and of the prior of Norwich.[5] The said prior hath granted him the stewardship that his father had ... [6] he hath it under the convent

---

[1] The following extract from a letter written by Thomas Playter to John Paston explains the crime committed by this person and his servant (January 1463): 'Please yor maistrship wete, that as for my Lord of Norwich cosyn's deth, Thomas Gurnay's man hath confessed that he slewe hym by comāundmēt of his maistr, and confessed ovr, that ye same dager he slewe hym wyth he kest [*cast*] it in a sege, whiche is founden and taken up all to bowyd [*bent together*], for he cowde not breke it, and in prson is bothe he and his maistr.' The same letter then goes on, and says: 'Also on Thursday next aftr Cristemasse was a man slayn by whom no man woot, nor what he is that slayn, no man knowe, his face is so mangled.' 'Clerk convict' means that he had been convicted, but had claimed benefit of clergy as being able to read; the master's life was thus spared and the man was hanged.

[2] He had been leading a somewhat ineffectual life at Court.

[3] Henry, son of John Heydon, Recorder of Norwich.

[4] Walter Lyhart.

[5] John Mowth, prior from 1453 to 1471.

[6] Dots here and in the following lines indicate gaps in the manuscript.

seal, and Spilman [1] is his tutor to learn him how he should be demeaned. . . . It is said about Baconsthorpe that Harry Heydon should have said that it were well done that men of the . . . should make ready their ball bats and their clouted shoen [2] and go fetch home their knights of shire. . . . Berney; and it is promised him that he shall be met withal because of his language. . . . us a good world and a peaceable. I shall purvey for all things that ye have sent to me for, so that I ween ye shall be pleased. The Blessed Trinity have you in His keeping. Written in haste, the Wednesday next . . . Saint Agnes.

Your

MARGARET PASTON.

[19th January 1463]

## 221. RICHARD CALLE TO JOHN[(1)] PASTON [J. G.]

*To my right reverend and worshipful master, my master John Paston, in the Inner Temple at London.*

Pleaseth your good mastership to wit that there came down to the under-sheriff of Norwich a writ to attach Mr John P. the younger,[3] whereof I send you a copy closed herein; but I understand there is come another writ to the under-sheriff of Norfolk both for him and me, and for all those that be indicted. Wherefore I purpose me to ride to Honing to the sheriff this day, to understand how he is disposed, and to desire him to show favour to your poor tenants; and as I feel him disposed I shall send your mastership answer.

And as for tidings here in this country, we have none but there be many Frenchmen upon the sea and do much answer upon the coasts. Mr Yelverton knew of the coming up of the *teste* within two days after they were gone, etc. My right reverend and worshipful master, the Blessed Trinity preserve and keep you farther in all your matters.

Sir William Willoughby was at Rising Castle, and yesterday he came home again. One Tenthale hath entered into a part of Felbrigg livelode, and a court holden, and the tenants returned. Item, as for the court that Debenham should hold at Calcot, we hear not of it.

Your poor servant and beadsman,

R. C.

[1463]

---

[1] Henry Spilman, afterwards Recorder of Norwich.
[2] Shoes shod with thin plates of iron.
[3] This copy is preserved. It charges John Paston, junior, with certain felonies and transgressions committed in Suffolk, possibly in connection with events described in No. 187, page 193.

222. MARGARET PASTON TO JOHN[1] PASTON

*To my right worshipful master, John Paston, in haste.*

Right worshipful husband, I recommend me to you, desiring heartily to hear of your welfare, praying you to wete that I have spoken with Strange's wife of the matter that ye spoke to me of. And she saith plainly to me, by her faith, that she knew never none such, nor never heard of none such, and told to me in like wise as she had said to James Gloys. And she said to me, if she could inquire of any other that she thought should have knowledge of any such, she should wete of them and let me have knowledge thereof; and if ye suppose that any other be in this country that ye think should have knowledge of this foresaid matter, if ye will send me word thereof, I shall do my part therein.

Also, I have been at Swainsthorpe and spoken with Coket; and he saith that he will do like as ye bade me that I should say to him for to do. And I have spoken with the sexton,[1] and said to him as ye bade me that I should do; and he asked me right faithfully how ye sped in your matters.

I told him that ye had fair behests, and I said I hoped that ye should do right well therein; and he said he supposed that D.[2] would do for you, but he said he was no hasty labourer in none matter. He said, by his faith, he wist where a man was that laboured to him for a matter right a long time, and always he behested that he would labour it effectually, but while he sued to him he could never have remedy of his matter. And then when he thought that he should no remedy have to sue to him, he spake with Fynes,[3] that is now Speaker of the Parliament, and prayed him that he would do for him in his matter, and gave him a reward; and within right short time after his matter was sped. And the said sexton and other folks that be your right well-willers have counselled me that I should counsel you to make other means than ye have made to other folks, that would speed your matters better than they have done that ye have spoken to thereof before this time. Sundry folks have said to me that they think verily but-if ye have my Lord of Suffolk's good lordship, while the world is as it is, ye can never live in

---

[1] i.e. the sacristan of Norwich priory.

[2] Perhaps John Damme.

[3] No Speaker of this name is met with during this period. A new Parliament met on 29th April 1463, and on the following day the Commons elected John Say as their Speaker. Margaret Paston seems to have confused his name with the family name of William Fiennes, Lord Say. There is no evidence of any relationship between these two men.

peace without ye have his good lordship. Therefore I pray that with all mine heart that ye will do your part to have his good lordship and his love in ease of all the matters that ye have to do, and in easing of mine heart also; for by my troth I am afraid else, both of these matters the which ye have in hand now, and of other that be not done to yet, but-if he will do for you and be your good lord. I pray you heartily send me word how ye do, and how ye speed in your matters. And I pray you as for such things as James hath a bill of, that I may have them as hastily as ye may; and that ye will vouchsafe to buy a piece of black buckram for to line with a gown for me. I should buy me a murrey gown to go in this summer, and lay in the collar the satin that ye gave me for an hood; and I can get none good buckram in this town to line it with. The Holy Trinity have you in His keeping, and send you health and good speed in all your matters.

Written at Norwich, on the Friday next after Crouchmas day.[1]

Yours,

Margaret Paston.

[6th May 1463]

223. James Gresham to Margaret Paston

*To my right worshipful mistress, my mistress Margaret Paston, at Caister.*

Please it your good mistress-ship to wete that a *fieri facias* [2] is come out of the Exchequer for Hugh Fenn to the sheriff of Norfolk to make levy of two hundred marks of the proper goods and chattels of my master, as executor of Sir John Fastolf; of which *fieri facias* we sent my master word, which sent us word again by Berney that we should let the sheriff understand that my master never took upon him as executor, and so for that cause that writ was no warrant to take my master's goods; and also that my master made a deed of gift of all his goods and chattels to Master Prouet and Clement Paston and other, so that my master hath no goods whereof he should make levy of the fore-said sum; and if the sheriff would not take this for none answer, that then my master would he should be letted in Master Prouet's and Clement Paston's name. Nevertheless we spake with the sheriff this day, and let him understand the causes aforesaid; and he agreed, so that he might have surety to save

---

[1] Crouchmas day, the feast of the Invention of the Holy Cross, falls on 3rd May.

[2] A writ directed to the sheriff, commanding him to levy the debt or damages against the unsuccessful party in an action for debt or damages.

him harmless, to make such return as my master of his counsel could devise. And because my master wrote by Berney that he would not find the sheriff no surety, we would not appoint with him in that wise. And so we took advice of Thomas Green; and because the under-sheriff shall be on Monday at Heigham, by Bastwick Bridge end, he and we thought that it was best that Master Prouet should meet with the sheriff there, and require and charge him that by colour of the foresaid *fieri facias* that he make no levy of any goods and chattels of the said Prouet's and Clement Paston's against the said John Paston's, letting him wete that such goods as the said Paston had be now the said Prouet's and Clement Paston's by virtue of a deed of gift made to them almost two years ago; and if the sheriff will be busy after that to take any chattel, that he be letted in Master Prouet's name, and Clement Paston's, by Dawbeney and other; which business of the sheriff shall be on Tuesday or Wednesday, and, as we understand, at Hellesdon. Wherefore ye must send thither Dawbeney with Peacock, and they may get them there more fellowship by the advice of master Sir John Paston.[1]

JAMES GRESHAM.

[1463]


## 224. THE DUKE OF NORFOLK TO JOHN[(1)] PASTON

*To our right trusty and entirely well-beloved servant, John Paston, the elder.*

### THE DUKE OF NORFOLK

Right trusty and entirely well-beloved servant, we greet you heartily well, and specially praying you that ye will be with us at Framlingham on Sunday next coming, that we may commune with you there, and have your sad advice in such matters as concerneth greatly to our weal, which shall be ministered unto you at your coming.

Praying you that ye fail not hereof, as our special trust is in you; and our Lord preserve you in His keeping.

Written at Framlingham, the 31st day of August.

NORFF.[2]

[1463]

---

[1] Paston's eldest son appears to have been knighted in the course of 1463.
[2] Paston, whose younger son John was a member of the duke's household, was one of Norfolk's confidential advisers.

## 225. The Abbot of Langley to Sir John Paston[1]

*To the right worshipful Sir John Paston, knight, be this delivered.*

Right worshipful sir, and tenderly beloved in our Lord God, I commend me to you, sending you knowing that I did your errand to my brother the parson of Blofield [2] on Wednesday was se'nnight, after the understanding that I had of you and from you by this bringer; which man I felt right well and favourably disposed to you-ward, and more favourable will be than to any other gentleman living, the will of the dead performed, and his conscience saved; and more things said favourably for you, which I entitled in a scroll to have certified to your servant Calle, if he had come as ye sent me word he should have done, and should, as ye behested me, have brought me our farm for Hellesdon, which not done, causeth me to write, praying your gentleness that I send no more therefore, for it is unpaid for the year afore the Hallowmas that my master Fastolf died, and for the same year that he died in, and since for two years, and five shillings unpaid of a year, and come Michaelmas next shall be another year unpaid. Thus is four years unpaid and five shillings, and at Michaelmas next shall be five years and five shillings.

This thus kept from Holy Church, that is Holy Church's good, may not be without great peril of soul; where the peril is God knoweth, I pray God amend it, and give them grace that have His goods so to dispose them, that they and the dead both may be out of peril. And the Trinity have you in His merciful keeping. Written at Langley, on Sunday at even late, next after Saint John's day Decollation.[3]

By your well-willing,

Abbot of Langley.

[4th September 1463]

## 226. R.C.V.C. to John[(1)] Paston

*To my worshipful master, Master Paston, the eldest.*

Right worshipful master, I recommend me unto your mastership. And of one matter, at reverence of God, take heed, for in truth I hear much talking thereof, and that is both in Norfolk, Suffolk, and Norwich among all men of worship, as well that love you as other; and that is of my master your son, Sir John, because

[1] John[(2)] Paston will be described henceforward in the letter-headings as Sir John Paston.
[2] Thomas Howes.
[3] The Decollation of St John the Baptist falls on 29th August.

he is so at home, and none other wise set for.[1]   Some say that
ye and he both stand out of the King's good grace, and some say
that ye keep him at home for niggard cheap, and will nothing
ware upon him, and so each man say his advice as it please him
to talk.   And I have inquired, and said the most cause is in part
for cause ye are so much out, that he is the rather at home for the
safeguard of the coasts.   But at the reverence of God, eschewing
of common language, see that he may worshipfully be set for
either in the King's service or in marriage; for as for touching
the Lady Chamberlain [2] that matter is done, for I spake with the
parson thereof, and I heard by him that that matter will not
proceed.

No more, but God speed you as well in all matters as I would
ye should do, I beseech you that this letter be kept secret.

By your beadsman,

R.C.V.C.

[? 1463]

## 227.   MARGARET PASTON TO JOHN[(1)] PASTON

*To my right worshipful husband, John Paston, be this letter
delivered in haste.*

Right worshipful husband, I recommend me to you.   Please
you to wete that I was at Norwich this week, to purvey such
things as needeth me against this winter; and I was at my
mother's, and while I was there, there came in one Wrothe, a
kinsman of Elizabeth Clere's, and he saw your daughter, and
praised her to my mother, and said that she was a goodly young
woman.   And my mother prayed him for to get for her one
good marriage if he knew any; and he said he knew one should
be of a 300 marks by year, the which is Sir John Cley's son, that
is chamberlain with my Lady of York,[3] and he is of age of

---

[1] It appears that Sir John Paston had not returned to Court since Margaret
wrote to her husband on 19th January (No. 220, page 226).

[2] Anne, daughter and heiress of Sir Robert Herling, Kt, by Jane,
daughter and heiress of John Gonvile, Esq.   She married first Sir William
Chamberlain, K.G., who died in 1462.   She was at this time his widow,
and inherited from her father a very considerable fortune.   She afterwards
married Sir Robert Wingfield; and after his decease she became the wife of
John, Lord Scrope, of Bolton.   As Lady Scrope she founded and endowed
a fellowship in the college of Gonvile and Caius at Cambridge, originally
founded by one of her ancestors.   She was born in 1426, and was alive in
1502.   At the time this letter was written she must have been nearly forty
years old, while Sir John Paston could not have been much above twenty.

[3] Cecily, Duchess of York, widow of Richard Plantagenet, Duke of York,
and mother of Edward IV.

eighteen year old. If ye think it be for to be spoken of, my
mother thinketh that it should be got for less money now in this
world than it should be hereafter, either that one, or some other
good marriage.

Item, I spake with Master John Estgate for Pykering's matter
after your intent of the matter of the letter that ye sent home;
and he said to me he should write to you how he had done
therein, and so he sent you a letter, the which was sent you by
John Wodehouse's [1] man with other letters.

As for answer of other matters, Dawbeney telleth me he wrote
to you. I beseech Almighty God have you in His keeping.
Written at Caister, the Sunday next after St Martin.

By your

M. PASTON.

[13th November 1463]


228.  MARGARET PASTON TO SIR JOHN PASTON

*To my well-beloved son, Sir John Paston, be this delivered in haste.*

I greet you well, and send you God's blessing and mine, letting
you wete that I have received a letter from you, the which ye
delivered to Master Roger at Lynn, whereby I conceive that ye
think ye did not well that ye departed hence without my knowledge.[2] Wherefore I let you wete I was right evil paid with
you. Your father thought, and thinketh yet, that I was assented
to your departing, and that hath caused me to have great
heaviness. I hope he will be your good father hereafter, if ye
demean you well and do as ye ought to do to him; and I charge
you upon my blessing that in anything touching your father that
should be his worship, profit, or avail, that ye do your devoir and
diligent labour to the furtherance therein, as ye will have my
good will, and that shall cause your father to be better father to
you.

It was told me ye sent him a letter to London. What the
intent thereof was I wot not, but though he take it but lightly,
I would ye should not spare to write to him again as lowly as ye
can beseeching him to be your good father; and send him such
tidings as be in the country there ye beeth in, and that ye ware
of your expense better and ye have been before this time, and be
your own purse-bearer. I trow ye shall find it most profitable
to you.

[1] John Wodehouse, Esq., of Kimberley; he died in 1465, and was buried
in the chancel of the church there.
[2] Sir John had evidently tired of home life. It does not appear where he
was at this date.

I would ye should send me word how ye do, and how ye have shifted for yourself since ye departed hence, by some trusty man, and that your father have no knowledge thereof. I durst not let him know of the last letter that ye wrote to me, because he was so sore displeased with me at that time.

Item, I would ye should speak with Wykes, and know his disposition to Jane Walsham. She hath said since he departed hence, but she might have him she would never be married; her heart is sore set on him. She told me that he said to her that there was no woman in the world he loved so well. I would not he should jape her, for she meaneth good faith; and if he will not have her, let me wete in haste, for I shall purvey for her in other wise.

As for your harness and gear that ye left here, it is in Dawbeney's keeping; it was never removed since your departing, because that he had not the keys. I trow it shall appeyr but-if it be taken heed at betimes. Your father knoweth not where it is.

I sent your grey horse to Ruston to the farrier, and he saith he shall never be nought to ride, neither right good to plough nor to cart; he saith he was splayed, and his shoulder rent from the body. I wot not what to do with him.

Your grandam would fain hear some tidings from you. It were well done that ye sent a letter to her how ye do as hastily as ye may. And God have you in His keeping, and make you a good man, and give you grace to do well as I would ye should do.

Written at Caister, the Tuesday next before Saint Edmund the King.

Your mother,

M. PASTON.

I would ye should make much of the parson of Filby, the bearer hereof, and make him good cheer if ye may.

[15th November 1463]

## 229. MARGARET PASTON TO JOHN[1] PASTON [J. G.]

*To my right worshipful husband, John Paston, be this letter delivered in haste.*

Right worshipful husband, I recommend me to you. Pleaseth you to wete that John Geney was here with me this day, and told me that ye desired that I should do make a ditch at Hellesdon; and the season is not for to do make no new ditches, nor to repair none old till it be after Christmas, as it is told me, and so I sent you word in a letter more than a month ago. I wot not whether ye had the letter or not, for I had none answer thereof from you. Joan Dyngane recommendeth her to you, and prayeth you for God's sake that ye will vouchsafe to speak to Hugh Fenn for her. For it is so that certain livelode which her husband had in Engham was cast in the King's hand in her husband's life, and, as she understandeth, it was done in his father's life; of the which her husband spoke to Hugh Fenn thereof in his life to help that he might be discharged thereof. And Hugh Fenn promised him verily that he had made an end therein and discharged him, and that he should never be hurt nor troubled therefor; and now the last week Barnard, the under-sheriff, sent down a warrant to seize the land for the King, and so, but-if he have twenty shillings for a fine within short time, he will not suffer her to have the avail of the lands. Wherefore she prayeth you, for God's sake, that ye will purvey a means that Hugh Fenn may save her harmless, inasmuch as he promised her husband to purvey therefor in his life; and if it please not you to speak to him thereof, that it please you to do John Paston or Thomas Playter or some other, that ye think that can understand the matter, for to speak to the said Hugh Fenn thereof in her name, and to search the King's books therefor, if ye think that it be for to do, and she will bear the cost thereof. As for the matter that ye would I should speak to William Worcester of touching the false forged evidence,[1] I cannot speak with him yet; his wife saith alway that he is out when that I send for him. Your farmer at Swainsthorpe hath found surety for your duty, as Richard Calle telleth me, so that ye shall be pleased when ye come home. And the Blessed Trinity have you in His keeping. Written in haste on the Monday next after St Andrew. By your,

M. P.

[December 1462-3]

230. HENRY BERRY TO JOHN[(1)] PASTON[2]

*To my right worshipful cousin, John Paston, Esquire, be this letter delivered.*

Right worshipful and reverend cousin, I recommend me unto you with all mine heart as your faithful kinsman and orator, desiring to hear of the good prosperity and welfare of your worshipful mother my lady and cousin, with your wife, Sir John Paston, your brethren William and Clement, with all your sons and daughters, to whom I beseech you heartily that I may be

---

[1] This probably refers to the dispute over Sir John Fastolf's will.
[2] This letter refers to the state of the monastery of St Augustine, in Canterbury. Henry Berry was a religious there, and a relation of Agnes Paston.

recommended. God of His high mercy preserve you all unto His mercy and grace, and save you from all adversity.

Worshipful cousin, my special writing and heart's desire before rehearsed, nature naturally so me compelleth,

What though I be put far out of conceit and sight,
I have you all in remembrance both day and night;

beseeching you, gentle cousin, to tender my writing. I take God to my witness I would as fain do that might be unto your honour, worship, and profit as any earthly man can think.

Wherefore, now late died the abbot [1] of our monastery, and left us in great debt; the bringer hereof is my special friend. The oldest brother in our place never heard nor saw our church in that misery that is now; we have cast the perils amongst us, and there is none other help, but every brother that hath any worshipful kin or friends, every man to do his part to the welfare and succour and relief of our monastery.

Therefore, worshipful cousin, I, a brother of that worshipful monastery wherein begun the faith of all this land, meekly beseecheth you in the reverence of Almighty God to render help, and succour us in our great necessity; for in London lieth to wed many rich jewels of ours, with other great debts, which my brother will inform you of.

Pleaseth your goodness, for God's sake, and all the saints of heaven, and at my simple request, to have compassion upon us, ye having due surety both in obligations and pledges.

In the reverence of Almighty God, do your alms and charity; it shall cause you to be prayed for, and all your kin, as long as the church standeth; and by this means I trust to Almighty God to see my cousin William, or Clement, to be steward of our lands, and so to have an interest in Kent, to the worship of God and you all, which ever have you in His keeping. Amen.

Written at Canterbury in haste the 28th day of January.

Also I beseech you, show the bringer of this letter some humanity and worship, that when he cometh home he may report as he findeth.

This is the cause every while they put my kin in my beard, saying I am come of lords, knights, and ladies. I would they were in your danger 1,000 marks, that they might know you, etc. [2]

By your cousin and beadsman,

HENRY BERRY.

[1464]

---

[1] James Sevenoke.
[2] This last paragraph is crossed out in the original manuscript.

231.    JOHN[3] PASTON TO JOHN[1] PASTON[1]

*To my right reverend and worshipful father, John Paston, dwelling in Caister, be this delivered.*

Right reverend and worshipful father, I recommend me unto you, beseeching you lowly of your blessing, desiring to hear of your welfare and prosperity, the which I pray God preserve unto His pleasance, and to your heart's desire; beseeching you to have me excused that ye had no writing from me since that I departed from you. For so God me help, I sent you a letter to London anon after Candlemas, by a man of my Lord's; and he forgot to deliver it to you, and so he brought to me the letter again, and since that time I could get no messenger till now.

As for tidings, such as we have here I send you.

My Lord and my Lady[2] are in good health, blessed be God, and my Lord hath great labour and cost here in Wales for to take divers gentlemen here which were consenting and helping unto the Duke of Somerset's going; and they were appealed of other certain points of treason, and this matter. And because the King sent my Lord word to keep this country, is cause that my Lord tarrieth here thus long. And now the King hath given my Lord power whether he will do execution upon these gentlemen or pardon them, whether that him list; and as far forth as I can understand yet, they shall have grace. And as soon as these men be come in, my Lord is purposed to come to London, which I suppose shall be within this fortnight. The men's names that be impeached are these: John Hanmer and William his son, Roger Puleston, and Edward of Madoc; these be men of worship that shall come in.

The commons in Lancashire and Cheshire were up to the number of 10,000 or more, but now they be down again; and one or two of them was headed in Chester as on Saturday last past.

Thomas Daniel[3] is here in Cheshire, but I wot not in what place; he hath sent three or four letters to Sir John Howard since my Lord came hither.

And other tidings have we none here, but that I suppose ye

[1] In November 1462 the Duke of Norfolk was at Holt in Denbighshire, where he was proposing to spend Christmas (No. 217, page 223). Early in December, he was summoned by the King to serve against the Scots (No. 218, page 223), and John Paston, the younger son, returned home for a while. The duke was at Framlingham in August 1463 (No. 224, page 231), but he had returned to Holt before March 1464, and young Paston had rejoined his household there, as appears from this letter.
[2] The Duke and Duchess of Norfolk.
[3] He had a reversionary grant of the constableship of Rising Castle in 1448. He married Margaret, daughter of Sir Robert Howard, and sister of Sir John, afterwards Duke of Norfolk.

have heard before. I suppose verily that it shall be so nigh Easter [1] ere ever my Lord come to London, that I shall not mowe come home to you before Easter; wherefore I beseech you that ye will vouchsafe that one of your men may send a bill to mine uncle Clement, or to some other man, who that ye will, in your name, that they may deliver me the money that I am behind of this quarter since Christmas, and for the next quarter, in part of that sum that it pleased you to grant me by the year. For by my troth, the fellowship have not so much money as we weened to have had by right much; for my Lord hath had great costs since he came hither.

Wherefore I beseech you that I may have this money at Easter, for I have borrowed money that I must pay again after Easter.

And I pray to Almighty God have you in keeping.

Written in the castle of the Holt, in Wales, the first day of March.

Your son and lowly servant,

JOHN PASTON, the Youngest.

[1464]

## 232. CLEMENT PASTON TO JOHN[1] PASTON [J. G.][2]

*To my right worshipful brother, John Paston, Esquire.*

Right worshipful brother, I recommend me to you. After all due recommendations, etc., please it you to wete that after that I heard say that the parson of Blofield [3] was come to town, I went to him to his inn; and he bade the messenger say that he was not within, and I bade him say again that I came thither to him for his own worship and avail and that I was sorry that I came so far for him. And after that he sent for me, and he could not find me, and I heard say thereof. And then I wrote a letter, reciting how he was sworn yesterday for to say the truth of all manner of matters concerning Sir John Fastolf, advised him to remember what his witness had said for his sake, and what shame it should be to him to say the contrary; and also, if he said the contrary, ye would hereafter prove the truth and contrary to his saying, and prove him in a perjury. And also I bade him remember

---

[1] In 1464 Easter Sunday fell on 1st April.

[2] This letter was written in April 1464, when witnesses began to be examined concerning Fastolf's will. These examinations were taken at intervals during the years 1464, 1465, and 1466, and the suit was not terminated when John Paston died.

[3] Thomas Howes, who had disagreed with John Paston about the executorship of Sir John Fastolf's will.

with what manner of men he dealt with, and I rehearsed how untruly they had done. And notwithstanding this, after I met in the street and spake with him, and I found him passing strangely disposed and sore moved with conscience that ye should have the land and found the college but with an hundred marks, notwithstanding he might find in his conscience by the will that the college should be founded in another place but with an hundred marks, and the remnant of the livelode sold so that he might purvey the money. So I felt by him that all his strangeness from you is for he deemeth that ye would part from nothing; and I told him the contrary thereof to be true, as this day he is examined upon a book to say the truth of all things as the judge will ask him, for the judge's information; which I trow will not be good. Also they have put in *testes* against you threescore or fourscore men. Master Robert Kent would say that ye should get you two licences of the prior's of your witness, Master Clement and the monk, with an ante-date bearing before the coming up; for that must ye needs have. Also he would say that ye should come to this town. Methought by Sir Thomas that they have answered in manner that ye shall have no licence for your foundation. An' they be about to get a licence to found the college in another place, methinketh that would hurt. Their colour is for cause ye can get no licence to found it at Caister; wherefore though your will were true, they might lawfully found it in another place. My Lord Chancellor [1] is gone to York and will not be here of all this term. Written on Wednesday next before St George.

The King hath been in Kent, and there be indicted many for Isley's death; and he will come to town this day again and he will not tarry here but forth to York straight.

By

CLEMENT PASTON.

[18th April 1464]

233. MARGARET PASTON TO JOHN[(1)] PASTON

*To mine right worshipful husband, John Paston, be this delivered in haste.*

Right worshipful husband, recommend me unto you. Pleaseth you to wete that I sent yesterday Loveday to Norwich to speak with the vicar of Dereham [2] for the matter between Master Constantine and him; and he saith that as for that matter,

[1] George Neville, Bishop of Exeter, afterwards Archbishop of York.
[2] Constantine Dalby was instituted to the vicarage of East Dereham in 1451, and was succeeded in 1458 by Robert Sheringham.

Master Constantine sued him for faith and troth breaking, and he sued Master Constantine in the temporal court upon an obligation of £10. And there was made an appointment between them by the advice of both their counsels, before Master Robert Popy, that each of them should release other; and so they did, and the suits were withdrawn on both parties, and each of them acquittanced other. And as for any copy of the plea, he had never none; nor he nor Master John Estgate, that was his attorney, remembereth not that it was registered. And Master John Estgate saith, if it should be searched in the register it would take a fortnight's work, and yet peradventure never be the nearer.

Sir [1] Thomas Howes hath been right busy this week at Blofield, in writing and looking up of gear; and John Russe hath been with him there the most part of all this week, and this day was Robert Lynne there with him. What they have done I wot not, but I shall wete if I may.

It was told me that Sir Thomas desired of John Russe to make him a new inventory of Sir John Fastolf's goods. John Russe might not be spoken with yet for the letter that he should have written, which ye sent me word of.

Item, it is told that the Duke of Suffolk is come home, and either he is dead,[2] or else right sick, and not like to escape. And Sir John Howard is come home; and it is said that the Lord Scales and he have a commission [3] to inquire why they of this country that were sent for came not hastilier up after they were sent for. It is reported that the King is greatly displeased therewith.

At the reverence of God, arm yourself as mightily ye can against your enemies, for I know verily that they will do against you as mightily as they can with all their power.

It is told me that Sir Thomas shall come up in haste, and other, such as he can make for his party.

Also, for God's sake, beware what medicines ye take of any physicians of London; I shall never trust to them, because of your father and mine uncle, whose souls God assoil!

The Blessed Trinity have you in His keeping, and send you health and good speed in all your matters. Written in haste, on the Friday next before St Barnabas,

By yours,

M. P.

All the gentlemen of this country that went up to the King

---

[1] *See* footnote 1, page 44.

[2] John, Duke of Suffolk, did not die till 1491.

[3] This refers to a proclamation dated 11th May 1464, by which all men between the ages of sixty and sixteen were ordered to attend the King.

are countermanded, and are come home again. It is told me that Rous of Suffolk is dead.[1] If John Gayn might have any release of his son, if it might do him ease, it were a good turn for him.

[8th June 1464]

## 234. RICHARD CALLE TO JOHN[(1)] PASTON [J. G.][2]

*To my right worshipful my master, John Paston, be this delivered in haste.*

Pleaseth it your good mastership to wit that I have been with my Master Calthorpe [3] for the matter ye wrote to him for, wherein I have found him right well disposed and favourably. Nevertheless, he told me that William Jenney hath been his good friend and have been of his counsel this two year in all his matters touching the law, but he said lever he had lose the lesser friend than the great friend; and so he hath granted favour according to your desire, and wrote a letter to the under-sheriff of Norfolk that he should take surety sufficient to save him harmless, and that done, to write a letter to the under-sheriff of Suffolk and let him wit that he hath taken surety that ye shall appear in the *crastino Animarum* [4] upon the exigents returnable, or else to bring a *supersedeas* lawful before that day, charging him that he do cease the calling of the writs, and to return that ye appeared the first day. Which surety is taken, and a letter written to the under-sheriff of Suffolk according hereto.

Item, as for Sir Thomas Howes, he lieth most at Norwich. I can think he come not up to London till Michaelmas.

Item, I rode over to Titchwell when that I was at Master Calthorpe's, for to have money of the farmers; and Yelverton and Sir Thomas hath sent to them that they shall pay to you no more money, for that they had payed to you they should pay it again to them. Wherefore I went for to distrain them; and so they said that I might not distrain them, for I came before the day, for their day is at midsummer. Nevertheless I would let, for that Simon Miller and other promised to Mr William Cotyng and to me that I should have the money after midsummer, so

¹ Reginald Rous, Esq., of Denington in Suffolk, ancestor of the earls of Stradbroke.
² This letter refers to a suit brought by Jenney against Paston in 1464 and arising out of the dispute as to Fastolf's will. Paston, relying on the influence of his friends, failed to appear either in person or by counsel at four several county courts. Calthorpe did not fulfil the promise mentioned in this letter; Paston was outlawed in the following September, and committed to the Fleet prison on 3rd November.
³ William Calthorpe, sheriff of Norfolk and Suffolk.
⁴ The day after All Souls' day, i.e. 3rd November.

that I brought with me a quittance of such money as ye have received of them, or else a general quittance; and the one I purposed to do in haste by the advice of the said Master W. Cotyng. For, an' I turned, I can think it should hurt. I am purposed to let it in your name to other folks or to them again, and surety found to you, etc. And Almighty God preserve and keep you. Written at Norwich on St Peter's even.

Your poor servant and beadsman,

RIC. CALLE.

[28th June 1464]

## 235. EDWARD IV: THE FOUNDATION OF CAISTER COLLEGE[1]

*Appointment of the King for the foundation of a college at Caister, etc.*

The King, for the sum of 300 marks of lawful money of England, or of silver plate to the value thereof, granteth to John Paston the elder, Esquire, to have licence lawfully made, to make and found a college of seven priests, and seven poor folk at Caister, in Flegg in Norfolk, for the soul of Sir John Fastolf, knight; they to be endued with certain rent, and otherwise after the intent and effect as is specified in a bill thereof signed by the King; and that he shall show his good grace, favour, and assistance to have the said foundation enacted and authorized in the Parliament next holden, and discharge the said John Paston and the said priests of any other fine or fee to be made in the Chancery for the said foundation; and that the King shall sign and grant warrants for said licence, and show his good grace and favour in the expedition thereof, what time he be sued to therefore by the said John Paston.

Also, the King granteth to be good and favourable lord to the said John Paston, and in especial in all things touching the execution of the will of the said Sir John Fastolf; and also to be good and favourable lord to the said John Paston in supporting and helping him, in that the King's highness may lawfully do, in such matters as are in debate atwixt the said John Paston and

---

[1] At the time when he should have appeared in the county court (*see* footnote 2, page 242), John Paston followed the King to Marlborough and obtained from him this licence for the erection of the college at Caister provided for in Fastolf's will. Along with this the King covenanted to give him a free pardon when required for all offences against the peace, but undertook at the same time to cause inquiry to be made into the substance of the accusations brought by Yelverton and Jenney. On the very day this document was issued Paston was declared outlawed, and on 3rd November he was committed a second time to the Fleet prison.

William Yelverton, or William Jenney, or any other, concerning the lands and tenements, goods or chattels, that were the said Sir John Fastolf's. Also the King granteth to help and support the said John Paston to obtain and have to the use of the said Sir John Fastolf such goods as were the said Fastolf's deceitfully eloined out of the possession and knowledge of the said John Paston; and that the King shall grant the said John Paston such lawful writings and letters from the King, directed to such persons as shall be behoveful for the same, what time the said John Paston sucth to the King's highness therefore.

Also where Yelverton or Jenney, or any justice of the peace of the shire of Suffolk hath recorded any riot, trespass, or offences to be done against the King's peace by the said John Paston, his servants, or tenants, or friends; or where any indictment or presentment is found against them, or any of them, before any of the said justices, for any such riot, offences, trespass, or for any other matter remaining of record in the King's Bench, or in any other place, the King granteth to the said John Paston, and all other persons named in the said records or indictments, or in any of them, and to all their borrows and pledges, and to each of them that will sue it, a pardon of all riots, trespasses, offences, felonies, forfeitures, done against the King's peace, and of fines therefore dempt or to be dempt, and of all other things generally, treason except, and that the King shall sign warrants lawful of the said pardons, what time his Highness be required by the said John Paston or his attorneys.

And also that his Highness shall do inquiry and examination be made whether the said record of the said justices, and presentments, and other informations or complaints made against the said John Paston, were done truly and lawfully or not; and if it be found that they were done otherwise than truth, law, or conscience will, then the King granteth to cause the doers thereof to recompense the said John Paston and the said other persons, as far as law and good conscience will in that behalf.

And that if it fortune any complaint to be made against the said John Paston, by any person in time coming, to the King, that he shall take no displeasure to the said John Paston till the time he come to his answer and be found in default.

And that the King shall receive £100 of the said 300 marks what time he send for it, and the remnant as soon as the said foundation take effect; and also that His Highness shall get the assent of the reverend father in God, the Archbishop of Canterbury, in such appointments as is made atwixt the King and the said John Paston, of such goods as were the said Sir John Fastolf's for the delivery thereof; and that if the said John

Paston refuse the administration of the goods and chattels that were the said Sir John Fastolf's, suffering other to take it upon them, the King, at the instance of the said John Paston, granteth to be good and favourable lord to such other as the course of the law, and assent of the said John Paston, shall take the said administration in execution of the said Fastolf's will, touching the administration of the goods and chattels foresaid, according to the same will; and that the King shall not claim nor desire any of the lands or tenements, goods or chattels, that were the said Sir John Fastolf's, against the said John Paston or any other executor, administrator, or feoffee of the said Sir John Fastolf, nor support or favour any other person in claiming any of the said lands or tenements, goods or chattels, against any of the said administrators, executors, or feoffees.

And the King granteth that whereas this bill is not sufficiently made in clauses and terms according to the intent thereof, that His Highness will take and execute the very intent thereof, notwithstanding the insufficience of any such terms and clauses in this bill. Written at Marlborough, the Monday next after the Nativity of Our Lady, the fourth year of the reign of the King.

[10th September 1464]

236.     ANONYMOUS TO JOHN[(1)] PASTON[1]

*To my right worshipful master and brother, John Paston, this letter be taken.*

Right worshipful and reverend master and brother, with all my service I recommend me unto you. Please it unto your great wisdom to have in your discreet remembrance the strait Order on which we be professed, and on which ye are bounden to keep your residence, and specially on this time of Christmas amongst your confrères of this holy Order, the Temple of Sion. For

---

[1] It is difficult, says Gairdner, to assign with confidence either a date or a meaning to this strangely worded epistle. The Order of the Temple of Sion is unknown to archaeologists, and the place from which the letter is dated cannot be identified. There seems, however, to be an air of irony about the whole communication which forbids us to construe any of its statements seriously. It is probably a mocking letter addressed to John Paston by one of the prisoners in the Fleet, where Paston was himself confined in 1464 (cf. footnote 1, page 243). His imprisonment on that occasion was probably of short duration, though there is no evidence as to the date of his release. It seems probable, however, that he was free by 3rd December of the same year; but some of his late fellow-prisoners, probably members of the Inner or Middle Temple like himself, who had formed themselves into an imaginary 'Order of the Temple of Sion,' and amused themselves by supposing that he would shortly return. Such, at any rate, is the theory of Gairdner, from whose preliminary note to this letter the foregoing remarks are condensed.

unless than ye keep duly the points of your holy religion, our Master Thomas Babyngton, master and sovereign of our Order, of the assent of his brethren, be advised to award against you right sharp and hasty process to do call you to do your observance, and to obey the points of your religion, which were unto me great heaviness. Wherefore I, as he that hath most greatest cause, and is most bounden unto your great gentleness, and also whom nature and kin most specially before every of all our brethren binden me to owe and will you good will and true heart, considering the great time of penance that ye have been in from soon upon Michaelmas hitherto, that is to say in relieving and sustenance of your even Christian and also in the charitable and meritory deed of alms-doing, that is to say, in plenteous and liberal gifts, which is more preciouser than gold or silver, which hath not been at all times to your great ease, neither heart's pleasance, but rather to your great disease and intolerable pain. And where God's law and man's law accord that it shall not be lawful to none earthly man to be so liberal and plenteous of that that God sendeth him, that he should so dispose it so that he should nought have to live by; and forasmuch as I have perfect knowledge of your frail and natural disposition so set unto them that be needy and hungry that of yourself we have no might, neither power, to abstain and rule yourself, but all so long as God sendeth and giveth you whereof to dispose and help your even Christian, ye must needs dispose it forth amongst your even Christian; I counsel you that in all so hasty and goodly time as ye can to come unto your holy brethren that be of this devout and close conversation, to the intent that ye might be advertised and learned by them the good rule and measure that ye ought and should have in the disposition and dealing of your alms.

And also, since ye have chosen you a place in this season of Advent, in which ye have had a reasonable leisure and space to do your penance in, which draweth fast to an end (which hath been a convenient place as for the season of the year, and now it draweth fast unto Christmas, on which time every true Christian man should be merry, jocund, and glad); and since there is no place which by likelihood of reason ye should find in your heart to be so glad and jocund in as ye should be in the place of your profession amongst your holy brethren (in which place in this season of the year it is accustomed to be all manner of disport, like as it is not unknown to your wise discretion); wherefore, as my simple reason leadeth me, your great discretion should rule you that ye should approach nigh the place of your holy religion in all so hasty time as ye could or might, of whose coming all your said brethren would be glad and fain, and in especial I your servant and brother, like as I am most singular bounden to the increase of your prosperity and welfare, which I shall ever desire with God's mercy, which have you under His blessed and favourable protection. Written in the Temple of Sion, the third day of December, in great haste.

By your servant and brother,

T.

[? 1464]

### 237. JOHN[1] PASTON TO MARGARET PASTON AND OTHERS [J. G.]

*To my mistress Margaret Paston, and to my well-beloved friends, John Dawbeney and Richard Calle.*

I pray you, see to the good governance of my household and guiding of other things touching my profit, and that ye, with Dawbeney and Richard Calle, and with other such of my friends and servants as can advise you after the matter requireth, weekly take a sad communication of such things as be for to do, or oftener an' need be, taking advice of the master, and of the vicar [1] and Sir James,[2] that is for to say, as well for provision of stuff for mine household as for the gathering of the revenue of my livelode or grains, or for setting a-work of my servants, and for the more politic means of selling and carrying of my malt, and for all other things necessary for to be done; and that when I come home I have not an excuse, saying that ye spoke to my servants, and that Dawbeney and Calle excuse them that they were so busy they might not attend. For I will have my matter so guided that if any man may not attend another shall be commanded to do it; and if my servants fail, I had lever wage some other man, for a journey or a season, than my matter should be unsped.

As for my livelode, I left with Dawbeney a bill of many of my debts, whereby ye all might have been induced whether ye should have sent for silver.

It liketh me evil to hear that my prests and poor men be unpaid, and that no money sent to more than ten marks by Berney of all this season; and yet thereof tell Richard Calle he sent me eight nobles in gold for five marks, and that as long as gold was better payment than silver I had never so much gold of him at once. And tell him that I will not that he shall keep that use, for I trow my tenants have but little gold to pay.

---

[1] If this be the vicar of Paston, it was William Warner, who succeeded Robert Williamson in 1464.

[2] James Gloys, the priest. For the honorific, *see* footnote 1, page 44.

Also, remember you, in any household, fellowship, or company that will be of good rule, purveyance must be had that
every person of it be helping and furthering after his discretion
and power, and he that will not do so without he be kept of alms
should be put out of the household or fellowship.

Item, where ye desire me that I should take your son [1] to
grace, I will for your sake do the better, and will ye know he
shall not be so out of my favour that I will suffer him to mischief
without by eftsoons his own default. And howbeit that in his
presumptuous and indiscreet demeaning he gave both me and
you cause of displeasure, and to other of my servants ill example,
and that also guided him to all men's understanding that he was
weary of biding in mine house, and he not ensured of help in
any other place; yet that grieveth not me so evil as doth that
I never could feel nor understand him politic nor diligent in
helping himself, but as a drone among bees which labour for
gathering honey in the fields, and the drone doth nought but
taketh his part of it. And if this might make him to know the
better himself and put him in remembrance what time he hath
lost, and how he hath lived in idleness, and that he could for this
eschew to do so hereafter, it might fortune for his best. But I
hear yet never from no place that he hath been in of any politic
demeaning or occupation of him. And in the King's house he
could put himself forth to be in favour or trust with any men of
substance that might further him; nevertheless, as for your house
and mine, I purpose not he shall come there, nor by my will
none other but-if he can do more than look forth and make a
face and countenance.

Item, send me word whether my glazier hath done at Bromholm and at the friars of the South Town,[2] and whether he be
paid such money as I sent home word he should be paid; and if
he have done all, he must have more money, but I remember not
certainly what, till I come home, for I remember not what his
bargain was for the work at the South Town. I trow Mr
Clement can tell, and also feel himself and send me word. Also
that ye and Richard Calle and Dawbeney see that Mr Clement
and Mr Brackley [3] (which hath great need, I wot well) and my
prests and poor men be paid, and also all other men. And that
ye see that I be not called on, for that is my duty. Also that ye
see amongst you that that is owing me be not lost nor forborne
for lewdness, for that shall both hurt me and do my tenants

[1] This refers to the displeasure given by Sir John Paston to both his
parents by leaving home without warning or permission in 1463. (*See* No.
228, page 234.)
[2] South Town, Yarmouth, where there was a house of Austin Friars.
[3] John Brackley, O.F.M.

harm. Let Richard Calle remember that my farmer of Swains-thorpe is fallen in great debt for default of calling upon but by one year; and I deem that both John Willeys and my farmer of Snailwell are like to be in the same case, and peradventure Aleyn of Gresham and other.

Item, remember you, ere ever I had to do with Fastolf's livelode, while I took heed to my livelode myself, it both served mine expenses at home and at London and all other charges, and ye laid up money in my coffers every year, as ye know. And I wot well that the payment of my prests and other charges that I have for Fastolf's livelode is not so great as the livelode is, though part thereof be in trouble. And then consider that I had nought of my livelode for mine expenses at London this twelve month day; ye may verily understand that it is not guided wittily nor discreetly. And therefore I pray you heartily put all your wits together and see for the reformation of it. And ye may remember by this how ye should do if this were yours alone, and so do now.

And that ye will remember I have sent you all many letters touching many matters, and also a bill now last, by Peacock, of errands, desiring you to see them all together and send me an answer articlerly; and such as ye cannot speed at this time, let them be sped as soon as ye may, that ye see over my said letters ofttimes till they be sped.

Item, I remember that mine hay at Hellesdon the last year was spent and wasted full recklessly and coloured under my sheep.[1] I pray you see that I be not served so this year.

Item, Peacock told me of a farmer that would have had Mauteby Marsh, paying twelve marks as it went afore; and Richard Calle told me of one that would pay more. Burgess paid me first twelve marks 6s. 8d., and I had the reeds and the rushes, and he found the shepherd's hire at shack-time [2] for my fold; and since, he brigged away the shepherd's hire and then the noble, and I trow he occupieth no longer himself. And I remember he told me seven years ago that my marsh should alway appeyr till the prime were past the number of nineteen, and then it should amend a nine or ten years, promitting me that he would then amend my farm. I pray you help to let it as well as ye can, rather to him than another man if he will do as well, and that ye commune with Peacock.

Item, as for the matter that I wrote of to the vicar and other good fellows, desire them that they be not too excessive hasty in the matter for none need, but to do that they may do therein

---

[1] i.e. on the pretence that it was used for my sheep.
[2] Shack, in Norfolk and Suffolk, was liberty of winter pasturage for the lord of the manor on his tenants' lands.

goodly and wittly as soon as they may; and as for the respite of the matter here, let them not care therefor. I shall do well enough, tell them; for certain, the matter is in as good case as any such matter was this twenty winter, as my counsel telleth me. But I will be sure of all ways that I may have, and specially of the declaration of the truth of my matter and of my friends.

Item, as for the matter atwixt the parson of Mauteby, Constantine,[1] and the vicar of Dereham,[2] whether it were small matter or great I care not; but I am sure that two witnesses which I know were apposed therein before a judge spiritual, which as I suppose was Master Robert Popy or some other. The vicar of Dereham can tell, and, as I trow, can John Winter of Mauteby, or other parishioners, tell where the suit was atwixt them, and I can think it was in the chapitle. If ye can easily get me what the witnesses said, I would no more; but do no great cost over it.

Item, recommend me to Master Robert Popy, and tell him, as for anything said against him in my matter then, mine adversaries meant untruly; they proved nought but that he is a good man and a worshipful and a true.

Item, if I had any oats beside my stuff, or may any buy after 13d., spare not; and take good measure of barter for some other chatters, and send me word how much ye may buy.

Item, it is told me ye make no wood, neither at Caister nor Mauteby, whereof I marvel; remember you we must burn wood another year.

Item, I send you a titling that I made while I was at home, what malt I had by estimation set at the least. Wherefore see that Brigge make a reckoning of his malt, and cast ye my book and look what ye can amend it; and appeyr it shall not, if all folks have done truly. But I suppose few of you have taken any heed at it as much as I did.

Item, I may sell here for 6s. 8d. a quarter clene fyed after Royston measure, which is less than the water measure of London. Cambridgeshire malt is here at 10s. Cast ye what I may sell of new and old, saving stuff for mine own house. Item, to remember that Guton malt must be shipped at Blakeney. Item, Lynstead's malt at Wolcote may be shipped there; therefore cast amongst you what malt may best be sold.

Item, if one man may not attend to gather silver, send another; and send me word what hath been received and spent.

---

[1] Constantine Dalby had been rector of Mauteby from 1453 to 1460, and appears also to have had the vicarage of East Dereham from 1451 to 1458. He was succeeded at Mauteby by Thomas Howes from 1460 to 1465, and then by Robert Cutler, who must be the 'parson of Mauteby' spoken of just before.

[2] Robert Sheringham, who was vicar of East Dereham from 1458 to 1467.

Item, that I have an answer of all my letters and of every article in them.

Item, but-if ye make such purveyance that my prests be paid and poor men, beside other charges, and purvey money for me beside, either ye gather shrewdly or else ye spend lewdly.

Item, I sent a letter by Ralph Greenacre to James Gresham and to you, which he promised me should be at Norwich on Wednesday after Twelfth day, and therein were divers matters; and in especial of a matter that should be in communication on Tuesday last past betwixt Yelverton and Robert Wingfield, as in the letter is specified. It is so that the said Robert shall be here within this two days; if anything ye have espied of it, send me word. Item, young Knevet telleth me that he is my good friend, and he is come riding homeward on Friday last was. I pray you, lay watch whether ye hear anything that he meddleth him at that matter, and send me word; for I would understand whether he were just and true or not, and that done it shall not lie in his power to hurt me. But take ye heed and inquire and know other men's purpose, and keep your intent as close as ye can; and whatsoever boast be made, work it wisely and set not by it, but send me word what ye hear.

Item, Calle sendeth me word that Sir Thomas Howes is sick and not like to escape it, and Berney telleth me the contrary. Wherefore I pray you take heed thereat, and let me have knowledge; for though I be not beholden to him, I would not he were dead for more than he is worth.

Item, take the vicar the bill that I send you herewith.

Item, that ye, if ye can find the means, to espy what goods Edmund Clere [1] escheateth of any man's.

Item, remember well to take heed at your gates on nights and days for thieves, for they ride in divers countries with great fellowship like lords, and ride out of one shire into another. Written at London, the Tuesday next after St Hilary.

Item, that Richard Calle bring me up money, so that my prests be paid; and that he come up surely with other men and attorneys.

[15th January 1465]

---

[1] Edmund Clere was escheator of Norfolk and Suffolk from November 1464 to November 1465.

238.     JOHN WYKES TO MARGARET PASTON

*Unto my mistress Margaret Paston, be this letter delivered in haste, etc.*

Right worshipful mistress, I recommend me unto your good mistress-ship. Please it you to wit that my master your husband, my mistress your mother, my master Sir John, Mr William, Mr Clement, and all their men, were in good health when this letter was written, thanked be Jesu. And also their matters be in a good way, for my Lord Chancellor is their singular good lord in this matter at this time; and that it proveth, for he was yesterday in the Exchequer, and all the serjeants, and there argued whether that the barons of the Exchequer should award any such commission or not, and upon that the said commission shall be brought upon Friday into the Chancery and there to be proved whether it be lawful or not, etc.

Item, and if it please you to give Dawbeney knowledge that there is judgment given upon the condemnation against Hall,[1] that he claimed for his bondman; and the judgment is given against Dawbeney, Ric. Calle, and Thomas Boon. And there is come out process for to take their bodies this same day; and if they or any of them be taken they shall never go out of prison unto the time that they have satisfied the party of eight score marks, and therefore let them beware. The Holy Trinity have you in His keeping. Written at London, upon Thursday next after the Purification of Our Lady, etc.

By your servant,

JOHN WYKES.

[7th February 1465]

239.     MARGARET PASTON TO JOHN[1] PASTON [J. G.][2]

*To my right worshipful husband, John Paston, be this delivered in haste.*

Right worshipful husband, I recommend me to you. Please you to wete that I send you a copy of the deed that John Edmonds of Taverham sent to me, by the means of Dorlet. He told Dorlet that he had such a deed, as he supposed, that would do ease in proving of the title that the Duke of Suffolk claimeth in Drayton;

[1] Robert Hall. In Trinity term, 1463, he brought an action against Dawbeney, Calle, and Boon (all of Norwich) for having unlawfully imprisoned him at Norwich for three hours on 20th February 1461, until he gave them a bond of £100 for his ransom.

[2] This is the first of a number of letters bearing upon the Duke of Suffolk's claim to the manors of Drayton and Hellesdon.

for the same deed that he sent me, the seal of arms is like unto the copy that I send you, and nothing like to the Duke of Suffolk's ancestors.

Item, the said Edmonds saith, if he may find any other thing that may do you ease in that matter he will do his part therein.

Item, John Russe sent me word that Barker and Harry Porter told him in counsel that the Duke of Suffolk hath bought one Brightlede's right, the which maketh a claim unto Hellesdon, and the said duke is proposed to enter within short time after Easter; for insomuch the said Russe feels by the said Barker and Porter that all the feoffees will make a release unto the duke and help him that they can into their power, for to have his good lordship.

Item, if it please you, methinketh it were right necessary that ye send word how that ye will your old malt be purveyed for; for, and any hot weather come after that it hath lain this winter season, it shall be but lost but-if it be sold betimes, for as for the price here, it is sore fallen. I have sold a hundred comb of malt, that came from Guton, to James Golbeter (clene fyed, and strek met, and none inmet),[1] for 2s. 2d. the comb, and to paid at Midsummer and Lammas.

Item, there be divers of your tenantries at Mauteby that had great need for to be repaired, but the tenants be so poor that they are not apower to repair them; wherefore, if like you, I would that the marsh that Burgess had might be kept in your own hand this year, that the tenants might have rushes to repair with their houses. And also, there is windfall wood at the manor that is of no great value, that might help them with toward the reparation, if it like you to let them have it that hath most need thereof. I have spoken with Burgess that he should heighten the price of the marsh; or else, I told him that he should no longer have it, for ye might have other farmers thereto that would give therefor as it was late before, and if he would give therefor as much as another man would, ye would that he should have it before any other man; and he said he should give me answer by a fortnight after Easter. I can get none other farmer thereto yet.

Item, I understand by John Pampyng that ye will not that your son be taken into your house, nor holpen by you, till such time of year as he was put out thereof, the which shall be about St Thomas-mass.[2] For God's sake, have pity on him; remember you it hath been a long season since he had aught of you to help him with, and he hath obeyed him to you and will do at all times, and will do that he can or may to have your good fatherhood. And at the reverence of God be ye his good father, and have a

---

[1] cleansed, and strike-measure, and not in-measure.
[2] Probably the feast of St Thomas of Canterbury, 29th December.

fatherly heart to him; and I hope he shall ever know himself the better hereafter, and be the more wary to eschew such things as should displease you, and for to take heed at that should please you. Peacock shall tell you by mouth of more things than I may write to you at this time. The blessed Trinity have you in His keeping. Written at Caister in haste, the Monday next after Palm Sunday.

Your

M. P.

[8th April 1465]

# APPENDIX

## LETTER No. 3

*To my Worshepefull housbond W. Paston be þis lettere takyn.*

Dere housbond I recomaunde me to yow &c. blyssyd be god I
sende yow gode tydyngges of þe comyng and þe brynggyn hoom
of þe Gentylwomman þat ye wetyn of fro Redham þis same
nyght acordyng to poyntmen þat ye made þer for yowr self,
and as for þe furste aqweyntaunce be twhen John Paston and
þe seyde Gentilwomman she made hym Gentil cher in Gyntyl
wyse and seyde he was verrayly yowr son. And so I hope þer
shal nede no gret trete be twyxe hym. þe parson of Stocton
toold me yif þe wolde byin her a goune here moder wolde yeve
ther to a godely furre, þe goune nedyth for to be had, and of
colour it wolde be a godely blew or erlys a bryghte sanggueyn.
I prey yow do byen for me ii pypys of gold. Your stewes do
weel. The holy Trinite have yow in governance. Wretyn at
Paston in hast þe Wednesday next after Deus qui errantibus for
defaute of a good secretarye &c.

Yowres

AGN: PASTON.

## LETTER No. 14

*To my Ryght Wurchepfull Cosyn John Paston esquier.*

Right worchepful cosyn, I recomaunde me to yow, thankyng
yow as hertyly as I kan for my selff &c., and specially for þat
ye do so moche for oure Ladyes Hous of Walsyngham which I
trust veryly ye do the rather for þe grete Love þat ye deme I
have þerto, for trewly if I be drawe to any worchep or wellfare
and discharge of myn Enmyes daunger I ascrybe it unto our Lady
Preyng yow þerfore þat ye woln ben as frendly to our Ladyes
hous as I wote well ye have alwey ben, and in especyall now
þat I might have of yow the report certeynly be your letter of
þat that Naunton your cosyn informyd yow and told yow be
mouthe of all maters touchyng oure ladyes hous of Walsyngham.
For me thynkyth be þat I have herde be oure Ladys prest of
Walsyngham, if I understode weell þat mater, þat it shuld do

moch to the gode spede of the mater, and dought yow not my
Lady shall quyte it yow and here poer priour here aftyr as he
may &c. Preyng yow also cosyn and avysing, for the ease of us
both and of our frendes and of many oth(e)r þat ye be at London
betymes þis terme, and if we spede well now All well all þis
yere aftir, for I knowe veryly þer was nevyr made gretter labour
þanne shall be made now and þerfore I prey to our Lady help
us and her blissid sone which have you in his holy kepyng.
Wreten at your poer place of Bayfeld on sent Fraunces Day in
hast.

Yo(u)r Cosyn,

WILLIAM YELVERTON, *Justic.*

LETTER No. 30

*To owre ryght trusty and welbelovyd frend Ser Thomas Todenham.*

Ryght trusty and welbelovyd frend, we grete you well, hertely
desyryng to here of your welfare which we pray God preserve
to your hertes desyre, and yf yt please you to here of owre
welfare we were in goud hele atte þe makyng of þis lettre,
praying you hertely þ(a)t ye wyll considere owre message, which
owre chapleyn mayster Robert Hoppton shall enforme you of;
fore as God knowyth we have gret besynesse dayly and has had
here by fore þis tym(e), wherfore we pray you to considere þe
purchas þ(a)t we have made wyth on(e) John Swysshcotte
squere of lyncoln Shyre of lxxx & viii li by yere, whereuppon us
must pay þe last payment þe moneday nexte aftyre Seynt
martyn day, which sum ys cccc and lviii li, wherfore we pray
you wyth all owre herte þ(a)t ye wyll lend us x li ore twenty
ore what þe seyd mayster Robert wants of hys payment as we
may do fore you in tym(e) fore to come, and we shall send yt you
ageyn afore newyersday wyth þe grace of God, as we are trew
knyght.

For þere is noman in your cuntre þ(a)t we myght wryght to
fore trust so well as un to yo(u), fore as we be enformyd, ye be
owre well wyllere, and so we pray you of goud contynuaunce.

Wherfore we pray you þat ye consydere owre entent of this
mony as ye wyll þat we do fore you in tym(e) to com(e), as God
knowyth, who have you in hys kepyng.

Wreten atte London on all Salwyn day Wyth Inne owre
loggyng In þe Grey frers Wyth Inne newgate.

## LETTER No. 99

### THE DUCHESSE OF NORFF.

*To oure right trusti and welbelovid John Paston esquier.*

Right trusti and welbelovid, we grete you hertili weel, and for as muche as it is thought right necessarie for divers causes þ(a)t my Lord have at this tyme in the parlement suche persones as longe unto him and be of his menyall servauntz, wherin we conceyve your good will and diligence shal be right expedient; we hertili desire and pray you that at the contemplacion of thise oure l(ett)res as our special trust is in you ye wil geve and applie your voice unto our right welbelovid cosin and servauntz John Howard and Sire Roger Chambirlayn to be knyghtes of the Shire, exorting all suche othir as be your wisdam shal mow be behovefull to the good exployte and conclusion of the same. And in your faithful attendaunce and trewe devoyre in this partie ye shal do unto my Lord and us a singler pleasir and cause us heraftir to thank you therfore as ye shal holde you right weel content and agreid with the grace of god who have you evere in his keping.

Wreten in Framlyngham Castel the viii day of Jun(e).

## LETTER No. 129

*Unto my ryght wurchipfull Cosyn Margaret Paston þis letter be delyverid in haste.*

Ryght wurchipfull & my moste beste beloved maystres and cosyn I Recomaund me unto you as lowly as I may, Evermore desyring to here of your gode welfare, þe whiche I beseche Almygthy Jhesu to preserve you and kepe you to his plesure and to youre gracious hertes desyre. And yf it plese you to here of my welfare, I was in gode hele at þe makyng of þis l(ett)re, blessed be God; praying you þ(a)t it plese you for to send me worde yf my fadyr were at Norwiche w(i)t(h) you at þe Trenite masse or no, and how þe matyr dothe be twene my maystres Blawnche Wychyngam and me, and yf ye sopose þ(a)t it schall be brought a bowte or no and how ye fele my fadyr yf he be wele wyllyng therto or no, prayng you lowly þ(a)t I may be recomaund lowly unto my maystres Arblasteris wyfe and unto my maystres Blawnche her dowgther specially. Ryght wurchipful cosyn, yf it plese you for to here of suche tydinges as we have

here, þe Basset of Burgoyne schall come to Calleis þe Saturday
eftyr corpus chr(ist)i day, as men say v honderd horse of hem.

Moreover on Trenite Sonday in þe mornyng come tydynges
unto my lord of Warwyke þ(a)t þere were xxviii<sup>ti</sup> sayle of
Spaynyards on þe Se and wherof þere was xvi grete schippis of
forecastell, and then my lord went and manned fyve schippis
of forecastell and iii Carvell and iiii Spynnes; and on þe monday
in þe morning eftyr Trenite Sonday we met to gedyr afore
Caleis at iiii at þe clokke in þe mornyng, and fawgthe to gedyr
till x at þe clokke, and there we toke vi of her schippis and they

xx
slowe of owre me(n) about iiii and hurt a ii hondred of us ryght

(x)x
sore and there were slayne on theyr parte abowte xii and hurt
a v honderd of them.

And haped me at þe fyrste abordyng of us, we toke a schippe
of iii ton and I was left therein and xxiii men w(i)t(h) me; and
thei fawgthe so sore þ(a)t our men were fayne to leve hem and
then come they and aborded þe schippe þ(a)t I was in, and there
I was taken and was p(ri)soner w(i)t(h) them vi houris and was
delyverid agayne for theyre men þ(a)t were taken before me
and as men sayne there was not so gret a Batayle upon þe Se
þis XL wyntyr, and for sothe we were wele and trewly bette,
and my lord hathe sent for more schippis and lyke to fygthe to
gedyr agayne in haste. Nomore I write unto you at þis tyme,
but þ(a)t it plese you forto recomaund me unto my Ryght
Reverent & Wurchipfull Cosyn your husbond and myn ownkill
Gournay and to myn awnte his wyfe and to alle gode maysters
and frendes where it schall plese you; and eftyr þe writyng I
have from you I schall be at you in alle haste.

Wreten on Corpus Chr(ist)i day in gret haste.

Be your owne emble Servant and Cosyn,

JOHN JERNYNGAN.


LETTER No. 135

*To my right worshipfull and right entierly welbelovid cousin the
Viscount Beaumont.*

Right worshipfull and right entierly welbelovid cousin, I
comaunde me to you w(i)t(h) alle my herte, desiring to here and
verile to knowe of your worshipfull estate, profite, hele and good
prosperite, the whiche I beseche our Lord Ihesu ever to mayn-
tene and preserve in alle worship to his plesaunce and to your

hertes ease. Please it you cousin to witte þat your welbelovid servaunt Roger Hunt and a servaunt of my moost dred Lord my husbond on William, yoman of his ewry, have comend to gedre and ben fully thorgh & agreid þat þe said William shall have his office if it may please your good lordship. Wherfore cousin I pray you as my speciall truste is in you, þat ye will at thinstaunce of my praier and writing, graunte by your l(ett)res patentes to þe said William the forsaid office with such wages and fees as Roger your said servaunt hath it of you; trustyng verile þat ye shall fynde the said William a faithfull servaunt to you, and can and may do you right good service in þat office.

And cousin, in thacomplesshment of my desire in þis mater, ye may do me a right good pleaser as God knowith, Whom I beseche for his merci to have you ever in his blessed governaunce, and send you good lyfe and Long, with muche worship.

Writen at Framlyngham the viii[th] day of Marche,

ELIANORE, the Duchesse of Norff.

# GLOSSARY

*Abiden, to be,* to be delayed
*Adoubted,* suspicious
*Advert,* advise
*Advise you,* take care
*Aglets,* pendant ornaments of metal
*A-great,* as a whole
*Aknow, be,* acknowledge
*Alderbest,* entirely
*Aley on their bodies,* be beaten
*Amortise,* settle by the statute of mortmain
*An',* if
*Anemps,* in the sight of
*Apaid,* content
*Apower,* able
*Appeyr,* harm, deteriorate
*Articlerly,* in detail
*Asseal,* seal
*Audacity,* confidence
*Avail,* doff
*Avaunt,* boast
*Avoid,* remove, depart
*Avoidance,* vacancy
*Aythe,* ever

*Basetry* }
*Basset* } embassy
*Bawdrick,* belt
*Bear a hand,* accuse, impute to
*Behove,* advantage
*Beset,* bequeathed
*Bever,* supply of drink
*Bill,* weapon
*Blavered,* prated
*Bogey,* budge fur
*Borrows,* sureties
*Bosart,* buzzard
*Botew,* a kind of boot
*Both,* also
*Brethel,* whore
*Briber,* pilferer
*Bribery,* pilfering
*Briganders (brigandines),* coats of leather or quilted linen with small iron plates attached
*Bronde,* upbraid
*Brothel, company of,* pack of scoundrels
*Bushment,* ambush
*But-if,* unless
*But-that,* only

*Calked,* calculated
*Carte,* expense
*Cast the perils,* consider the dangers
*Cause* (Nos. 166, 317), prevent
*Certain,* number, batch
*Chapitle,* chapter-house
*Charge,* value
*Chatters,* bargains
*Chavil,* jaw-bone
*Chevisance,* provision, arrangement, interest on a loan
*Chevise,* provide, arrange, borrow at interest
*Cleped,* called, named
*Closet,* enclosed pew
*Clothing,* livery
*Coffer. See* TRUSSING COFFER
*Coisy* (= *queasy*), unsettled
*Colour, by,* under pretence
*Comfort,* support, encouragement
*Con,* know how to
*Con thank,* be grateful to
*Conceit,* estimation
*Condeneth,* gives satisfaction
*Confetered,* in agreement
*Coningclose,* rabbit-warren
*Content again,* repay
*Conversement,* acquaintance
*Copschotyn,* too fond of the bottle
*Corons, raisins of,* currants
*Costuous,* costly
*Counsel, in,* in secret, confidentially
*Countery,* counting-board
*Couth,* known

261

*Coverchief*, head-dress
*Covetise*, covetousness
*Crased*, sick
*Creancer*, creditor
*Crod*, wheeled
*Crome*, pole with a hook at one end
*Crone*, discuss
*Cunning*, understanding

*Danger*, debt
*Delyverst*, nimble
*Demean*, act
*Dempt*, adjudged
*Depart*, part (with), separate
*Detray*, betray
*Disparbled*, dispersed
*Doles*, boundary marks
*Dormant*, beam
*Dorter*, dormitory
*Do to wete*, inform
*Draught-chamber*, withdrawing-room
*Dronchyn*, drowned
*Duty*, due

*Easy*, small, inadequate, of little value
*Eloined*, removed
*Eme*, uncle
*Endangered*, indebted
*Enfect*, infected
*Entress*, interest, concern
*Estrager*, falconer
*Even Christian*, fellow christian
*Eyer*, lay eggs

*Failed*, wanted
*Farcy*, disease in horses, similar to glanders
*Fardel*, bundle, parcel
*Farm barley*, barley paid as rent
*Fastingong*, Shrovetide
*Fathered*, arranged for
*Fault*, fail
*Fautorer*, supporter, abettor
*Ferd*, dealt
*Fery over*, defer
*Fetis*, well made
*Flight-shot*, distance covered by a light arrow

*Flygge*, ripe
*Fode forth*, put off
*For-because*, in order that
*Forborn*, spared
*Force not*, care not
*Forcer*, chest
*Fordell*, advantage
*Fotte*, fetched
*Free*, willing
*Fronture and forcelet*, stronghold

*Galingale*, a kind of ginger
*Gan*, have been
*Garees*, finery
*Garnish*, set of pewter
*Geer*, burden, anxiety
*Gelt*, gold
*Gisering*, battle-axe
*Glaive*, broadsword
*Good*, goods, money, cost (but often in its modern sense)
*Gree, in*, favourably
*Guiding*, conduct, behaviour
*Gypcer*, purse

*Halvendele*, half-share
*Hant*, dragged
*Happe*, wrap
*Harness*, defensive armour; fittings (Nos. 161, 266)
*Haubergeon*, sleeveless coat of chain-mail or plate armour
*Haulte*, high
*Hayward*, one who guarded crops at night
*Head, to*, to behead
*Hedermoder*, hugger-mugger
*Helle*, cover
*Hight*, named
*Hosecloth*, cloth for hose
*Hostlements*, offensive weapons
*Hutch*, coffer or chest on legs

*Importable*, insupportable
*Imprended*, imprinted
*Inbassat, of*, on embassy
*Incontinent*, immediately
*Indifferent*, impartial
*Inforce*, strengthen
*Inkyr*, inquiry
*Insurance*, betrothal

*Jape*, futility, disappointment

*Journey*, (day of) battle. *See* MALE JOURNEY

*Kersche of cr'melle*, kerchief of worsted

*Krott*, crack or chip

*Lachesed*, neglected

*Langedebief*, a kind of sword

*Lesings*, lies. *Make lesing* = tell a lie

*Less-than*, unless

*Let*, prevent, delay

*Lever*, rather

*Levest*, dearest

*Lewd*, unrefined, illiterate

*List*, phase, care

*Livelode*, income-bearing property, inheritance, estate(s), rents

*Loader*, carrier

*Lobster*, stoat

*Lust*, good pleasure

*Lusteth*, pleaseth

*Magery*, management

*Mak*, wife

*Male journey*, ill-fated day

*Mate*, match (No. 392)

*Maun*, may

*Mean*, mediator

*Mell of*, meddle with, concern oneself with

*Meny*, company, servants, entourage

*Mickle*, much

*Moaned*, lamented

*Morken*, marked

*Mote*, have you

*Mowe* (*mown*), be able to. *Mown coming* = be able to come

*Musterdevelers*, a grey woollen cloth

*Ne nor* (*not*), neither

*Ne force*, no matter

*Ne were*, were it not

*Noiseth*, complaineth of

*Nonage*, minority

*None erst*, no earlier

*Nor had*, had not

*Novelties*, news

*Nowche*, button, brooch, etc.

*Noy*, call, summons

*Obligation*, written acknowledgment of a debt

*Ordain*, order

*Or then* (*than*), before

*Overmore*, also

*Owch*, jewel

*Parclose*, low door of enclosed pew

*Passagers*, passage boats

*Passel*, in lots, bit by bit

*Pavise*, large shield

*Pawntements*, terms of agreement

*Peaced*, held their peace

*Pensily*, heavily

*Percase*, perhaps

*Peyse*, weigh

*Pill*, pillage

*Pillion*, Doctor of Divinity's cap

*Pine*, pain, annoyance

*Plancher*, floor

*Polronds*, shoulder-pieces

*Prat*, practice

*Prest*, borrowed sum

*Pretend*, in mind, consider

*Purfeled*, trimmed, edged

*Quarrels*, square pyramids of iron shot from crossbows. [But sometimes in the modern sense]

*Queasy*, unsettled

*Qwethword*, promise to pay

*Rathe*, early, soon

*Rather*, earlier, sooner, more readily

*Rathest*, most readily, soonest

*Reareth*, rouseth

*Refute*, convenience

*Rejoice* (*rejoy*), enjoy

*Rents*, rags

*Rewly*, grievous

*Ride against*, ride to meet

*Rowth*, *he had not*, he cared not

*Rutters*, throwers

*Sacring*, mass

*Sad*, serious, sombre

*Savation*, safety, protection
*Schitel*, unstable, erratic
*Set by*, esteem
*Shent*, abashed, ashamed
*Shrew;* rogue
*Shrewd*, evil, venomous, irksome
*Singularly*, inaccurately
*Skeusacion*, excuse
*Skilled*, availed
*So-but*, unless
*Sojourn*, stay as a guest
*Sojournant*, guest
*Sote*, sweet
*Sowde*, pay
*Sowter*, shoemaker
*Speed*, succeed
*Spere*, inquire
*Sperred*, shut
*Stews*, fishponds
*Sticked*, stabbed
*Stilled*, remained silent
*Strange*, undesirable (No. 101)
*Strange man*, outsider (No. 102)
*Such*, these
*Sure*, betrothed; made sure (No. 323) =arrested. [Sometimes also in modern sense]
*Swive*, have sexual intercourse with
*Syse*, lawsuit

*Teles*, part of a crossbow
*Tender*, favour, approve
*Teynes*, burning material
*Than*, unless
*Thar*, need
*Then*, before
*Thorough*, agreed
*Titling*, estimate
*Tonnen, do*, cause to be turned
*To-you-ward*, on the way to you

*Trussing coffer*, clothes-chest
*Twain, be*, be at loggerheads

*Under-nemyng*, reproving
*Unethe*, scarcely
*Unlikely*, unsuitable
*Unset*, unexpected
*Ure*, practice, use
*Uttered*, talked about

*Wage*, hire
*Wappes*, a short time
*Ware*, spend
*Wared*, spent
*Wateth*, knoweth
*Wed*, lie to, lie in pawn
*Weened*, thought
*Wenged*, avenged
*Wete(n)*, know, learn, inquire
*We(e)ting*, knowledge
*Wewe*, widow
*Whole*, well
*Whylghe*, how long
*Wifels*, battle-axes
*Wight*, account
*Windacs*, part of a crossbow
*Wis*, know
*Wist*, knew
*With-more*, moreover
*Withset*, distrain
*Wode*, furious, mad
*Wost*, knew
*Wot*, know
*Wreyth*, reveal the contents of
*Wryghe*, misshapen, bent
*Wyte*, blame

*Yarn*, closely
*Yed (yeden)*, went, gone, departed
*Yeld*, reward

L.5

PD1883

−3. JUL. 1973